Kawamata Project on Roosevelt Island

Kawamata Project on Roosevelt Island, July 15-December 1, 1992 was conceived and organized by Claudia Gould in cooperation with the artist and the project team: Mika Koike, Elizabeth O'Donnell, Jane Gregory Rubin, and Andrea Schwan.

on the table, inc./New York is an organization formed to create the installation at the Small Pox Hospital, the publication, partial filming of a MICA TV video, and the exhibition/installation of concepts and models October 13-November 6, 1992 at The Arthur A. Houghton Jr. Gallery of The Cooper Union for the Advancement of Science and Art.

The Kawamata Project on Roosevelt Island has received generous support from **The Japan-United States Friendship Commission, The Bohen Foundation, The Japan Foundation, The LEF Foundation, France R. and Thomas H. Dittmer, Werner and Sarah Ann Kramarsky, and anonymous donors in New York and Japan.**

This project was developed in cooperation with the **Roosevelt Island Operating Corporation** with permission from the **New York City Landmarks Preservation Commission.**

on the table, inc./New York extended project team:
Alan Stuart Braverman, accountant/ Braverman CPA
Ann Bremner, publication editor/ english
Peter J. Galdi, structural engineer
Claudia Gould , project director, curator
Tadashi Kawamata, project artist
Mika Koike, project coordinator/ Japan, graphic design, publication editor/ japanese
MICA TV, Carole Ann Klonarides and Michael Owen/ video production
Elizabeth O'Donnell, architect, project coordinator/ New York
Jane Gregory Rubin, attorney/ Lankenau Kovner & Bickford
Andrea Schwan, media consultant/ The Kreisberg Group

primary structure construction team:
(under the direction of Regele Builders)
Carl Alston
Bernardo Suarez Arbelaez
Thomas J. Bas
Messias DeOliveira
Bill Greenlee
Jim Johnson
Pierre Lavesque
J. J. Lima
Tim McCarthy
Mike P. Michael
Vincent J. Pelliccione
James M. Raglione

artistic structure construction team:
Matthew Abbott
Edip Agi
Takahisa Araki
Harold Dean
Andrew Kennedy
Minoru Kimura
Alexander Knox
Katsuhiro Kono
Joey Kötting
Keisuke Kudo
Curtis Lewis
David Lindberg
David McWeeney
Exavier Wardlaw Muhammad
Bernard Naylon
Nial O'Sullivan
Brad Peebles
Fernando Rebollo
Charles Schick
Kazuma Shimizu
Thomas Towle
Mark von Schlegell

カワマタ・プロジェクト・オン・ルーズヴェルト・アイランドは、クロゥディア・ゴールドがアーティスト川俣正とプロジェクト・チーム、小池美香、エリザベス・オドネル、ジェイン・グレゴリー・ルービンおよびアンドレア・シュワンとの協力のもとに考案され、1992年7月15日より12月1日のあいだに実現された。

オンザテイブル・ニューヨークは、スモールポックス病院でのインスタレーション制作とその広報活動、MICA・TVの撮影ビデオおよびクーパーユニオンのアーサー・A・ヒュートン・ジュニア・ギャラリーで1992年10月13日から11月6日まで開かれた展覧会のコンセプトおよび模型の設置を行うために設立された。

このルーズヴェルト・アイランドにおけるカワマタ・プロジェクトは、日米友好基金、ボーエン・ファンデーション、国際交流基金、LEFファンデーション、フランス・Aおよびトーマス・ディトマー、ワーナーおよびサラ・アン・クラマースキー、そしてこのほかにも多数の支援をニューヨークおよび日本の方々から受けた。

このプロジェクトはニューヨーク市史跡保存委員会の許可の下に、ルーズヴェルト・アイランド・オペレーティング・コーポレーションとの協力で実現された。

オンザテイブル・ニューヨーク、拡張プロジェクト・チーム

アラン・スチュアート・ブレイヴァーマン、会計士、ブレイヴァーマン公認会計士
アン・ブレムナー、英文編集
ピーター・J・ガルディ、構造エンジニア
クロゥディア・ゴールド、プロジェクト・ディレクター、キュレイター
川俣正、プロジェクト・アーティスト
小池美香、日本側プロジェクト・コーディネーター、グラフィック・デザイン、編集
MICA・TV、キャロル・アン・クロナリデスおよびマイケル・オーウェン、ビデオ制作
エリザベス・オドネル、建築家、ニューヨーク側プロジェクト・コーディネーター
ジェイン・グレゴリー・ルービン、弁護士、ランカノウ・コヴナー&ビックフォード
アンドレア・シュワン、プレス担当コンサルタント、クライスバーグ・グループ

基礎構造設営チーム（レギェレー・ビルダースの監督のもとで）

カール・アルストン
メシアス・デオリヴェイラ
ピエール・ラヴェスク
マイク・P・マイケル
ベルナード・スアレス・アルベレス
ビル・グリンリー
J・J・ライマ
ヴィンセント・J・ペリッチオーネ
トーマス・J・バス
ジム・ジョンソン
テイム・マッカーシー
ジェイムス・M・ラグリオーネ

美術構造設置チーム

マセュウ・アボット
ハラルド・ディーン
アレクサンダー・クノックス
工藤圭介
デイヴィッド・マクウィーニー
ネイル・オサリヴァン
チャールズ・シック
マーク・ヴォン・シュレーゲル
エディプ・アジ
アンドリュー・ケネディ
河野勝弘
カーティス・ルイス
エグザヴィエ・ワードロウ・ムハメド
ブラッド・ピーブルス
清水和真
荒木隆久
木村稔
ジョーイ・コティング
デイヴィッド・リンドバーグ
バーナード・ネイロン
フェルナンド・レボロ
トーマス・トウェル

Authors:
Yve-Alain Bois
Elizabeth A. Frosch
Claudia Gould
Kostas Gounis
Tadashi Kawamata

Editors:
Minoru Kimura
Mika Koike
Mitsuyoshi Sakano

Ann Bremner
Naomi Kondo

Supervisor for Design:
Tsuyoshi Aruga

Translations:
Yoko Hayami
Momoyo Kamiya
Zuika Go
Daniel John O'Brien
Kyoko Suzuki

Producer:
Fram Kitagawa

Publishers:

Gendaikikakushitsu Publishers
2-2-5 Sarugaku-cho, Koshin Bldg. 302,
Chiyoda-ku, Tokyo 101 Japan
phone 03.3293.9539, fax 03.3293.2735

on the table, inc.
249 West 11th Street 4W,
New York, New York 10014 U.S.A.
phone 212.924.2104, fax 212.633.9685

June 1993

Printing:
Artecs Hakushindo

Distributed by
Princeton Architectural Press
37 East 7th Street,
New York, New York 10003 U.S.A.
phone 212.995.9620, fax 212.995.9454

Partial funding for this publication has been provided by: The Japan-United States Friendship Commission, Art Front Gallery, Kodama Gallery, and on the table, Tokyo.

Printed in Japan

ISBN 0-9636372-0-7

Kawamata Project on Roosevelt Island

Claudia Gould

Gendaikikakushitsu Publishers

on the table, inc.

Contents

目次

Kawamata Project on Roosevelt Island

Claudia Gould

The dictionary defines ''miracle'' as ''an extraordinary event manifesting divine intervention in human affairs; an extremely outstanding or unusual event, thing, or accomplishment.'' For the team members and other individuals involved with the Kawamata Project on Roosevelt Island, this installation was—is—a miracle. Its realization may not be attributable to divine intervention, but in its ''unusualness'' the event that took place in the middle of New York City has come to seem truly miraculous to us.

Story of the Project

The southern tip of Roosevelt Island, the location of the Kawamata installation and the ruins of the former Small Pox Hospital, first attracted my attention as a potential site for artists' projects when, from 1984 to 1986, I worked at P. S. 1 in Long Island City. Coincidentally, it was during this same period that I first met Tadashi Kawamata, who was a resident artist in P. S. 1's International Studio Program. As a commuter traveling daily across the East River, I found myself looking at, and thinking about, Manhattan from the outside. Out of Manhattan, but overwhelmed by Manhattan—even more so by being out of the center—Long Island City and, indeed, all of the venues that surround it exist in relation to the citadel of Manhattan. To anyone who has stared at Manhattan from the highways, airways, or cities that encircle it, Manhattan represents an apex of mystery and power. Like the spires of a medieval cathedral, the skyscrapers of Manhattan dominate the geography of their surroundings and, metaphorically, the imagination of the world.

Viewed from midtown Manhattan across the East River, the Small Pox Hospital ruin rises from the island as an ironic, crumbling counterface to some of the world's most spectacular real estate. The notion of a ruin in view of a great city is more familiar in a European context than in that of the ''new world,'' although in many American cities today abandonment and devastation have created an erosion as destructive as the effects of time or war on older cultures. The Small Pox Hospital is a different kind of ruin—proud and poetic, it is a silent but grand memorial to the social concerns of the era in which it was built. Yet one can read the dark allegory of this romantic ruin in many ways: as a symbol of the disfunctions of disease, city structures, or cultural ideals—a viewer's choice there on an aggressive promontory in the middle of the East River.

Intrigued by this site, I first contacted the Roosevelt Island Operating Corporation (RIOC) in late 1985 and proposed a variety of projects by artists for the island. In June of 1987, I invited Kawamata to propose a project for this building site after viewing *Destroyed Church*, his installation for Documenta 8. Constructed around a church abandoned since the Second World War, *Destroyed Church* possessed the chaotic energy of a tornado—and the stillness of death, its silent aftermath. That quality of silence and death had a direct correlation to the Small Pox Hospital site.

At the time of these initial contacts, RIOC, a governing body, was unaccustomed to reviewing art proposals, and I, too, had an incomplete understanding of the complex issues we would be confronting together. Nonetheless, we slowly moved ahead, establishing the necessary procedures as we went along. By the end of 1987, the Roosevelt Island projects had been reviewed and accepted by a committee of art professionals and island residents. Because no organization was specifically involved in funding or sponsoring these projects, I decided to concentrate on only one of the proposals—Kawamata's. This was how the Kawamata Project on Roosevelt Island came to be. Always working in close collaboration and friendship with Tadashi Kawamata, I would serve as the curator and director of the project, with responsibility for the organization of a sponsoring corporation and fundraising for all components of the project. Mika Koike assumed responsibility for all aspects of development, public awareness, and coordination in Japan and would act as designer of all print materials and as the Japanese editor of the publication we planned to document the project. During this early period and through 1990, Maria del Rio, my friend and former colleague at P. S. 1, assisted and guided the project through the difficult logistics of public art in New York City.

In fall of 1989, the New York City Landmarks Preservation Commission and RIOC stipulated that architectural planning be integrated in all project work in order to safeguard the Small Pox Hospital structure. Architect Elizabeth O'Donnell was hired and became an invaluable member of our team, working with Kawamata to address the interface between the installation and the existing ruin. O'Donnell suggested the addition of structural engineer Peter J. Galdi to work on the armature that would be built as the primary structure. His drawings and engineering reports ensured that Kawamata's installation would neither touch nor otherwise impact the original landmark structure.

Over the next two years, many meetings were held by our team, the Landmarks Commission, and RIOC to work out the unimaginable details of a contract governing work on this unique site. Andrea Schwan, a public relations consultant with The Kreisberg Group in New York, joined our team to negotiate the contract with RIOC, and Andrea, in turn, brought in our last team member, attorney Jane Gregory Rubin. By November of 1991 the contract with RIOC was signed, and we incorporated **on the table/New York** as organizer and sponsor of the project. With Elizabeth O'Donnell as project coordinator and Andrea Schwan as media consultant, we set an official date for the project, September 1992, and arranged for an exhibition of models and photographs associated with the project to be held at The Cooper Union for the Advancement of Science and Art in October of 1992.

The long spiral of planning, negotiating, fundraising, and organizing began to close in August of 1992, when Kawamata's artistic team from Japan and New York began work in and around the primary structure constructed by Regele Builders. At the end of this labyrinth the figurative deconstruction of the site—and the actual construction of the installation—commenced, and another kind of situation began.

Installation and Site

History exists as long as an object is in use; that is so long as form relates to its original function. However when form and function are severed, and only form remains vital, history shifts into the realm of memory. When history ends memory begins.... History comes to be known through the relationship between a collective memory of events, the singularity of place (locus solus)*, and the sign of the place as expressed in form.*

Peter Eisenman

The former Small Pox Hospital, the site of the Kawamata Project on Roosevelt Island, was built by architect James Renwick, Jr. in 1854-56. Having lost its function through transformation and eventual abandonment in the 1950's, the hospital ruin exists now as a memory, but a memory of what? In his introduction to Aldo Rossi's *Architecture of the City* Peter Eisenman writes of *locus solus*, the singularity of place (or, by extension, event), and his comments suggest the knot that binds Kawamata's 1992 installation to Renwick's nineteenth-century sanatorium.

Kawamata's work always has a direct relationship to its site, whether urban corner, park, or island, and this sense of connectedness reflects the artist's basic way of existing in the world. To Kawamata, his projects are organic constructions, which he refers to as *cancers*, shaped by existing conditions—physical characteristics, past and present uses, and less definable qualities of spiritual essence—with few elements predetermined. He infuses each project with awareness and acceptance of that site's particularity, its "singularity of place." In this case, he responded to both the history/memories of the Small Pox Hospital and the present circumstances of the site in New York City.

This island, remote for most inhabitants of the the world's most combustive city, has long been a place of quarantine. Isolated geographically from the rest of New York, the nineteenth-century institutions that occupied the island were themselves defined in terms of various segregating categories. A 1985 essay by Elizabeth Frosch describes Roosevelt (then Blackwell's) Island as "a divided territory with lunatics, paupers and petty thieves at one end and hardened criminals and the infectiously ill at the other."[1] And this is not the first time temporary wooden structures occupied the Small Pox Hospital site. Historian Elizabeth Montgomery notes that prior to the construction of the hospital, patients were cared for in "a pile of poor wooden shanties on the banks of the river."[2]

In 1992, Kawamata's project could be seen by many as a metaphor for the isolation and political quarantining of the AIDS epidemic. Others could understand the project as a metaphor for destruction and indifference to the fate of our poor and the cities where they live; still others could find in the project signs of rebirth and hope in the face of the Golgotha of our contemporary culture.

For Kawamata, however, this was a private piece as much as a vehicle for social and political commentary. Temporality and the dialectic of construction and deconstruction are recurrent issues in his work—a response to the rapid changes, the growth and decay, that take place in so many cities, most notably Tokyo, today. Yet the island as a quiet refuge, a remote place, was equally on his mind while developing this installation. In discussing the Small Pox Hospital ruin and the project he created around it, he described the installation as delicate and gentle, and I suspect he saw his own role as that of a careful guest who did not want to disturb the present calm of the site or violate the memories embedded there. The water that surrounds and isolates the site also played a significant role in the artist's interpretation of the work. To him, the water contributed to the sense of subtle sensuality he hoped to convey even while acknowledging the more tragic aspects of the

site's history. He contrasted the living presence of water with the abandoned shell of the hospital, a metaphor for death or disease, and called his installation "moisture around the ruin," a kind of slight, life-giving condensation from mist or breath. He also referred to the fairy tale of Sleeping Beauty, with the ruin being gently awakened from its long sleep by the "soft contact" of his structure. But unlike the prince on a white horse of the fairy tale, Kawamata awakened the slumberer to a less than perfect world. He wished not only to touch New Yorkers with the poetry of his installation but also to direct their attention to issues such as AIDS, homelessness, and the racial/sexual/religious prejudices that he feels are consuming this world.

Although this installation was Kawamata's largest to date, it was a transitional work. Conceived in the immediate aftermath of his project for Documenta 8, the installation on Roosevelt Island integrated the elegiac grandeur of his large, commissioned works with the provisional fragility of his more-personal works, his guerrilla projects or *Field Work*: small shanty-like structures assembled on urban corners, which look unconstructed, "like accumulated garbage that drifted to the town."[3] Other more recent but commissioned Kawamata works in this vein include the Favela (the Portuguese word for slum) pieces, *Favela in Houston* (1991) and *Favela in Ushimado* (1991), as well as *Sidewalk in Columbus* (1990) and Documenta 9's *People's Garden* (1992). All of these projects involved free-standing, independent installations with direct relationships to the ground where they stood: Houston's high contrast skyscrapers and river, pathways crossing a university campus in Columbus, and, at Documenta 9, small private garden houses in a Kassel park. "The sites where Kawamata has constructed his Favelas have no historical connections with slums. He is more concerned with horizontal space, the expansion of the work in the city, than with vertical time, or history. The outward appearance of the Favela suggests a very primitive form of human dwelling within the city, and Kawamata seems to have become interested in living space and the ways human beings inhabit the urban landscape."[4]

At Roosevelt Island, Kawamata combined sensitivity to historical associations with his more recently developed interest in "the ways human beings inhabit the urban landscape." The latter idea was expressed, in part, through the materials he incorporated into the project. From July to September Kawamata's assistants scoured many New York neighborhoods for scrap wood, which was used in constructing some sections of the installation. Such cycles of use and reuse are essential to Kawamata, both as a reflection of his ideas about urban life and as a way to build a sense of history and memory into his works. He often utilizes materials scavenged from the environs of a particular project or salvaged from past works, and additional lumber for the Roosevelt Island installation, for example, was recycled from *Sidewalk in Columbus*. At the end of the project, part of the lumber was distributed among squatters in New York City, for their use in constructing shelters and living spaces.

Visually, the Kawamata Project on Roosevelt Island reflected the chaos of the city but stood apart from it. Intended to be viewed primarily from afar, the installation occupied the south facade of the ruin, facing downtown Manhattan, and spilled over to the traditional ''front'' and ''back'' facades, facing midtown Manhattan to the west and Long Island City to the east. The selection of these locations redirected the orientation of the remaining hospital edifice, temporarily shifting attention to the main installation area as the perceived ''front'' of the composite structure. The installation addressed not only Roosevelt Island, but Manhattan and the entire metropolis surrounding Manhattan.

From its immediate environs on the island, Kawamata's structure appeared to be imploding, falling in on the viewer, and it was difficult to find a comfortable perspective. When seen from the distance, from Manhattan, Long Island City, or a boat on the water, however, it stood like a figurehead at the prow of a ship. Once ''inside'' the installation other relationships unfolded. One could note obvious connections to a medieval city complete with castle, moat, and small dwellings or shacks. From another perspective one might see analogies to a Hollywood movie set, a temporary building with temporary sets on a rather tenuous site—the perfect architectural folly. One could also identify potential links to an eclectic assortment of historical precedents (Antonio Gaudi's organically baroque architecture, Kurt Schwitters' *merzbilder* and *merzbau*, Robert Rauschenberg's combines) and contemporary parallels (the memory-laden density of Ilya Kabakov's environments, the intricate layering of Rei Kawakubo's designs). Despite the seeming disparity of these references, however, the overriding impression left by Kawamata's construction was of intricate harmony.

Walking tours of the installation conducted three-to-five days a week followed a consistent itinerary. The tour groups entered the site from the north end, where visitors immediately would be struck by the monumentality of the gray castle-like structure clothed in its architectural couture. Layer upon layer of fine wooden lath, all scavenged, hugged and dressed the primary structure, which at times rose to 30 feet in height. The first perspectives resembled those of a cave or a tunnel and induced a disorienting claustrophia as the viewers proceeded under and through the labyrinth constructed adjacent to the building on the south side. As they left this maze, however, the visitors were able to see the open sky over Manhattan and the water of the East River, which counteracted the earlier sense of claustrophobia. Proceeding south along the west side, the groups turned a corner and encountered a surprising vista of Kawamata's city unfolding with countless shanties and walls. Proceeding up into this village, viewers found a more-intimate and less-disorientating perspective from which they were able to comprehend the size and magnitude of the project as a whole. They could look down into the cave or peer at the intricate lace work, look up and see the sheets of plywood overhead, or stand on the far east hill and glimpse the project from a distance. At every viewing point, and there were many, Kawamata and his team had constructed simple wooden benches where visitors could sit, view, and take a rest. From a bench at the far eastern corner of the site they could see how the lace work continued around to the Long Island City side of the Small Pox Hospital. Walking in that direction, away from the starting point, they would end up, eventually, back where they began.

What made this project unique for Kawamata (its large scale, independent effort, and years of negotiations not withstanding) was the unusual visual framework of the piece. The wood scavenged from New York neighborhoods included not only the artist's familiar thin stripes of lath but also colored doors, strip moldings, window frames, and wall segments, some already plastered with old posters, which were woven in and around the rational skeleton to create a flexible skin.

Since only a limited number of visitors could take part in the walking tours, the exhibition at The Cooper Union for the Advancement of Science and Art, on view from October 13 to November 6, was intended to give the general public a closer look at the Roosevelt Island project, in the form of a parallel installation or conceptual recreation. A giant model of the project filled the walls, floor, and ceiling of the Arthur A. Houghton Jr. Gallery with a wooden labyrinth simulating the actual Roosevelt Island installation. All the walls of the gallery were left white, and some of the wood was also painted white, allowing the installation to almost disappear into the gallery space. The fourth wall of the gallery, which is made of glass and overlooks the library at Cooper Union, remained in its original state; to Kawamata the transparent glass served as a reminder of the water of the East River surrounding the island. In the hallway outside the gallery 150 black-and-white photographs depicted the process of the installation at the Small Pox Hospital.

The Kawamata Project on Roosevelt Island concluded on December 1, 1992, and the installation—like the Small Pox Hospital—then passed from history into memory. In an interesting twist on Kawamata's ideas of recycling materials, about half the wood from the project was donated to RIOC for use in efforts to stabilize the Small Pox Hospital ruin, further enmeshing the installation in the continuing identity of the island. Nourished by the singularity of this place, the project itself has become part of the island's *locus solus*, at the Small Pox Hospital site and in the memories of those who saw it.

Acknowledgements

In the seven years this project was in process, numerous individuals and institutions contributed to its development and so share credit for its success. On behalf of Tadashi Kawamata and myself, I would like to begin by thanking **The Roosevelt Island Operating Corporation**; without RIOC's willingness to work with us on a continual basis this project would not have existed. I am most grateful to **Alyce Russo**, Director of Planning and Development, whose tenacity always helped us move forward, and her assistant **Terry Arcarola**, as well as **Barry Chafetz**, Vice President of Operations; **Jerry Lieber**, Director of Engineering Services; counsel **Debra James**, and publicist **Leslie Gottlieb**. **Jean Lerman** inherited the project when she became President of RIOC in 1991; I thank her for not disinheriting us. I would also like to acknowledge the **Department of Public Safety on Roosevelt Island** for watching out for the team and crew's well-being at the site. Several individuals no longer affiliated with RIOC also contributed over the years to our successful cooperation and have our sincere gratitude: **Harvey Harth, Martha Sickles, Maxanne Resnick, Martha Thomas, Lynn Abraham**, and, especially, former President **Rosina K. Abramson**.

At **The New York City Landmarks Preservation Commission** we are extremely fortunate to have worked with **Elizabeth Frosch**, who was enthusiastic about the project from the beginning. Her personal knowledge and interest in this site enlightened us all. I would also like to thank Elizabeth for the essay she contributed to the news sheet-project guide and to this publication. In addition, I would like to thank the other contributors to the catalog, **Yve-Alain Bois**, for his perspective on Kawamata in relation to art and architectural history, and **Kostas Gounis**, for his view of Kawamata's relationship to the city as both outsider and insider.

This publication has been the effort of many individuals most notably from

on the table, Tokyo whom have assumed total responsibility for organizing the book. **Fram Kitagawa** accepted our tight production condition, more importantly he assumed the risk of producing this book in collaboration with his company **Gendaikikakushitsu Publishers**. The visual documentation of the project was the work of many people who visited and worked at the site this past summer; the beautiful and courageous photos taken by **Hisayasu Kashiwagi** and **Andrew Moore** constitute a large portion of this publication. The translations from English to Japanese and Japanese to English have been accomplished with clarity and respect for the originals by **Yoko Hayami** and her group, I would like to thank them for their fine efforts. From her home in Columbus, Ohio, **Ann Bremner** has assumed the responsibility of copy editing all of the English essays; I thank her for taking on this laborious task. This book will assume another life when it is distributed world wide by **Princeton Architectural Press**. Kawamata and I would like to acknowledge with gratitude **Kevin Lippert** and **Ann C. Urban** from Princeton Architectural Press for their personal interest in making this possible.

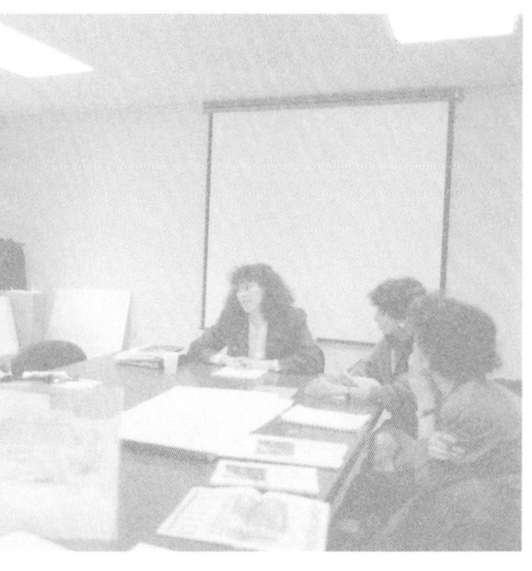

Since 1988, Kawamata and I have planned to have MICA TV produce a video of the project, and the video will be completed as a final phase of the project. In this regard, I would like to thank **MICA TV, Carole Ann Klonarides and Michael Owen**, for their long-term support of the project. In addition, the installation was documented daily by **Takahisa Araki**, an assistant to Kawamata, and I thank him for his dedication and his generosity in making his videotape footage available for various documentary and publicity efforts.

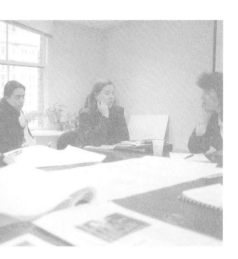

The Cooper Union for the Advancement of Science and Art played an essential role in the project through collaboration on the exhibition at the **Arthur A. Houghton Jr. Gallery**. At Cooper Union, I am grateful to President **John Jay Iselin**, Director of Institutional Relations **Beverly Wilson**, and the entire staff of the President's Office; **Richard Henderson** Associate Dean, Irwin S. Chanin School of Architecture; **Rosemary Wright**, former Assistant Dean at the School of Art; **Camilla Brooks**, Senior Development Officer; **Ingrid Bacci**, Public Affairs Director; **Mindy Lang**, Director, Center for Design and Typography; and **Edip Agi**, Exhibition Assistant.

Technical assistance and countless other contributions, including introducing us to the team at Cooper Union, came from architect and project coordinator **Elizabeth O'Donnell**. Her three-year dedication to this project was invaluable as each day she went far beyond the call of duty. In addition, I would like to thank **Paul Segal Associates** (with whom Elizabeth is associated) for their patient support throughout the project and **Martha Smith** for lending her expertise and assistance to the production of construction drawings.

Elizabeth worked closely with structural engineer **Peter J. Galdi**, whose skill guaranteed a safe and complementary relationship between Kawamata's artistic structure and the existing building. We would also like to mention **Andrews & Clark, Inc.**, who performed a site survey. Fabrication of the primary structure was skillfully accomplished by **Regele Builders**. From Regele, I would like to acknowledge **Joe Regele**, **Heather McGregor** in the office, and the wonderful crew under the brilliant direction of **Jim Raglione**.

In negotiating a contract with RIOC for this project, attorney **Jane Gregory Rubin** employed her special leadership skills with grace and ease. I would also like to thank her for helping us to create ***on the table/New York*** and obtain insurance coverage, which was pivotal for the completion of the project. In this latter regard I should also acknowledge the services of **Michelle Holmes** of **Huntington Block**. **Alan Braverman**, our accountant, also has played a special and crucial role in attending to many details involving the corporation. At Braverman CPA I would also like to thank **Sheleigah Grube**, **Howie Seligman**, and **Betty Tchou**.

Andrea Schwan's expertise is in writing and working with the media, and her direct position with the Kawamata project unfolded in the six months prior to its completion. Her overall competence and ingenuity, however, have guided me for the past two years, and I would especially like to thank her for her continual humor and encouragement on all subjects. From her office at **The Kreisberg Group**, I would like to thank **Victoria Beneitez**. A special acknowledgement also should go to **Luisa Kreisberg** for her willingness to allow activity about this project to be produced and created in her offices; we are very grateful for all her generosity and the numerous meetings the team held in The Kreisberg Group's conference room.

Graphic designer and public art advocate **Melissa Feldman** also contributed significantly to public awareness of the project by including Tadashi Kawamata in a lecture series at The Municipal Art Society.

I was fortunate to have **Brad Peebles** assist me in the office on several occasions, and I would especially like to thank him for the clear and organized research he conducted for this essay.

Naturally, funding for an installation such as this is critical, and the project would have been impossible without the financial assistance and trust we received from many organizations and individuals. Thus I acknowledge with gratitude: **The Japan-United States Friendship Commission, Washington D.C.**; **The Bohen Foundation, New York City and Chester Springs, Pennsylvania**; **The Japan Foundation, New York City**; **The LEF Foundation, St. Helena, California**; **Werner H. and Sarah Ann Kramarsky**; **Frances R. and Thomas H. Dittmer**; **Bill Smith**, and **anonymous donors in New York and Japan**. In addition to his generous financial support, I would like to thank Bill Smith and the staff of the **Bill Smith Studio** for welcoming Mika Koike into their office. Also outstanding in his generosity is **Anthony Slayter-Ralph**, who has assisted with fundraising efforts for **on the table/New York** over the past several months. **Kodama Gallery** in Osaka, Japan has supported the Kawamata Project on Roosevelt Island since 1989 by purchasing all models and drawings about the project produced in Japan. We would also like to acknowledge the cooperation of **Harvestworks inc** in administering grant funding. This publication has been specifically funded in part with the generous support of **The Japan-United States Friendship Commission, Art Front Gallery, Kodama Gallery**, and **on the table, Tokyo**.

Many other individuals, companies, and groups have been ''friends'' to this project over the years, and Kawamata and I would like to thank them for their service, support, advice, and/or personal inspiration. They are: **Cee Brown, Laurence Cabrolie, Bryan Cain, Germano Celant, Wendy Coad, Maria and Daniel del Rio, Jane Dickson, Elizabeth Diller, Tom Finkelpearl, Marge Goldwater, Keith Hanadel, Seth Hauser, Alanna Heiss, Fred Henry, Howard Hirsch, Hoover Treated Wood Products, Machiko Ichihara, Annely Juda Fine Art, Kamitori Gallery, Kaneko Art Gallery, Gallery Kobayashi, Richard Lanier, *Mariner III*, Amerigo Marras, Andrés Mencke, Mimi and Hiromitsu Morimoto, The Municipal Art Society, Shirin Neshat, Anna O'Sullivan, Catherine Owens, Kyong Park, Carol Parkinson, Annie Philbin, Nancy Princenthal, Lauren Krantz Reiter, Johannes Schaub, Linda Shearer, Kiki Smith, Nancy Spector, Jolie Stahl, Galerie Brenda Wallace**, and **Susan Wyatt**.

Finally, if it were not for the remarkable vision of **Tadashi Kawamata**, the extraordinary coordination and dedication of **Mika Koike**, and stalwart nature of both Tadashi and Mika, this project would have been inconceivable.

December 1992

1. Elizabeth A. Frosch, *The Abandoned Structures of Roosevelt Island, New York City and Their Place among the Ruins of America* (New York: Columbia University, 1985), p. 63.

2. Elizabeth V. Trump Montgomery, *A Separated Place* (Middletown, Connecticut: Chris Montgomery, 1988), p.195.

3. Tadashi Kawamata, ''Prologue,'' *Field Work* (Tokyo: on the table, 1991), unpaged.

4. Jun-ichi Shioda, *Urban Environment and Art in Japan/My Home Sweet Home in Ruins* (Tokyo: Setagaya Museum of Art, 1992), pp.119-120.

Jessica Harris <jessaharris@gmail.com>

クト

Fri, Aug 21, 2009 at 6:05 PM

事柄に神性のものが介入し
物事、あるいは業績。」と
ったチーム・メンバー、
レーションはまさに奇跡
だが、我々の目に真の奇
ニューヨーク市のほぼ中
である。

スモールポックス病院の廃
トたちのプロジェクトに
1984年から1986年にか
のPS1に勤務しており、
デント・アーティストで
を渡って通勤しているう
ることに気づいた。マンハッタンから外れていながら、むしろ市街から外れているからこそ、マンハッタンに圧倒され、ロング・アイランド・シティとそれを囲んでいるすべての土地が、マンハッタンという一種の城との関連の上に存在している。ハイウェイや航空路、そして周囲の街からマンハッタンを眺めるすべての人の目に、マンハッタンは謎と力の頂点として映る。中世の大聖堂の尖塔さながら、マンハッタンの摩天楼は周囲の地勢や、さらに言うなら、世界の空想を支配するのである。

マンハッタンの中心部からイースト・リヴァー越しに眺めると、そこに浮かび上がるスモールポックス病院の廃墟は、世界に名だたる壮観な不動産群に立ち向かい、脆くも崩れようとする皮肉な存在として映る。大都市のただ中にある廃墟という概念は、アメリカという「新世界」よりはヨーロッパ的状況にいっそう馴染むと思われるが、現在、多くのアメリカの都市は、放棄と荒廃によって、長い時の流れを経たり、旧文化における戦闘で破壊されたのとそっくり同じように浸蝕されつつある。その中でもスモールポックス病院は一風変わった廃墟である。それは誇りに満ちて、詩的でさえある。何も語ろうとしないが、建築された時代の社会的関心を示す偉大な記念碑であることに違いはない。しかしながらもこの叙情的な廃墟に秘められた隠喩は様々に読み取ることができる。病気や都市構造、もしくは文化的理想が機能不全に終わったことを象徴するものとして、この廃墟はイースト・リヴァーの真ん中に挑戦的に突き出た岬の上にあるが、それが象徴するものの解釈は見る者に委ねられている。

この場所に興味をいだき、1985年に私はルーズヴェルト・アイランド・オペレイティング・コーポレーション（RIOC）と連絡をとり、この島に様々なアーティストによる複数のプロジェクトを展開する提案をした。1987年6月、川俣の第8回ドクメンタ展でのインスタレーション「デストロイド・チャーチ」を見た私は、彼にこの場所にプロジェクトを計画しないかと誘った。第二次世界大戦後、長い間放置されていた教会を取り囲むように組み立てられた「デストロイド・チャーチ」は、竜巻のような混沌としたエネルギーをもちながら、同時に死の静けさ、沈黙の余韻を保っていた。この沈黙と死という特質は、スモールポックス病院の現場とすぐに結びついた。

連絡をとるようになった初めのうちは、管理母体であるRIOCが、芸術的な提案を吟味することに慣れていなかったし、私自身もこれから彼らと共に直面していくことになる複雑な問題点を十分理解していなかった。しかし、我々は徐々にではあるが前進し、必要な手順を整えていった。1987年の末までに、このルーズヴェルト島プロジェクトは美術の専門家と島の住民からなる委員会において検討され、受理されることとなった。ところがこれらの計画に資金援助をしたりスポンサーになろうとする機関が全くなかったため、私はいくつかあるプロポーザルの中から一つだけ選んで、それに集中することにした——それが川俣のものだった。こうしてルーズヴェルト・アイランドにおけるカワマタ・プロジェクトが実現することになったのである。以来、川俣正とは常に協力しあい親友として仕事をしてきたが、このプロジェクトで私はキュレイターとディレクターとしての役割を受け持ち、後援してくれる機関の総括とプロジェクトのあらゆる面での資金調達との責任を持つこととなった。小池美香はプロジェクト進行上の各段階での一般への呼び掛けと日本での調整の責任を引き受け、印刷物すべてのデザインとプロジェクトを詳細に報告する出版物の日本での編集を受け持った。また、計画当初から1990年に至るまで、私の友人でありPS1での同僚でもあったマリア・デル・リオが協力してくれて、ニューヨークのパブリック・アートに関わる難題を切り抜けられるように導いてくれた。

1989年秋、ニューヨーク市史跡保存委員会とRIOCは、スモールポックス病院を保護するため、建築上のプランがプロジェクト作業のすべての段階に組み込まれるべきだと規定を下した。そこで、建築家エリザベス・オドネルが起用され、我々のチームに欠かすことのできないメンバーとして川俣と協力し、インスタレーションと現存する廃墟の間にインターフェイスを組み込んだ。オドネルは、基本的構造体としての骨組建築のために、構造エンジニアのピーター・J・ガルディにも加わってもらうことを提案した。彼の設計図とエンジニアリング・リポートによって、川俣のインスタレーションはこの歴史的建造物の構造に触れることも影響を与えることもないということが保証された。

それからの2年間、我々のチームとニューヨーク市史跡保存委員会及びRIOCは何回となく会合を開き、他に例を見ないこのユニークな場での作業を管理するために信じがたいほどの細部に至る契約書を作り上げた。このRIOCとの契約交渉に、ニューヨークのクライスバーグ・グループの渉外コンサルタント、アンドレア・シュワンが、我々のチームに加わって協力することになった。そして今度はアンドレアが、我々のチームに加わった最後のメンバーである弁護士ジェーン・グレゴリー・ルービンを連れてきた。1991年11月までに、RIOCとの契約が締結され、我々はこのプロジェクトのオーガナイザー兼後援者としてオンザテイブル・ニューヨークを会社組織にするに至ったのである。エリザベス・オドネルをプロジェクト・コーディネーターに、アンドレア・シュワンをプレス・コンサルタントに定めて、プロジェクトの公式日程を1992年9月に設定し、プロジェクトに関する模型と写真の展覧会を1992年10月にクーパー・ユニオンで開催することを決めた。

日本とニューヨーク双方からの川俣のアーティスティック・チームがレギェレー・ビルダースが建てた基本構造のまわりに作業を開始した1992年8月、計画、交渉、資金調達、組織化という一連の長い作業が終わろうとしていた。迷路のすえに、現場の象徴的な解体——そして実際のインスタレーション制作が開始され、いままでとは違った状況が始まっていった。

インスタレーションと場

「歴史は物件が使用されている限り存在する。すなわち、形が元の機能と関連している限りということである。しかし形と機能が分断され、形だけが生き続けると、歴史は記憶の領域に移っていく。歴史が終わるとき、記憶が始まる……。歴史とは、出来事の記憶の寄せ集めと、場所の特異性（locus solus＝唯一の場所）と、形の中に表現された場における記号とのそれぞれの関係を通じて明らかになる。」

ピーター・アイゼンマン

ルーズヴェルト・アイランドにおけるカワマタ・プロジェクトの現場となったかつてのスモールポックス病院は、1854年から56年にかけて建築家ジェイムズ・レンウィック・ジュニアによって建てられた。1950年代に行われた公共施設の移動と実際の建物の遺棄によって当初の機能を失ってしまった今、この病院の廃墟は記憶として存在している。ではそれは一体何の記憶なのだろうか。アルド・ロッシ著『都市の建築』への序文でピーター・アイゼンマンはlocus solus、すなわち場所（拡大解釈すれば、出来事)の特異性について述べている。この言及は川俣の1992年のインスタレーションとレンウィックが建てた19世紀の療養所とをつなぐ結び目を示唆していると言えるであろう。

川俣の作品は都市の街角であろうと公園であろうと島であろうと、その場と直接結びついたもので、この場との関連性こそが川俣というアーティストの世界における基本的な在り方を映し出している。川俣にとってプロジェクトは、あらかじめ予定された要素がほとんどないその場での条件、例えば物理的な特徴や過去と現在における利用のされかた、あまりはっきり定義できない精神的要素などによって形作られる有機的な構造物であり、彼はそれを癌のようだと述べている。川俣は場の特質、「場所の唯一性」に対する意識と認識をそれぞれのプロジェクトに注ぎ込む。このプロジェクトの場合、それはスモールポックス病院の歴史もしくは記憶と、ニューヨークにあるこの現場の現状との両方に向けて感応された。

世界で最も激しやすいこの都市の住人のほとんどにとって、この島は遠隔の地であり、長いこと孤立した場となっていた。地形的にニューヨークの他の部分から離れていたこの島の大部分は、19世紀に建てられた諸施設によって占められているが、これらの諸施設は様々な差別的カテゴリーに分類されていた。1985年にエリザベス・フロッシュがエッセーの中で、ルーズヴェルト島(と、ブラックウェル島)のことを「一方に狂人、貧者、こそ泥が集まり、もう一方には極悪人や感染病患者が集まる、隔絶された土地」[1] だと説明している。さらに、スモールポックス病院の敷地に仮設の木造構築物が建てられたのはこのプロジェクトが初めてのことではない。歴史学者エリザベス・モンゴメリーは、ここに病院が建てられる以前には、患者たちは「川岸にあるみすぼらしい木の堀っ建て小屋で」[2] 手当てを受けていたと記している。

1992年、カワマタ・プロジェクトを孤立とエイズの政治的隔離を象徴するものとして捉える人が多かった。また、このプロジェクトを破壊と現代社会の貧困、人々の住んでいる都市の運命に対する無関心を象徴するものだと理解する人々もいた。あるいは、現代文明がゴルゴダへ向かう中での復活と希望の兆しだと見る人々もいた。

しかし川俣にとっては、このプロジェクトは社会的、政治的論評の媒体となるものであると同時に、極めて個人的な作品でもあった。構築と解体という一時性と弁証性は、彼の作品にくりかえし出てくる主題である。そこでは現在の多くの都市、特に東京で起こっている目まぐるしい変化、成長と衰退というものがくりかえし取り上げられている。しかし、静かな隠れ家、離島としてのこの島のイメージは、インスタレーションを進める一方で常に彼の念頭にあった。スモールポックス病院の廃墟とそれを囲むようにして作り出したプロジェクトについて語った中で、彼は慎重に言葉を選びながら、このインスタレーションを繊細で優美なものとして説明している。おそらくは、その場を妨げたり、そこに埋め込まれた記憶を乱すということはしたくない、という

注意深いよそ者として自分の役割を川俣は考えていたのだと思う。島を取り囲み、現場を孤立させている水流は、彼のこの作品を解釈する上で重要な役割を果した。水流は、今よりもっと悲惨な状態にあったこの地の過去を踏まえながらも、彼が本当に伝えようとした繊細で官能的な感覚に寄与するものであった。彼は水のもつ生き生きとした存在感を死と病の象徴である遺棄された病院の残骸と対照させ、自分のインスタレーションは「廃墟を取り巻く潤い」であり、靄や息から生み出される微かな、生気を与えるような何ものかの凝結だと言う。彼はまた、自分の作る構造物が病院の廃墟に「やさしく触れる」ことによって、廃墟が永い眠りから覚めていくのだとも述べ、眠り姫のおとぎ話を引き合いに出している。しかし、おとぎ話に登場する白馬の王子とはちがって、川俣は眠っていた者を叩き起こして、完璧とはほど遠い世界へと追い立てる。インスタレーション作品の持つ詩情性によってニューヨーカーの心を打つばかりでなく、彼はこの世を食い尽くすエイズ、ホームレス、人種や性や宗教の差別といった問題にも彼らの心を向けようとしたのであろう。

このインスタレーションは、今までででは川俣の作品の中でも最大のものだが、過渡的な作品でもある。第8回ドクメンタ展のためのプロジェクト直後に考え出されたルーズヴェルト島のインスタレーションは、これまでに彼に委ねられた大型な作品に見られる哀調に満ちた壮麗さに、もっと個人的でゲリラ的なプロジェクト或いはフィールド・ワークといった一連の作品の持つ一時性を統合したものである。彼の「フィールド・ワーク」とは「町の中に吹き溜まったゴミが寄り集まった物」[3]とでも言えそうな、構築されていない、街角にしつらえられた小さな堀っ建て小屋のことである。またその他のでも最近の作品に、ファヴェーラ(ポルトガル語でスラムの意)というのがある。「ファヴェーラ・イン・ヒューストン」(1991年)、「ファヴェーラ・イン・牛窓」(1991年)、コロンバスの「サイドウォーク」(1990年)、第9回ドクメンタ展の「ピープルズ・ガーデン」(1992年) などがそれである。これらのプロジェクトはすべて、設置された場と直接の関係をもちながらもフリースタンディングな独自のインスタレーションである。ヒューストンの摩天楼と川がおりなす対比、コロンバスの大学のキャンパスを横切る通路、そして第9回ドクメンタ展に見られるカッセルの公園の小さいプライベート・ガーデン・ハウス群……。「設置場所にもファヴェーラを指示するような歴史的事実は付着していない。特定の場所に関わるプロジェクトにおいて、その場所の歴史性、言い換えれば垂直な時間性が問題にされていたとすれば、ここではむしろ、都市の中でのある広がり、水平的な空間性とでもいうべきものに関心が移っているようでもある。ファヴェーラの外形が模されるのはそれが都市における人間の居住の最も原初的な形態を伝えているからである。都市風景の中での居住、人間の暮らしに関心が注がれ始めたように思う。」[4]

ルーズヴェルト島において、川俣は自らの歴史に対する感性を、最近特に興味を抱くようになった「都市の風景の中で人がいかに住まうか」というテーマと結びつけた。このより新しい主題は、彼がこのプロジェクトに組み込んだ材料を通して部分的に表現されている。7月から9月にかけて、川俣のアシスタントたちがニューヨークの近隣を廃材を求めて走り回った。この廃材は、今回のインスタレーションの様々な部分に使われている。こうした利用・再利用のサイクルは川俣にとっては欠くことのできない本質的要素であり、都市生活についての彼の考えを写し出すものであると同時に、歴史と記憶の感覚を作品の中にとり入れる手段でもある。彼はよく特定のプロジェクト現場周辺から集めた廃品を用いたり、過去の作品の材料を活用する。例えば、ルーズヴェルト島のインスタレーションに後から追加した木材の中には、コロンバスの「サイドウォーク」の時のものも含まれている。また、このプロジェクトの終りに建材の一部はニューヨーク市の不法居住者たちに配分され、彼らの住居を設営するのに使われた。

視覚的には、このルーズヴェルト・アイランドにおけるカワマタ・プロジェクトは都市のカオスを反映したものであるが、位置的にはそれから分離されている。遠くから見られることを配慮して、インスタレーションはマンハッタンのダウンタウンと向き合うように廃墟の南側ファサードを占め、そこから昔のままの「正面」と「背面」のファサードにまで広がり、西にマンハッタンの市街地を見て、東はロング・アイランド・シティと向かい合うように作られている。こうしたロケーションを設定したことによって現在残された病院の方位は変更され、構築物に認識上の「正面」を作ることで人々の意識は主要なインスタレーションへ向けられる。インスタレーションはルーズヴェルト島のみならず、マンハッタンやこの島を取り巻く街全体に語りかける。

この島のカワマタ・プロジェクトを直接取り巻く周辺地域からは、川俣の構築物は見る者の上に崩れて落ちてくるかのようで、どこから見ても心地よく眺めることなどとてもできない。しかし、マンハッタン、ロング・アイランド・シティ、川面の船など遠く離れたところから見ると、それは船の舳先についている船首像のようだ。またインスタレーションの「中へ」入ると、今度は別の繋がりが見えてくる。城、濠、小規模な住宅、堀っ建て小屋などから成り立っていた中世の都市と、はっきりした関連性があることがわかるであろう。さらに別の角度から見ると、ハリウッドの映画のセット、脆い敷地に作られたセットの中の仮の建物——単なるばかげた大建築のようだと言えなくもない。また、過去の先例（アントニオ・ガウディの有機的なバロック建築、クルト・シュヴィッタースの「メルツビルダー」と「メルツバウ」、ロバート・ラウシェンバーグのコンバイン・ペインティング）や、同時代のアーティストの特質（イリヤ・カバコフの作品周辺に見られる記憶の密度や川久保玲のデザインのもつ複雑なレイヤリング）など、様々な折衷的なものに合い通じると見ることもできるだろう。これらの引用は一見不つりあいに思われるかもしれないが、いずれにしても川俣の構築物が与える圧倒的な印象は、複雑な調和であった。

ガイド付きでインスタレーション内を歩いて回るツアーが週に3回から5回行われたが、いつも決まった順路で回るようになっていた。ツアーの一行は北の端から敷地内に入り、そこでまず建築的な衣装をまとった灰色の城のような構造体のモニュメンタリティーに心を打たれる。整然と仕上げられた細い板を次々に重ねたものが、基本構造を抱え込むような形で、30フィートもの高さになっているところがある。最初に見たときには、洞穴やトンネルのように見え、建物の南側に近接して建てられたこの迷路の下や中を通って進んでいくうちに、どこにいるかわからないような感覚に陥る。しかしこの迷宮を抜けると、一気にマンハッタンの上空に広がる大空とイースト・リヴァーを見渡すことができる。この眺望は、初めの閉所恐怖症的な感覚と対照的である。そしてさらに西側に沿って南へ進み、角を曲がると、数えきれないほどの小屋と壁の並ぶ川俣の町の意外な展望が目の前に広がる。このヴィレッジの中に入っていくにつれ、先程よりは違和感も、自分の居場所を見失ったりということも次第になくなり、そこからプロジェクト全体の大きさを把握できることに気が付く。洞穴の中を見下ろしたり、複雑なレース細工を覗きこんだり、頭上の合板のシートを見上げたり、丘の東端に立って離れたところからプロジェクト全体を眺めたりすることもできる。ビュー・ポイントはたくさんあるが、どこから見るにしても、見に来た人たちが腰を下ろして眺めたり休んだりできるように、川俣のチームはシンプルな木のベンチをたくさん設置しておいた。現場の東の隅に置かれたベンチからレース細工がスモールポックス病院のロング・アイランド・シティの側まで続いているのがよく見える。出発点から多少距離のあるそちらの方向に歩き続けていくと、最終的には出発点に戻ってくるというしかけである。

川俣にとってこのプロジェクトが他に類を見ないものとなったのは、(作品の規模、孤立無援の努力、堪え難いほど長い交渉の年月)、この作品のもつ視覚的な背景があったからだと言える。ニューヨークの近隣から寄せ集められた木材の中には、川俣がこれまでにもよく使った細い貫板材ばかりでなく、ペイントされたドア、細長い蛇腹、窓枠、あるいはしっくい処理が施されたりその合理的な骨組の内外に古いポスターが貼られたままの壁材などもあった。

ガイド・ツアーに参加できる人数は極限られていたため、クーパー・ユニオンで10月13日から11月6日まで開催された展覧会では、概念的に改造した装置を置いて、一般の人々にもこのルーズヴェルト島でのプロジェクトを身近に見てもらえるように企画された。プロジェクトの巨大な模型がアーサー・A・ヒュートン・ジュニア・ギャラリーの壁・床・天井を埋め尽くし、実際にルーズヴェルト島で行われたインスタレーションに似せた木材の迷路を作り出した。ギャラリーの壁はすべて白いまま、木材の一部も白く塗られて、インスタレーションがギャラリーの空間に吸い込まれるように設置された。ギャラリーの壁のうち一面はガラスで、クーパー・ユニオンの図書館を見下ろすようになっていたが、そこだけは手を付けずそのままにしてあった。川俣にとって、その透明なガラスは島を取り巻くイースト・リヴァーの水を想起させるものだった。ギャラリーの外の廊下には、スモールポックス病院のインスタレーションのプロセスを示す白黒の写真150枚あまりが展示された。

ルーズヴェルト・アイランドのカワマタ・プロジェクトは1992年12月1日に終結し、そのインスタレーションはスモールポックス病院同様、歴史から記憶へと移行した。素材を再利用するという川俣のアイディアをひとひねりして、プロジェクトで使用した木材のおよそ半分はRIOCに寄付され、スモールポックス病院の廃墟を保存するのに使われることになった。こうしてこのインスタレーションは、永続的な島のアイデンティティーに組み込まれていくことになる。この場の持つ特異性に育まれて、プロジェクト自体がスモールポックス病院の敷地においても、また、それを見た人々の記憶の中でも、島における唯一の場所（locus solus）の一つとなったのである。

謝辞

このプロジェクトが進行した7年の間に、数え切れないほど多数の方々が、個人としてまた機関としてこのプロジェクトに寄与し、成功へ向けて支援してくれた。川俣正に代わって、また私自身からも、まずルーズヴェルト・アイランド・オペレーティング・コーポレーション（RIOC）に感謝したい。RIOCの継続的な惜しみない協力がなければ、このプロジェクトは存在していなかったはずである。常に粘り強く我々を助けてくれた開発計画ディレクターのアリス・ルッソー氏には特に感謝している。彼女のアシスタントのテリー・アルカローラ氏、オペレーションの副知事バリー・シャフェッツ氏、エンジニアリング・サービス・ディレクターのジェリー・リーバー氏、顧問のデブラ・ジェームズ氏、広報官レスリー・ゴトリーブ氏にも謝意を表したい。ジーン・ラーマン氏が1991年にRIOCの知事になった時からこのプロジェクトを引き継いで、最後まで我々とつきあってくれたことに感謝したい。また、ルーズヴェルト・アイランド・パブリック・セイフティーの方々は我々のチーム・メンバーが敷地内で安全に作業できるように配慮してくれた。現在はRIOCから離れてしまった方々もまた、長年にわたってこの協業に力をかしてくれた。その中でもハーベイ・ハース氏、マーサ・シックルズ氏、マクサンヌ・レズニック氏、マーサ・トーマス氏、リン・アブラハム氏、そして前知事のロジーナ・K・アブラムソン氏に特にここで謝意を表したい。

最初からこのプロジェクトに熱心に取り組んでくれた、ニューヨーク市史跡保存委員会のエリザベス・フロッシュ氏と出会えたことは我々にとって実に幸運なことだった。ルーズヴェルト島についての彼女の個人的な知識と関心は、我々にとって非常に参考になった。また、彼女がプロジェクト紹介の広報誌と本書にエッセーを寄稿してくれたことにも感謝したい。さらに、本書への寄稿者イヴーアラン・ボワ氏とコスタス・グーニス氏にも感謝している。イヴーアラン・ボワ氏は美術と建築史におけるこのカワマタ・プロジェクトの位置付けを、またコスタス・グーニス氏はニューヨーク市の構成員及び部外者にとっての市とカワマタ・プロジェクトの関係についての見解をそれぞれ明らかにしてくれた。

本書は数多くの方々の尽力の賜物であるが、特にオンザテイブル東京が本書をまとめる総括的な責任を担ってくれた。北川フラム氏は、我々の厳しい条件を受け入れてくれたばかりでなく、主宰する現代企画室と共に本書を刊行するためのリスクを負ってくれた。このプロジェクトのヴィジュアルな記録は、この夏現場を訪れたり作業をしたの人々の作品でもあるが、本書に掲載した多くの最も美しく雄々しい写真は、柏木久育氏とアンドリュー・ムーア氏が撮影したものである。速水葉子氏と彼女のグループは、原文に対して明快かつ適切な英訳及び和訳をしてくれた。この大変な作業を成し遂げてくれた彼女たちにも感謝したい。オハイオ州コロンバスの自宅で、すべての英文エッセイ編集という困難な仕事をしてくれたアン・ブレムナー氏にも感謝を述べたい。また、プリンストン・アーキテクチュラル・プレスによって世界中に配給されることとなり本書は新たな生命が与えられることとなったが、川俣と私自身、その実現を促してくれた同プレスのケヴィン・リッパートとアン・C・アーバンの両氏に感謝を述べたい。

1988年から、川俣と私はMICA・TVにこのプロジェクトのビデオ製作を依頼する計画をたてたが、そのビデオはこのプロジェクトの最終段階として完成される。MICA・TVのキャロル・アン・クロナリデス氏とマイケル・オーウェン氏が長期にわたってこのプロジェクトをサポートしてくれたことに感謝している。また、このインスタレーションは、川俣のアシスタントの一人だった荒木隆久氏が毎日カメラに収めたが、様々なドキュメンタリーや発行物にビデオ・フィルムを快く使わせてくれた。心から謝意を表したい。

クーパー・ユニオンは、アーサー・A・ヒュートン・ジュニア・ギャラリーでの展覧会に協力するという形でこのプロジェクトに欠くことのできない役割を果たしてくれた。クーパー・ユニオン理事長ジョン・ジェイ・イズリン氏、機関調整部長のビバリー・ウィルソン氏、そして理事長室スタッフ、アーウィン・S・チャニン建築学校の副学部長リチャード・ヘンダーソン氏、美術学校の前副学部長ローズマリー・ライト氏、主席開発官カミーラ・ブルックス氏、公事担当部長イングリッド・バッチィ氏、デザイン及びタイポグラフィー・センターのディレクターのミンディ・ラング氏、展覧会補佐のエディプ・アジ氏――にも謝意を表したい。

技術上の協力だけにとどまらず、我々をクーパー・ユニオンに紹介するなど数え上げたらきりがないほどの協力をしてくれたのが建築家でありこのプロジェクトのコーディネーター、エリザベス・オドネル氏だった。彼女の3年にわたるこのプロジェクトへの献身的な協力は価値を推し量ることのできない貴重なものであり、彼女は毎日、責務の範囲を越えた協力を惜しまなかった。また、エリザベスが共同運営するポール・シーガル・アソシエイツも、プロジェクトの初めから終りまで根気強く協力してくれて、その設計図制作担当者マーサ・スミス氏は、専門的な意見を聞かせてくれた。

エリザベスは構造エンジニアのピーター・J・ガルディ氏と親しかった。ピーターの卓越した技術によって、川俣の美術的な構造と現存する建物との関係は、安全で相補的なものとなった。用地の測量検分はアンドリュース・アンド・クラーク社が担当した。第一次構造はレギェレー・ビルダーズがその素晴らしい技巧で製作にあたった。特にジョー・レギェレー氏とヘザー・マグレガー氏、それにジム・ラグリオーネ氏の素晴らしい指揮の下、目覚ましい活躍をしたクルーにここで感謝の意を表したい。

このプロジェクトのためにRIOCと契約についての交渉をするうえで、弁護士ジェイン・グレゴリー・ルービン氏はその才能によって特殊なリーダーシップを優雅に、しかも悠々と発揮してくれた。彼女はまた、我々がオンザテイブル・ニューヨークを作り、プロジェクトに保険をかけるのにも力を貸してくれた。これこそ、プロジェクト完成のための中枢となるものだった。この件に関しては、ハンティングトン・ブロックのミシェル・ホームズ氏の尽力にも触れておきたい。我々の会計士アラン・ブレイヴァーマン氏はその会社を巻き込んでプロジェクトのあらゆる段階に参加し、特別かつ重大な役割を務めてくれた。そのブレイヴァーマンCPA社のシェレイア・グルーブ氏、ハウィー・セリグマン氏、ベティー・チョウ氏にも感謝したい。

アンドレア・シュワン氏の専門はプレスメディアで記事を書く仕事だが、カワマタ・プロジェクトに関しての彼女の役割はその完成の6か月前に拡張された。彼女の包括的な能力と才能は、この2年の間私を導いてくれた。彼女の巧まざるユーモアと、あらゆる問題についての励ましに特に感謝したい。クライスバーグ・グループの彼女のオフィスにいるヴィクトリア・ベネイテス氏にも感謝している。また、このプロジェクトの製作・創造に関する活動のために快くオフィスを提供してくれたルイーザ・クライスバーグ氏にも特に謝意を表さないわけにいかない。彼女の寛大な御好意で、我々のチームがクライスバーグ・グループの会議室で何度も会合を開くことができた。我々一同、心から感謝している。

グラフィック・デザイナーでパブリック・アートを支援するメリッサ・フェルドマン氏は市営美術協会でのレクチャー・シリーズに川俣正を招いて、より広範囲の人々の注目をこのプロジェクトに向けてくれた。

ブラッド・ピープルズ氏が様々な状況下にあってオフィスで私を助けてくれたことも幸運だった。このエッセーを書くために、明確に編成されたリサーチをしてくれたことに対して、特に感謝している。

このようなインスタレーションに出資することは当然ながらリスクを伴うが、我々が今回、多くの法人や個人から受けた経済的支援や信用なくしては、プロジェクトは達成不可能であった。そこで私は、その法人や個人の方々の名を感謝の心を込めてここに記しておきたい。ワシントンDCの日米友好基金、ニューヨーク市とペンシルヴァニア州チェスタースプリングスのボーエン・ファンデーション、国際交流基金ニューヨーク支局、カリフォルニア州セント・ヘレナのLEFファンデーション、ウェルナー・Hおよびサラ・アン・クラマースキイ夫妻、フランシス・RおよびトーマスH・ディトマー夫妻、ビル・スミス氏、そしてニューヨークおよび日本の数々の協力者たち。ビル・スミス氏の寛大な経済的援助と、小池美香を暖かく迎え入れてくれたビル・スミス・スタジオのスタッフの方々にも重ねて感謝したい。また、アントニー・スレイター・ラルフ氏も数か月にわたってオンザテイブル・ニューヨークのための資金調達に力を尽してくれた。彼の卓越した寛容さを特に記しておきたい。大阪の児玉画廊は1989年以来、このプロジェクトに関して日本で製作された模型とデッサンをすべて購入することによって、ルーズヴェルト島の川俣プロジェクトを支援してくれた。ハーベストワークス社は助成金管理に協力してくれた。また、本書は日米友好基金、アート・フロント・ギャラリー、児玉画廊そしてオンザテイブル東京により出資された。

ほかにも数多くの個人、法人、グループが長年にわたってこのプロジェクトの「友人」となってくれた。川俣と私にとって彼らの尽力・支援・忠告、さらに彼らが個人的に与えてくれたインスピレーションはこの上なく有り難いものだった。その方々は、シー・ブラウン、ローランス・カブロリエ、ブライアン・ケイン、ジェルマーノ・チェラント、ウェンディ・コード、マリアおよびダニエル・デル・リオ、ジェイン・ディクソン、エリザベス・ディラー、トム・フィンケルパール、マージ・ゴールドウォーター、キース・ハナデル、セス・ホーザー、アラナ・ヘイス、フレッド・ヘンリー、ハワード・ヒルシュ、フーバー・トリーテッド・ウッド・プロダクツ、市原真知子、アネリー・ジューダ・ファイン・アート、上通ギャラリー、かねこ・あーとギャラリー、コバヤシ画廊、リチャード・レニエ、マリナーIII、アメリゴ・マラス、アンドレス・メンケ、ミミとヒロミツ・モリモト、市立芸術協会、シリン・ネシャット、アナ・オサリバン、キャサリン・オーウェンズ、キヨン・パーク、キャロル・パーキンソン、アニー・フィルビン、ナンシー・プリンセンタール、ローレン・クランツ・ライター、ヨハネス・ショウブ、リンダ・シアラー、キキ・スミス、ナンシー・スペクター、ジョリー・スタール、ギャラリー・ブレンダ・ウォレス、スーザン・ワイアットの各氏である。

このプロジェクトの実現は、川俣正の素晴らしい視点と小池美香の特筆すべきコーディネーションと献身、さらに両者の固い信念がなければ、とても考えられないものだったことを最後に記しておきたい。

1992年　12月

1. エリザベス・A・フロッシュ「ルーズベルト島の廃棄された構造建築物、ニューヨーク市とアメリカの廃墟の中のその位置」コロンビア大学（ニューヨーク、1985年）、p.63

2. エリザベス・V・トランプ・モンゴメリー「隔離された場所」クリス・モンゴメリー（コネチカット州ミドルタウン、1988年）、p.195

3. 川俣正「プロローグ」フィールド・ワーク（オンザテイブル・東京、1991年）、ページ付なし

4. 塩田純一「都市と現代美術、廃墟としてのわが家」世田谷美術館（東京、1992年）、p.119－120（但し和文オリジナルはp.9）

The Small Pox Hospital, Roosevelt Island, New York City

Elizabeth A. Frosch

The Past

On March 23, 1976 the New York City Landmarks Preservation Commission designated the Small Pox Hospital, located at the southern tip of Roosevelt Island, New York, an individual New York City Landmark. Among the qualities for which it was recognized was its picturesqueness as a romantic ruin. However, this majestic gothic-style building with its crenelated roof and its bucolic setting was not designed as a ruin but as the first major hospital in the United States dedicated to the care of victims of smallpox.

In 1828 the city of New York purchased Roosevelt Island, then called Blackwell's Island, from the Blackwell family for $50,000. Within the same year the city began to construct a new penitentiary on the island, and over the next thirty years the city moved all of its charitable and correctional institutions from Manhattan Island to Blackwell's Island. These institutions consisted of the Penitentiary, the Alms-House, the Lunatic Asylum, the Work-House, the Small Pox Hospital, the Charity Hospital, and Strecker Memorial Laboratory. The architects commissioned to design these buildings were some of the most illustrious in nineteenth-century America: Minard LaFevre, A. J. Davis, and James Renwick, Jr.

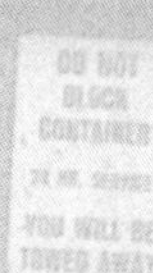

Why was this island chosen as a site for these facilities? Blackwell's Island was originally not as scenic a location as it is today. The island was once known as Hog Island, either for the large number of wild hogs found on the island or for some early settlers' practice of raising hogs there. The island itself can be found on an early map of the area, dated circa 1639, which indicates that it was owned by a Dutchman named Jan Claesson Alteras, who farmed it for the West India Company. In 1665 the island was taken over by the English and given to a Captain John Manning for the procurement of stone.

The ability to quarry gneiss, a good building stone, from the island gives us our first clue as to why the city picked this location for so many institutions. Here was a place where building materials were easily available and cheap. Furthermore, since putting criminals to work at hard labor — for example, in a stone quarry — was an acceptable practice in the nineteenth century, labor was also readily available. In September of 1828 the new penitentiary was completed on the island. From that time until the completion of the Strecker Memorial Laboratory in 1892, all of the institutional buildings on the island were constructed of local stone.

An additional reason to pick this site was its separateness from Manhattan Island. At the time, the people to be housed in the institutions on the island were seen as "undesirable," and that was enough to make the city want to keep them away from the mainstream of city life. Furthermore, the facilities at Bellevue Hospital, which housed a number of these institutions, were overcrowded and could not physically handle the growth in the resident population. Blackwell's Island, by contrast, offered ample space for new construction.

By 1850 the Penitentiary, the Lunatic Asylum, and the Penitentiary Hospital had been erected on the island. In this year James Renwick, Jr. became the architect for the Board of Governors of Charities and Correction of New York City. He would hold this position for the next twenty years.

Noted for his ability to blend traditional design motifs with new technological concepts, James Renwick, Jr. (1818-1895) was one of the most prolific architects of public buildings in nineteenth-century America. He is best known for Grace Church (1843-1846) and St. Patrick's Cathedral (1858-1879) in New York City; the Smithsonian Institution (1847-1855) and the original Corcoran Gallery (1859-1879) in Washington D.C.; and Vassar College (1863-1864) in Poughkeepsie, New York. Renwick also designed a variety of lesser-known public edifices such as hotels and charitable and correctional institutions in and around the New York City metropolitan area. During the twenty years he worked as the architect for the Board of Governors of Charities and Correction he designed eleven structures including three on Roosevelt Island: the Work-House (1850), the Small Pox Hospital (1854-56), and the Charity Hospital (1858-1861).

Renwick chose to design the Small Pox Hospital in the Norman Style, which not only was compatible with the picturesque location of the building at the southern tip of the island but also allowed for castellated detailing in the roof design, repeating a motif previously used in the design of the Penitentiary and the Lunatic Asylum on the island. This use of a common design element gave the complex of institutional facilities the appearance of a unit in function and form. However, the site for the Small Pox Hospital had been deliberately located away from the other island institutions, even separated by a wall, as isolation was necessary to prevent an epidemic.

The Board of Health took control of the Small Pox Hospital from the Commission of Charities and Correction in 1875, but the Commission regained control of the hospital building in 1886. At that time, facilities for the care of small pox patients were relocated to a new building on North Brother's Island, New York, and the former Small Pox Hospital building was converted into The Home for Nurses of the Maternity and Charity Hospital Training School, which was then housed in the Charity Hospital building. (Later known as City Hospital, the Renwick-designed Charity Hospital is the large building north of the Small Pox Hospital.) Two wings were added to the original Small Pox Hospital building, a southwest wing by the architectural firm of York and Sawyer in 1903-04, and a northwest wing by the architectural firm of Renwick, Aspinwall and Owen in 1904-05. Both wings are constructed of the island stone, and their design is very similar to the Norman castellated motif of the initial building. However, although compatible in design, they are bland in comparison to Renwick's original building.

Blackwell's Island continued to be a major location for New York City charitable and correctional institutions into the twentieth century, with health-care facilities assuming an increasingly prominent role after the turn of the century. Over time, however, changing attitudes and practical needs made the isolation of the island a less-appealing characteristic. The completion of the Queensboro Bridge in 1909 made access to the island somewhat more convenient. An elevator on the bridge gave access to the island, which previously could be reached only by ferry boat, but other transportation links were slow to develop.

By 1934 three more hospitals had been erected on the island, which New York City had renamed Welfare Island in 1921. But, also by the 1930's, complaints were being made about the poor conditions within the older buildings. The Parks Commissioner at the time, Robert Moses, was instructed to begin plans to turn part of the island into a public park. These plans were met with much resentment and opposition by the medical community, which felt that the money for planning the park would be better used in solving the problems of providing housing and care for the chronic sick who were currently living on the island. The medical community won this dispute. In December of 1935 plans were approved for the demolition of the penitentiary building and its replacement with a large health center for the chronically ill, Welfare Hospital for Chronic Disease, now called Goldwater Memorial Hospital.

New institutions, such as Goldwater Memorial Hospital, had almost completely taken over the sites of the nineteenth-century ones by the 1950's. Many institutions housed in the historic structures sought alternative locations, leaving most of the island's historic structures vacant. The City Hospital (formerly Charity Hospital) was relocated to the Borough of Queens in the 1950's. With this relocation, the Small Pox Hospital building, as well as the original Charity Hospital building, was abandoned.

In 1970, the New York State Urban Development Corporation hired Giorgio Cavaglieri, F.A.I.A., to structurally stabilize the remaining seven historic structures on the island. Some of the structures were extensively restored and rehabilitated: the Lighthouse, the Chapel of the Good Shepherd, which originally served the Alms-House, and the original Blackwell House. Other structures, such as the Small Pox Hospital building, were stabilized, their future pending construction bids for their reuse. These potential reuse proposals relied on the planned construction of a subway line to connect Manhattan Island to Welfare Island. This subway connection was only recently completed, and the Small Pox Hospital building has stood untouched since 1970, deteriorating into its current dilapidated and threatened condition.

The Present

The southern tip of the island houses three of the early nineteenth-century institutional structures, including the Small Pox Hospital. This area has been fenced off from the rest of the island for a number of years, with entrance possible only by permission of the Roosevelt Island Operating Corporation. Over the years a number of plans have been put forth for reusing the buildings, restabilizing them and creating a park around them, and demolishing them and constructing apartment buildings on the site. None of these plans has been put into effect. Ironically, the isolation that once made the island such an appealing site for charitable and correctional institutions has hampered later development significantly. Until recently, reaching the island remained quite inconvenient, with only limited access routes via car or tramway. However, now that the subway connection is completed, it is probable plans will go forward that affect these historic structures.

The Future

Some believe that the Small Pox Hospital should be demolished; others feel it should be reused or restabilized as a ruin. As it is now, it stands as a reminder of Roosevelt Island's history. As Norval White and Elliot Willensky wrote in their *AIA Guide to New York City* (New York, 1978):

Years of disuse and exposure to the elements have made this [The Small Pox Hospital] into a natural ''Gothik'' ruin. Its official landmark designation further encourages such a role. In quoting architectural historian Paul Zucker on the subject of ruins: ''... an expression of an eerie romantic mood... a palpable documentation of a period in the past... something which recalls a specific concept of architectural space and proportion.'' The designation suggests the structure possesses all of these. It does.

Elizabeth A. Frosch is Associate for Special Permits with the New York City Landmarks Preservation Commission.

ニューヨーク、ルーズヴェルト・アイランド、スモールポックス・ホスピタル

エリザベス・A・フロッシュ

過去

1976年3月23日、ニューヨーク市史跡保存委員会はニューヨークのルーズヴェルト島最南端にあるスモールポックス（天然痘）病院を単独で市の史跡に指定した。評価の対象となった特質の一つとして、そのロマンティックな廃墟の絵画的な美しさがあげられていた。とはいえ、屋根に狭間飾りを頂く堂々たるゴシック様式のこの建物と牧歌的な背景は、廃墟として意図されたわけではなく、天然痘罹病者の治療のための合衆国初の専門病院として設計されたものだった。

1828年にニューヨーク市は、当時ブラックウェルズ島と呼ばれていたルーズヴェルト島を5万ドルでブラックウェルズ一族から購入した。同じ年、市はこの島に新しい刑務所の建設を開始し、その後の30年間に慈善および更生関連のすべての公共機関をマンハッタンからルーズヴェルト島に移転させた。刑務所、救貧院、精神病院、感化院、スモールポックス病院、慈善病院、並びにストレッカー記念研究所などがそれである。そしてこれらの建築物の設計は19世紀アメリカの高名な建築家たち――ミナード・ラファーブル、A・J・デイヴィス、そしてジェイムズ・レンウィック・ジュニア――に依頼された。

なぜこの島がこうした施設の建設地として選ばれたのであろうか。元来ブラックウェルズ島は現在のような美しい風景の土地ではなかった。かつてはホグ・アイランド（豚の島）と呼ばれていたが、それは野生の豚が多数いたためか、あるいは一部の初期定住者がここで豚を飼育していたためであるらしい。島そのものは1639年頃からこの地域の地図に掲載されており、西インド会社のために農耕を請け負っていたオランダ人、ヤーン・クラーセン・オルトラスの所有地であったことが記されている。1665年に島はイギリス人の支配下に移り、石材の採掘のためにキャプテン・ジョン・マニングに委ねられた。

これほど多数の施設を設置する場所としてニューヨーク市がこの島を選んだ第一の理由は、優れた建築用石材となる片麻岩を切り出すことができたことであろう。すなわ

ちここは建築用材が容易に安価に手に入る場所であった。加えて、犯罪者を重労働に就労させること ──例えば石切り仕切り場で働かせること ──は、19世紀においては容認され得る慣習であったため、労働力もまたいつでも確保できた。1828年9月に、島に新しい刑務所が建設された。以来、1892年にストレッカー記念研究所が完成するまで、島の公的機関の建造物はすべて地元産出の石材で作られることになった。

市がこの土地を選択したもう一つの理由として、マンハッタン島から完全に隔絶していたことが挙げられる。（長い間、島に渡るには船を利用するしかなかった。）その頃、島の施設に収容されていたのは「好ましからざる者」と見なされていた人々であり、それだけで市が彼らを市民生活の表舞台から締め出したいと考えるには十分な理由であった。その上、こうした諸々の施設のうちの幾つかを構内に置いていたベルヴュー病院では、収容人数が過密状態となったため、それ以上の増加に物理的に対応できなくなっていた。対照的に、ブラックウェルズ島には新しい建設工事用に充分な土地の余裕があった。

こうして1850年までに刑務所、精神病院、そして刑務所病院が島に建てられた。この年、ジェイムズ・レンウィック・ジュニアはニューヨーク市慈善更生評議会指定の建築家となり、以後20年間この地位にとどまることになる。

ジェイムズ・レンウィック・ジュニア（1818―1879）は伝統的なデザイン・モチーフを新しい技術概念に融合させる能力に抜きんでており、19世紀アメリカの公共建築物を最も数多く設計した建築家の一人であった。彼の作品としてはニューヨーク市のグレース協会（1843―1846）とセント・パトリック教会（1858―1879）、ワシントンDCのスミソニアン協会（1847―1855）、初めのコーコラン・ギャラリー（1859―1879）、ニューヨーク州ポーキープシィにあるバサール大学などが大変よく知られている。レンウィックはこの他にもニューヨーク都市圏内外に、さほど有名ではないが様々なホテルや、慈善施設、更生施設といった公共の大型建築物なども設計している。慈善更生評議会指定の建築家の地位にあった20年間に、彼はルーズヴェルト島の感化院（1858―1861）、スモールポックス病院（1854―1856）、そして慈善病院（1858―1861）の3施設を含む建物11施設の設計をしている。

レンウィックはスモールポックス病院の設計にノルマン様式を採用した。それは島の南端のこの建物の絵画的なロケーションにふさわしいばかりでなく、この島に建ててきた刑務所や精神病院の設計に用いたのと同じモチーフを繰り返すことによって、屋根のデザインに城郭風ディテールの使用が可能になり、さらに、この共通のデザイン要素を使用することによって、複合施設としての機能と形態の統一性をもたらすことができた。但し、スモールポックス病院の敷地は意図的に島の他の施設とは離れた場所に設けられ、さらに壁で遮られた。伝染病を防止するためには隔離する必要があったためである。

1875年に保健局が慈善更生委員会からスモールポックス病院の管理権を引き継いだが、同委員会は1886年にその建物の管理権を再び取り戻している。その時、天然痘患者の療養施設はニューヨーク州ノース・ブラザース島の新しい建物に移された。そして、スモールポックス病院の建物は、当時慈善病院の建物内にあった慈善病院看護婦養成学校の宿舎として使用されることになった。(スモールポックス病院のすぐ北側にある大きな建物が、後に私立病院となったレンウィック設計の慈善病院である。)元のスモールポックス病院には二つの翼棟が増築された。南翼棟はヨーク・アンド・ソーヤー建築事務所が1903年から4年に掛けて、北の翼棟はレンウィック・アスピンウォール・アンド・オーウェン建築事務所が1904年から5年にかけ建築したものである。両翼棟とも島の石材で建造され、デザインは元の建物のノルマン風の城郭風モチーフと酷似したものとなっている。しかし増築した翼棟はデザインの継承はしているものの、レンウィック設計のオリジナルと比較すると面白みに欠けている。

今世紀になって衛生管理関係の施設がますます重要な役割を果たすようになったこともあり、ブラックウェルズ島は20世紀に入ってもなお、ニューヨーク市の慈善施設と更生施設の主要な地として存在し続けた。しかし時の経過と共に人々の考え方にも変化が生じ、また現実的な必要性にも迫られ、この島が孤立していることは格別都合のよい条件ではなくなってきた。1909年のクィーンズボロー・ブリッジの完成で、島へ渡るのは幾分か便利になった。この橋にあるエレベーターが以前はフェリーボートでしか辿り着けなかった島へ渡る足の便となったのだが、その他の交通手段の開発ははかばかしく進展しなかった。

1921年にニューヨーク市によりウェルフェア・アイランド(福祉の島)と名称を変えたこの島には、1934年までにさらに3つの病院が立てられた。しかし、1930年代には古くからある建物の内部の貧弱な状況に対して苦情が寄せられるようになった。当時の公園管理長官ロバート・モーゼスは島の一部を一般大衆向きの公園に造り替える計画を立案するように指示を受けた。しかしながらこの計画は医療関係者から猛烈な反発と反対を向けられることになる。医療関係者は公園開発資金は当時島で暮らしていた慢性病療養者に対する住居と治療を提供するためにこそ利用すべきだと考えた。そして医療関係者がこの紛争には勝利を治め、現在ゴールドウォーター記念病院と呼ばれる大型保険センター、「慢性病のためのウェルフェア病院」の建設が認可された。

SMALL-POX HOSPITAL.

1950年代までには、ゴールドウォーター記念病院をはじめとする新しい施設が19世紀の施設の敷地をほぼ完全に受け継ぐ形となった。歴史ある建物を占有していた多数の公的機関は別の場所を求めて移転し、島のほとんどの歴史的建造物は空き家のまま残された。私立病院（元の慈善病院）は1950年代にクィーンズ地区へ移転した。この移転に伴って、スモールポックス病院の建物は元の慈善病院の建物共々放置されることとなる。

MALE CONVICTS. PENITENTIARY BLACKWELL'S ISLAND.

FEMALE CONVICTS. PENITENTIARY BLACKWELL'S ISLAND.

1970年にニューヨーク州都市開発公団は島に残る７棟の歴史的建造物の構造軀体に安全処理を施すため、アメリカ建築学会特別会員ジョルジオ・キャヴァリエリを起用した。幾つかの建物——灯台、当初は救急貧窮院の為に設けられていた「良き羊飼いの礼拝堂」、そして元ブラックウェルズ屋敷——については徹底的な復元修理が行われた。スモールポックス病院を初めとするその他の建築物に対しても安全処理は施行されたが、その将来に関しては再利用を目的とした個々の建築工事の入札いかんにかかっていた。再利用計画案が実現される可能性はマンハッタン島とブラックウェルズ島を結ぶ地下鉄の建設計画次第であったが、この地下鉄路線はごく最近開通したばかりである。その間、スモールポックス病院は1970年以来手付かずのまま放置され、現在のように老朽化し崩壊の危機にさらされるまで荒廃するに至った。

現在

島の南端には19世紀初期の公的機関３施設の建造物があり、スモールポックス病院もその一つである。長年の間この地区は柵によって島の他の部分から遮断された状態で、ルーズヴェルト・アイランド・オペレーティング・コーポレーションの許可によってのみ立ち入ることが可能であった。ここ何年の間にも、幾つもの計画が提案されてきた。建物の再利用計画の他、保存して周囲に公園を造るもの、また取り壊して跡地にアパートを建てるものなどの案が上がった。だが、そのどれもが実行に移されないままだった。皮肉なことに、昔は慈善や更生目的の公的機関にとって絶好の立地条件とされたこの島の孤立そのものがその後の発展を著しく妨げたのであった。ごく最近まで島にわたるのには、車かロープウェイを使う限られたルートしかなく、非常に不便であった。しかし、地下鉄路線が完成した今日では、こうした歴史的建造物を活用する計画も進展を見ることであろう。

将来

ある人達はスモールポックス病院は取り壊すべきだと主張し、またある人たちは再利用すべきだ、或いは廃墟として保存するべきだと主張する。いまのところこの建物はルーズヴェルト島の歴史の証人として存在している。ノーヴァル・ホワイトとエリオット・ウィレンスキーは、著書『アメリカ建築学会編ニューヨーク案内』（ニューヨーク、1978）に次のように書いている。

「長年無人のまま風雨に晒され、ここ（スモールポックス病院）は自然にできた「ゴシック様式」の廃墟となった。公式に史跡に指定されたことで、この役割に一層の意義が認められるであろう。建築史家ポール・ズッカー氏の廃墟に関する項を引用すれば「謎めいたロマンティックな雰囲気の表現、過去の一時代に触れられる記録として、建築空間とそのプロポーションの特定コンセプトを呼び起こしてくれるもの」とある。今回の史跡指定はこの建造物がこうしたもの全てを兼ね備えていることをと示している。まさにそのとおりである。」

［エリザベス・A・フロッシュは、ニューヨーク市史跡保存委員会の特別許可担当官である。］

PEPSI

Keep Out: Construction Work

Yve-Alain Bois

Kawamata's project on Roosevelt Island is with Richard Serra's *Rotary Arc*, which sprawled for seven years at the Canal Street exit of Holland Tunnel, one of the two best public sculptures ever displayed in New York City. I will presently return to my odd association of those two works, one a heavy, opaque, curvilinear wall, the other looking elegant and fragile, at times almost calligraphic (that is, when seen from Manhattan). But I would like to state, at the outset, that I regard Kawamata's overall production as a major statement in the realm of public sculpture. If I had now the energy, time, and will to write a history of this art in the twentieth century, it would only consist of six chapters (probably following an historical introduction where Rodin's *Balzac* and *Bougeois de Calais* would have to figure prominently): the first on Brancusi's complex at Tîrgu Jiu; the second on Mathias Goeritz's *The Towers of Satellite City* in Mexico City, a terribly underrated "highway sculpture" (as the artist called it); the third on Smithson's sites/non sites (with a few addenda on various earth projects by other artists, although this would be stretching a bit the notion of public art); the fourth on Gordon Matta-Clark's cutouts; the fifth on Richard Serra's site-specific pieces; the sixth on Kawamata's nomadic enterprise.

Let me begin with my Serra/Kawamata comparison. The two works have more in common than it seems (it is not by chance that both immediately prompted in my mind a recollection of Auguste Choisy's brilliant architectural thought), but they also differ considerably. Both are ephemeral works (it was assumed from the start that *Rotary Arc*, unlike the ill-fate *Tilted Arc*, was only going to be temporarily installed). Yet the ephemeralness of Serra's work was contingent, incidental, it was not a part of its structure (in fact, I consider it a sad mistake not to have prolonged its existence ad infinitum). The topic of *Rotary Arc* was the transience of perception, the volatile definition of a simple shape in relationship to its site while it was beheld from various angles and at various speeds. Not so for Kawamata's project: seen by most from afar and frontally, it was made to disappear almost as soon as completed. *Rotary Arc* stood firm like a rock whose identity dissolved with your movement around it; Kawamata's project was, almost from its inception, an evanescent after-image (it was not so much the perception of it as the work itself that was fugacious). Serra's piece was a critique of the gestaltist theory of visuality that still governed minimalism, a phenomenological investigation; Kawamata's an elegy about the capitalist cycle of growth, deterioration, and rehabilitation that plagues the life of our cities. It perfectly translated Baudelaire's Haussmannian poem *To a Passerby* into a tangible language of decay that we can easily read as so many metaphors of the ills of our time in this last decade of the twentieth century.[1]

Note that Kawamata's piece is unnamed. Or rather, like all that he does, it bears only the name of its site. There too lies a fundamental difference from the work of Richard Serra, who has certainly been most articulate on the notion of site-specificity. Think again of *Rotary Arc*: everything was miraculously adjusted to the site, with the cars swirling around it when popping out from Holland Tunnel and the passersby venturing on the gravel that covers the large no-man's land where the sculpture stood, or hovering above it on the footbridge that connects Laight and Varick Streets. Anyone familiar with Serra's essay on that piece cannot but marvel at the way he had planned every detail of all possible sequences in its viewing (reading that essay, as well as hearing the sculptor speak of any of his site-specific works, either already done or still in the planning stage, one literally imagines a storyboard).[2] No one can doubt Serra's seriousness when he speaks about site-specificity (and his anger over the *Titled Arc* fiasco was fully justified). Yet there is an element of the site that Serra did not take into account, and that is its history. For all his attention to the temporal experience through which his outdoor sculptures unfold for the spectator, Serra has always been more concerned with the present tense of perception than with any notion of commemoration of the past. When one of his masterpieces, *Clara-Clara*, installed (once again, alas, temporarily) in the Tuileries Gardens, gave a lesson on urbanism that referred to a centuries-old debate concerning Paris's central axis, it was by chance, by happenstance, for the site was not that originally planned and the work had not been conceived as site-specific.[3]

All of Kawamata's large urban projects (by opposition to the multiple tiny shacks he builds with refuse materials in the rundown areas of the various cities he wanders through, and that he calls his ''field work'') purposively involve the social history of their sites—at least this is true of his projects outside Japan, where the rapid rhythm of construction/demolition induces a certain de-specification of any place, produces cities whose only history is that of a willful erasure of any historical trace. It is my contention that Kawamata is the only artist, so far, who has managed to inscribe convincingly the history of a site into his work. Note, first, the extraordinary care with which he chooses each of his urban sites for its specific past—ever since the *Destroyed Church* at Kassel (1987), which brought him international recognition. (I gather it is the artist that insists on the publication of a historical essay in each of the books devoted to a single piece of his—the most spectacular example in that respect being perhaps that on his gigantic yet intimate intervention upon the ''beguinage,'' a kind of convent, at Kortrijk in Belgium). In the case of the Roosevelt Island project, both the geographic situation and the history of the place (discussed by Elizabeth Frosch and by Claudia Gould in this book) play a major role in the work's signification. Located across the river from the UN and Lever House (the most expensive apartment building in Manhattan—from where, more that ten years ago, having tea in one of the upper floors, I marvelled at the desolate strip of land in the middle of the East River), Kawamata's shanty-like disorder faces luxury and international law; the site's memories of exclusion and quarantine confront the oblivious selfishness of the well-off; its silence and isolation oppose the turmoil and traffic of metropolis. Even the mode of visual access to Kawamata's project was connected to the *genius loci*: only its prow-like western facade was visible from Manhattan. To visit the piece, one had to make an appointment, have a chain-link gate opened, and be accompanied by one of the coordinators of the project—just as if you were going to visit a prisoner in a jail (the island once hosted one) or, in a hospital, the victim of a grave and contagious disease.

Francois-Auguste-René Rodin
The Burghers of Calais, 1886.

Of course, architects have spoken about memory and the *genius loci* for quite a long time. Since the end of the sixties, it has even been one of the main issues of so-called postmodernism in its various guises, so clear was the collapse of the modern movement's dream of a universal and autonomous prismatic space. But if the architects' words have been eloquent, I have never been impressed by their deeds regarding the matter. Take Peter Eisenman, for example, whose Wexner Center for the Arts is familiar to a large audience. The spatial urban contextualization of the building is bright and effective (the tilting of two grids at an acute angle, in both elevation and ground plan, being related to the two main axes that define the site in their non-congruence—that of the city of Columbus as a whole, that of the university campus, a pocket of calm and singularity amidst the general city grid). But the temporal signs of that contextualization are pitiful. Eisenman's markings, on the ground, of the previous location of an armory that once stood at the site (a mock archaeological ruin of foundation walls) are utterly rhetorical and require a long caption to be deciphered; and if the medievalizing brick towers that adorn the crystalline Center are more readable as a historical conundrum, it is as an overblown joke, not as a genuine tribute to the city's past.[4] Architects speak a lot about history, memory, and the like, but suffer from a total incapacity to deal with it: they build upon, so they efface—not only because their stones or concrete slabs materially cover up (or eventually engulf) the previous architectural tenants of any place, but because an existing construction is always more powerful, for better or worse, than a remembrance. So demonstrates, implicitly, Kawamata—and perhaps it was Eisenman's pretense that led the sculptor, when he was invited to participate in the opening exhibition at the Wexner Center (the theme was, appropriately, site-specificity), to turn his back on this apocryphal, Disneyland-type reconstruction of a past and to contextualize for the present Eisenman's distinctive trademark: the astounding mesh of white lattices that wrap his building. For a few weeks this minimalist and immaculate grid was parasited and extended by Kawamata's wooden scaffoldings, and they in turn were prolonged into a dissemination of shanties across the campus, along the very axes that had determined Eisenman's design. Walter Benjamin's phrase: "there is no document of civilization that is not at the same time a document of barbarism" is quoted much too often without necessity. But here its invocation is not ornamental: like Krzysztof Wodiczko, but in a very different manner, both more and less direct, Kawamata hinted that no museum could ever have been created, in the culture craze that served as an alibi for the urban gentrification programs that characterized the 1980's, without having produced at the same time its contingent of homeless.[5]

Richard Serra
St. John's Rotary Arc, 1980.

Kawamata chooses a site, and he chooses it well, I said. Doubtless because he is a stranger, the quintessential traveler, he always finds, in whatever city he happens to be invited to work, a knot of memory and forgetfulness, a place whose disjunctiveness, grounded in history, has gradually become invisible to its daily beholders.[6] He points his finger at it, asks us to pause and ponder over the roots of our social environment—this man without roots, this archetypal wanderer. That already would not be a small achievement, but there is more to it. What is it that makes Kawamata's call upon our collective memory more effective than that of any other artist or architect? This much: he underscores the deficiencies of our private memory and he commemorates without building a monument.

Robert Smithson
A Non-Site, 1968.

Detlef Mertins has perfectly described the perceptual process involved in all of Kawamata's large urban projects. At the beginning of the construction, there is no reaction, the planks and beams that appear against an old building or pile up on a previously empty lot, do so without fanfare, unnoticed; then the alluvia reach a quantitative point where they can't be ignored anymore. This is the second act—call it puzzlement: "Everybody knows that strange things sometimes happen at City Hall. But this was more than a mislabelled file. It just wasn't like any construction job I had ever seen: all scaffolding and no building. And nothing was straight. It looked like a wrecking operation in reverse."[7] This act is the longest, it takes up at least three-fifths of the whole operation, sometimes all of it. Let's imagine however, theoretically, that it leads into a third movement once the piece is "finished" (not the right word, of course, but there is none for its peculiar status then); that is, when Kawamata the builder-scavenger has decided that his gigantic pick-up-sticks heap is set and will admit no more addition (in Europe this game is called Mikado: does it have a Japanese origin?). Now comes the time of the visit, of the eventual wandering through the piece by especially interested or curious spectators: nothing of a climax, one could perhaps even say that it is a low point in the short life of a project. Then the destruction begins, much swifter than the construction (one-third of its length usually). But the grand finale is when nothing is there anymore, when everything is exactly as before Kawamata had even set foot on the site: have I dreamed? At the end of the elaborate construction job, there is no material trace of the activity of the team of workers that have been bustling everyday for months in a row with only a tiny interruption between assemblage and demolition: has time been suspended?

But of course there is a trace, and it is the core of Kawamata's art: this trace is in our minds, and it does not have to compete with a building that permanently obfuscates it on the spot. Architects believe they can call upon our memory through all sorts of orchidaceous devices (mock history, stylistic quotes), but they are bound to fail. Kawamata succeeds because, for him, our fleeting memory is the medium, not simply an idea he wants to illustrate: he tests our memory, teases it. Once everything is gone and the forgotten building he has put on the map by momentarily cannibalizing it is as naked as before his intervention, we begin to remember, first the beauty of Kawamata's toy-like structure, then perhaps the ancient magnificence and function of the dilapidated building itself. We begin to remember, and also to think of the future: can't something be done out of this ruin, again? "When a parasite attacks the grid," said the sculptor, "order is restored when it is repaired. After it is treated though, some of the grid changes. This is the chance for new possibilities to arise."[8] (The artist also often uses the metaphor of cancer: when a cancer is cured everything is back in order, but the cured patient, having skirted death, will never be the same.)

Mathias Goeritz (in collaboration with Luis Barragan), *The Towers of Satellite City*, 1957.

I visited Kawamata's project on Roosevelt Island only once (it was almost "finished"—I went literally a few hours before the "inauguration.") At first I felt annoyed (not guilty, for there was nothing I could do to bend my tight schedule this past fall) at not having found the opportunity to view it a second time. But soon it did not bother me anymore, although I had already agreed to write these pages. I was surprised at my casualness. I was deeply moved by this project, and I take the critic's task to heart (I rarely write without first obtaining a stern familiarity with the works I have endeavored to write about). What then could explain what might even be called my slight reticence concerning a possible second visit? It took me a while to understand this: I was dealing with a potential ghost, a would-be reminiscence. No double-checking would make it more tangible. Once again: it is because Kawamata does not attempt to erect a monument—he knows too well how impossible that is in a modern society—that he is able to memorialize.[9]

When I say that the time of the visit is perhaps the low point of a project's short life, this is of course an exaggeration. No caller to the Roosevelt Island project, especially in the rather tight conditions of spectatordom I've mentioned above, could have failed to be struck by the majesty of the site at the deserted tip of the island, in the midst of tall blades of grass and bushes covering the trash dumped there during the last decades, engulfed in the wind and the cries of the sea gulls and the flow of the river and the vastness of the sky: a romantic landscape opposite the shiny and intimidating great facade of the Upper East Side waterfront. Nobody could have failed to be surprised by the discrepancy between the frontal view of Kawamata's piece seen from a distance and the sometimes cavernous, sometimes labyrinthine aggregation of planks, posts, and beams—accentuated by the odd topography, which made Renwick's building, once dominant, seem sunk into a crater scooped out in the middle of a recent hill-like accumulation of debris.

But I maintain that this part of Kawamata's projects (the mazes where you get lost, the countless partial views, the jungle of sticks and passages you go through) is not where his strength lies. Here comes perhaps the major difference between his work and that of Serra: both of them are heirs to the tradition of the picturesque that Piranesi initiated, but while Serra understood this legacy as a perceptual inquiry about parallaxes and the uncertainty of our perception, Kawamata selected more tragic traits in the work of the Venetian engraver and that of his followers. Serra's Piranesi is cinematic (we owe Eisenstein a great essay on him); Kawamata's is the pessimist historian looking at the past and pointing at the twilight of reason.[10]

This leads me back to my early mention of Choisy, the great engineer and archaeologist whose *Histoire de l'architecture* was Le Corbusier's bedside book. I had a few reasons to have him in mind when strolling around Kawamata's rubble. The first was a quasi-hallucination: having climbed a hill separated by a small combe from another hill hiding the south facade of the building (and that Kawamata had populated with many small shacks, a sort of eerie village sprouting from the neo-gothic ruin), I felt I was confronted by a poor man's version of the Propylaea on the Acropolis. And further along, on yet another hill (this time at the level of the roofs of this "village," a frozen sea of not-so horizontal surfaces of every texture, color, and material), I felt again I was experiencing changes akin to the "architectural promenade" that Choisy so intelligently describes in speaking of the great Athenian site as a perfect example of what he calls the "Greek picturesque." Nothing there that I could not ascribe as well to Serra's best site-specific pieces.

Gordon Matta-Clark
Conical Intersect, 1975.

But there was a second twist, a second "choisism," so to speak. Kawamata's pieces are "all scaffolding and no building" writes, very perceptively, Detlef Mertins—but Choisy had demonstrated that maybe the two, scaffolding and architecture, were not necessarily distinct. What made Choisy famous indeed, at a rather young age, was his finding that the Roman mode of construction implied, for economic reason, the transformation of a temporary scaffolding in brick (itself supported by a cheap and rudimentary wood structure) into permanent support sunk in the mass.[11] There was, so to speak, an inversion of categories not identical to but of the same range as that performed by Kawamata (and it, too, concerned the nature of scaffolds).

Last choisism. I kept the best for the end, but it leads me to a slight critique of Kawamata's work in general. Choisy had a topological comparative method. He would say, for example:

> One can dispose buttresses in two very distinct ways. In one solution, one expels outside those embarrassing auxiliaries; in the other, on the contrary, one places the buttresses inside the room. The first solution if that of western architecture in the middle ages; the other that of Roman and Byzantine architecture. Both have their advantages and flaws. If one chooses the first, one sacrifices the space situated between two buttresses; if one chooses the second, one enlarges the covered surface of the room by all this space. The first solution gives a more limited interior space, but unencumbered and freer; the second a wider space, but full of obstacles.[12]

Choisy's method came from the comparative anatomy of Geoffroy Saint-Hilaire, the man who fought Georges Cuvier's functionalism and said that an animal lives either outside its skeleton (mammals, birds, fish) or inside it (insects).

This topological notion of space is also at work in Kawamata's oeuvre (he notes that ''the inside of a bag can be considered as the continuation of the outer surface'' and that the comment that struck him most about his work when he began to leave galleries and museums and intrude upon the public space was that ''the internal structure of the room was bulging out; that the inside looked as though it had been turned inside out''[13]). This ''turning inside out'' like a glove is what most of Kawamata's pieces seem to be doing to architecture (at least, for me, the truly successful ones); this is the effect of inversion they produce (and this effect in turn governs entirely Kawamata's subtle reflections upon the private and the public, the building and its context, the dweller and the homeless). Now, this prodigious illusion of a topological inversion is particularly enhanced if one is prevented from going into the building that is being parasited (which happens more often than not, usually for security reasons). This was especially clear at Roosevelt Island: Renwick's dangerous ruin could not be trespassed, but one could see through it and glance at the tentacles of Kawamata's ''cancer'' leaping through its doors and windows. It is breathtaking to look from the outside at an ''insided out'' structure, but not particularly interesting to enter it. This is why you can grasp Kawamata's site-specific works, unlike Serra's, even if you happen to only see them frontally and from afar. But it is also why his interior pieces seem almost mannered to me, too pretty, too delicate (while Serra's never suffer from their enclosure): the mock-up full-size ''model'' of Kawamata's Roosevelt Island project (rather, an interpretation of it) that the sculptor displayed at Cooper Union during the short intermission of the construction/demolition process, and through which one could wander, certainly did not convey much of the atmosphere of the actual thing. If I was allowed to give Kawamata some advice—but I'm not, a critic should not be—it would be to keep the spectator at bay as much as he can from the guts of the buildings he rescues from oblivion.[14] The beholder does not need to get in to cherish and muse over the specter that will haunt his memory.

Yve-Alain Bois is currently the Joseph Pulitzer Jr., Professor of Modern Art at Harvard University and an editor of the journal *October*. He has published numerous articles on abstract art in the 1920's and post-World War II American art, some of them reprinted in *Painting as Model*, a collection of his essays published by MIT Press in 1990.

1. The critical writing on Kawamata, though not extensive in English but overall of a surprisingly high quality, abounds in metaphorical readings. This is not the place to investigate this metaphorical compulsion which I take as a direct effect of Kawamata's non-dogmatic mode of urban intervention. For a strong metaphorical interpretation of the Roosevelt Island project, see Claudia Gould's essay in this volume.

2. Richard Serra and Clara Weyergraf, ''St. John's Rotary Arc'' (1980), reprinted in Richard Serra, *Interviews, Etc. 1970-1980* (Yonkers: The Hudson River Museum, 1980), pp.151-161.

3. See my essay ''A Picturesque Stroll around *Clara-Clara*'' and particularly the afterword I wrote about its installation in the Tuileries Garden, reprinted in *Richard Serra*, ed. Ernst-Gerhard Güse (New York: Rizzoli, 1987), pp. 40-59. What I say here about Serra's lack of interest in the history of the site involves as well its social present: I could not agree less with Douglas Crimp when he reads the sculptor's urban works as political agitprop gestures (''Serra's Public Sculpture: Redefining Site Specificity,'' in Rosalind Krauss, *Richard Serra/Sculpture* [New York: The Museum of Modern Art, 1986], pp. 40-56). The fact that *Terminal*, a sculpture installed in Bochum in 1977, became the object of a political slogan for the Christian Democrat Party that opposed it, has nothing to do with the structure of the piece. Serra is not Hans Haacke.

4. Chris Burden, in turn, appropriately mocked Eisenman's joke when he added brick-colored plastic foam crenelations to the Center's towers during the temporary exhibition I mention below. See *Breakthroughs: Avant-Garde Artists in Europe and America, 1950-1990* (New York and Columbus: Rizzoli and Wexner Center for the Arts, 1991), pp.194-197. For a critique of Eisenman's mode of historicizing, see my essay, ''Surfaces,'' to appear in the catalogue of the forthcoming exhibition devoted to the architect's ''Cities of Artificial Excavation'' at the Canadian Center for Architecture, Montreal, 1993.

5. On the connection between the art market, real estate, and homelessness as a major theme of Wodiczko's work, see Denis Hollier, ''While the City Sleeps'' in *Krzysztof Wodiczko: Instruments, Projections, Vehicles* (Barcelona: Tapies Foundation, 1992), pp.21-45.

6. On this aspect of Kawamata's work, see the beautiful essay by Geert Bekaert, ''The Stranger,'' in *Kawamata Begijnhof Kortrijk* (Kortrijk and Tokyo: Kanaal Art Foundation and Gendaikikakushitsu Publishing, 1991), pp.39-42.

7. Detlef Mertins, ''In Deference To Dis-Order,'' in *Kawamata: Toronto Project 1989* (Toronto: Mercer Union, 1989), p.47. Mertins's essay provides the best critical assessment of Kawamata's production.

8. ''Kawamata: An Interview with Linda Genereux,'' in *Kawamata: Toronto Project 1989*, op. cit., p.31.

9. The breakdown of the logic of the monument in our times, initiated with the rejection of Rodin's *Balzac* by those who had commissioned it, has been discussed by Rosalind Krauss in ''Sculpture in the Expanded Field'' (1978), reprinted in Krauss, *The Originality of the Avant-Garde and Other Modernist Myths* (Cambridge: MIT Press, 1985), pp.277-290. All the headlines of the six chapters of my hypothetical ''history of public sculpture in the twentieth century,'' from Brancusi's ensemble to Smithson's non-sites, involve a further distancing from the concept of the monument. For Brancusi and Smithson's specific cases, each involving a different mode of relationship to history, see Rosalind Krauss, ''Echelle/monumentalité—

Modernisme/postmodenisme: la ruse de Brancusi,'' in *Qu'est-ce que la sculpture moderne*, catalogue of an exhibition of the same title organized by Margit Rowell at the Centre Georges Pompidou, Paris, in 1986 (pp.246-253).

10. On Piranesi and Serra (as well as a short discussion of Choisy), see my ''Picturesque Stroll around *Clara-Clara*,'' op. cit. On Kawamata and Piranesi, see Detlef Mertins's ''In Deference To Dis-Order,'' op. cit.

11. *L'art de bâtir chez les Romains*, written in 1869 (Choisy was then 28 years old), appeared in 1873 (Paris: Ducher) and was widely praised. My long study of Choisy will appear in a forthcoming book on the history of axonometric projection.

12. Auguste Choisy, *L'art de bâtir chez les Byzantins* (Paris: Librairie de la Société Anonyme des Publications Périodiques, 1883), p.124.

13. Kawamata, ''Interview,'' in *Kawamata (Underconstruction)*, eds. Mika Koike, Motoi Masaki, and Makoto Murata (Tokyo: Gendaikikakushitsu Publishing, 1987), pp.37-38. Elsewhere Kawamata uses the same inside-out image when speaking of the skin of the mouth (Genereux, op. cit., p.29).

14. The success of Kawamata's project at Kortrijk seems to contradict my point here, but the situation was unusual, almost a direct opposite to those Kawamata deals with most of the time: the convent is visually sealed off from the town (and every night at nine o'clock, its small gate was closed), and Kawamata's scaffoldings, spread out in the courtyards and pathways of this ''village within the town'' were invisible from outside. Once you had entered the beguinage, you were in Kawamata's project but still outside the buildings his wood sticks parasited.

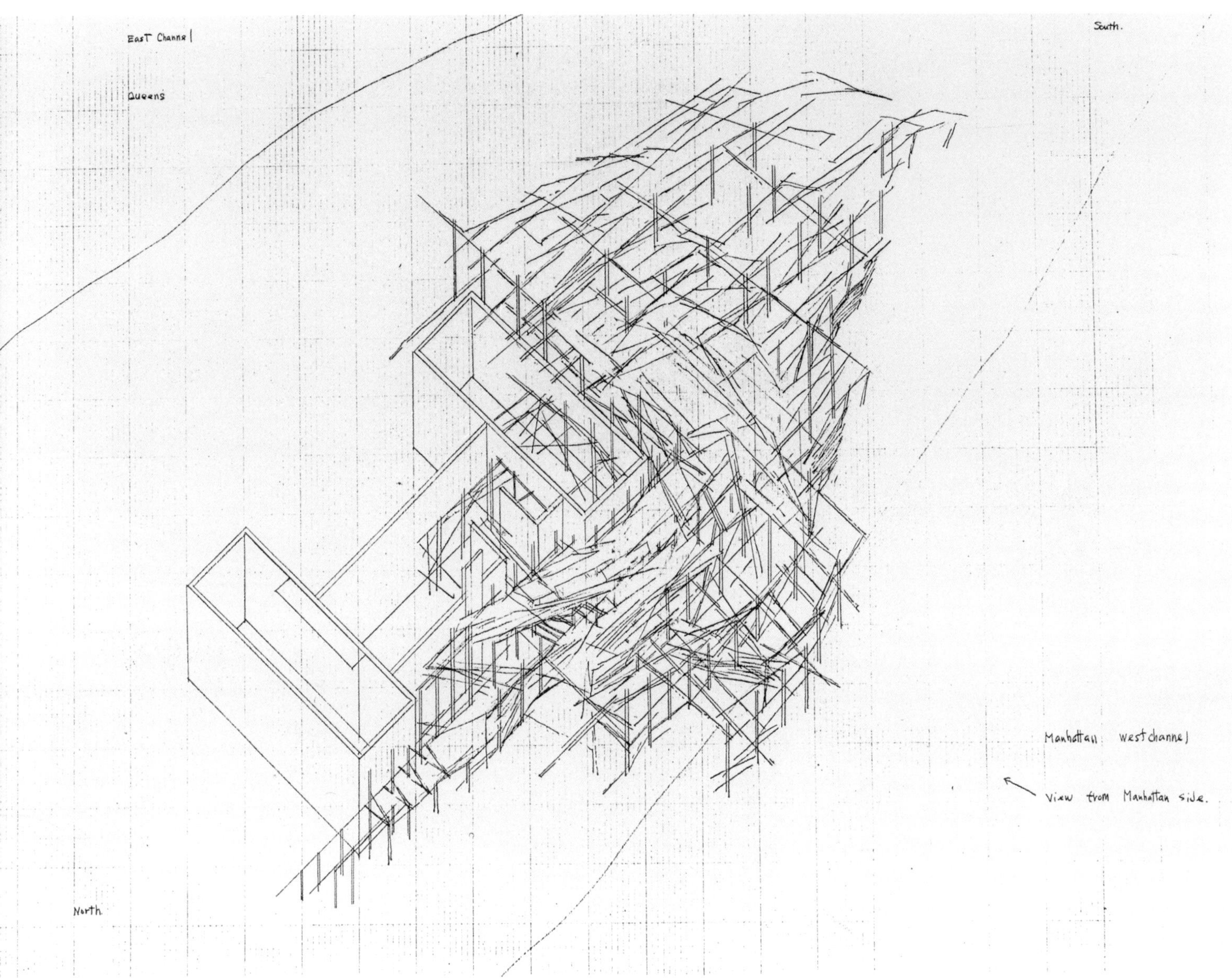
East Channel
Queens
South.
Manhattan west channel
View from Manhattan side.
North.

POST PLAN (1/S1)

STRUCTURAL SPECIFICATION

GENERAL

1. The Contractor shall report to the Engineer any condition(s) that prevents or otherwise alters the execution of the work as indicated on the construction documents. All members shown are as required for structural integrity and stability.
2. The latest editions of all codes and or regulatory agencies having jurisdiction shall be in effect for all components of the work.
3. The Contractor shall assume responsibility for shoring, erection sequencing, and stabilization of all work during construction. All structural work shall be coordinated with the architectural drawings, while construction personnel shall be thoroughly skilled in carpentry.
4. Wind loads based upon gross bay dimensions are as follows:

   Vertical Surfaces: 5 pounds per square foot
   Horizontal Surfaces: 5 pounds per square foot

   No vertical or horizontal bay surface shall be constructed so as to contain more than 30% area coverage by applied members. Maximum storey height and bay width are not to exceed eleven and one half feet. All columns and sills shall be founded upon undisturbed soil or backfill placed and compacted under the supervision of a Geotechnical Engineer.
5. No snow or occupant loads have been considered in design. The structure is not to be occupied after its construction has been completed, nor is the existing building to be used in any way for stability and/or shoring of the proposed sculpture.

STRUCTURAL STEEL

1. The design, fabrication, transportation, and erection of all structural steel shall be in conformance with the "Steel Construction Manual", the AISC.
2. Structural steel for hot rolled plates and shapes shall be ASTM A36.
3. Structural bolts shall be manufactured to ASTM A307, grade 5 and tightened snugly over a washer with a handwrench until all adjacent surfaces are in complete contact.

STRUCTURAL LUMBER

1. The design, transportation and erection of all structural lumber shall be in conformance with the "Timber Construction Manual", the AITC.
2. All structural lumber shall fire retardant and machine rated for the following properties:

   f(b) = 1,400 psi   f(v) = 80 psi   E = 1,400,000 psi

   f(t) = 825 psi   f(c) = 325 psi(perpen)   f(c) = 825 psi(para)

3. All lumber shall be surface dried to a maximum moisture content of 19%.
4. Sills, nailers and ledgers may be construction grade.

PETER J. GALDI
STRUCTURAL ENGINEER
125 FIFTH AVENUE
NEW YORK, NY 10003
212-529-0444

TADASHI KAWAMATA
ARTIST
CITY HEIGHTS AOBADAI #405
3-12-2 AOBADAI MEGURO-KU
TOKYO 153 JAPAN

SMALLPOX HOSPITAL PROJECT
ROOSEVELT ISLAND
NEW YORK

POST PLAN AND NOTES
S1

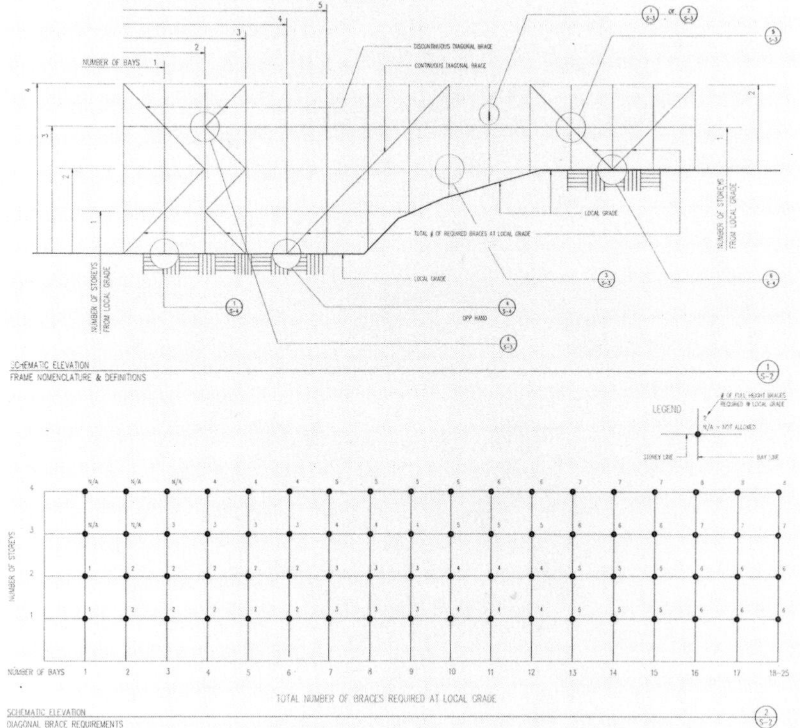

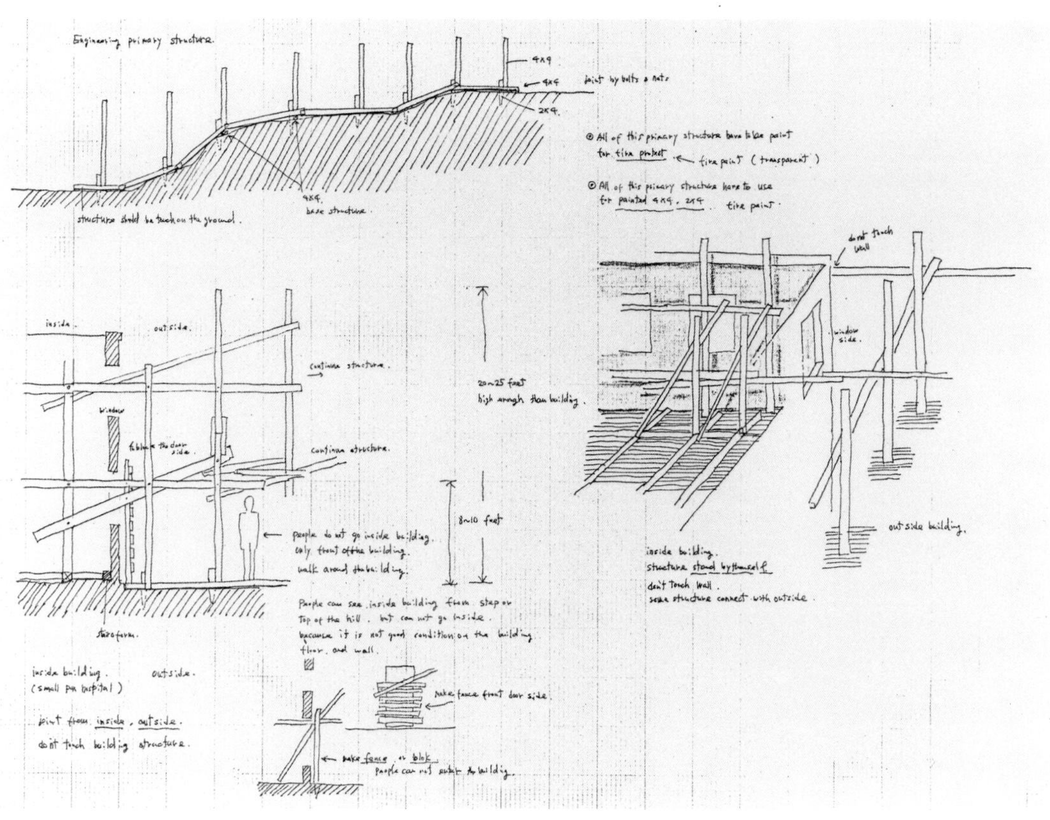
Engineering primary structure.
4x4
4x4
joint by bolts & nuts
2x4.
4x4.
base structure.
structure should be touch on the ground.
⊙ All of this primary structure have to take paint
for fire protect ← fire paint (transparent)
⊙ All of this primary structure have to use
for painted 4x4, 2x4. fire paint.
don't touch wall
window side.
out side building.
inside building.
structure stand by themself
don't touch wall.
some structure connect with outside.
inside.
outside.
continue structure.
window
to block the door side.
continue structure.
20~25 feet
high enough than building.
8~10 feet
people do not go inside building.
only front of the building.
walk around the building.
People can see inside building from step or
Top of the hill. but can not go inside.
because it is not good condition on the building
floor, and wall.
stiroform.
inside building.
(small pox hospital)
outside.
joint from inside, outside.
don't touch building structure.
make fence front door side.
make fence or blok
People can not enter the building.

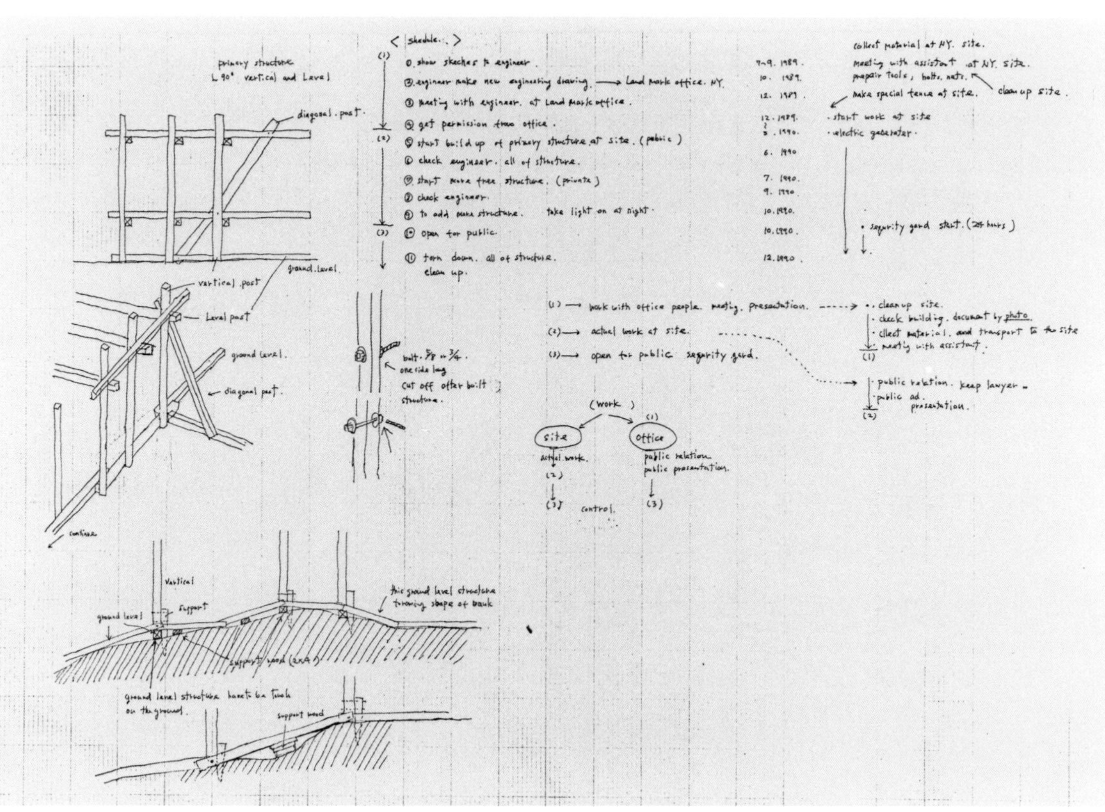
primary structure
L 90° vertical and Level
diagonal post.
ground level.
vertical post
Level post
ground level.
diagonal post.
continue
< shedule.. >
(1)
① show skeches to engineer.
② engineer make new engineering drawing. → Land mark office. NY.
③ meeting with engineer. at Land Mark office.
④ get permission from office.
(2)
⑤ start build up of primary structure at site. (public)
⑥ check engineer. all of structure.
⑦ start more free structure. (private)
⑧ check engineer.
⑨ to add more structure. take light on at night.
(3)
⑩ open for public.
⑪ torn down. all of structure.
clean up.
7~9. 1989.
10. 1989.
12. 1989.
12. 1989.
~
3. 1990.
6. 1990
7. 1990.
9. 1990.
10. 1990.
10. 1990.
12. 1990.
collect material at NY. site.
meeting with assistant at NY. site.
prepair tools, bolts, nuts.
make special fence at site.
clean up site.
· start work at site
· electric generater.
· segurity gard start. (24 hours)
bolt. 5/8 ~ 3/4.
one side long
cut off after built
structure.
(1) → work with office people. meeting. presentation.
(2) → actual work at site.
(3) → open for public segurity gard.
· clean up site.
· check building. document by photo.
· cllect material. and transport to the site
· meeting with assistant.
(1)
· public relation. keep lawyer.
· public ad.
presentation.
(2)
(work)
(1)
site
actual work.
(2)
(3)
control.
office
public relation
public presentation.
(3)
vertical
support
ground level
support wood (2x4)
this ground level structure
tracing shape of bank
ground level structure have to be touch
on the ground.
support wood

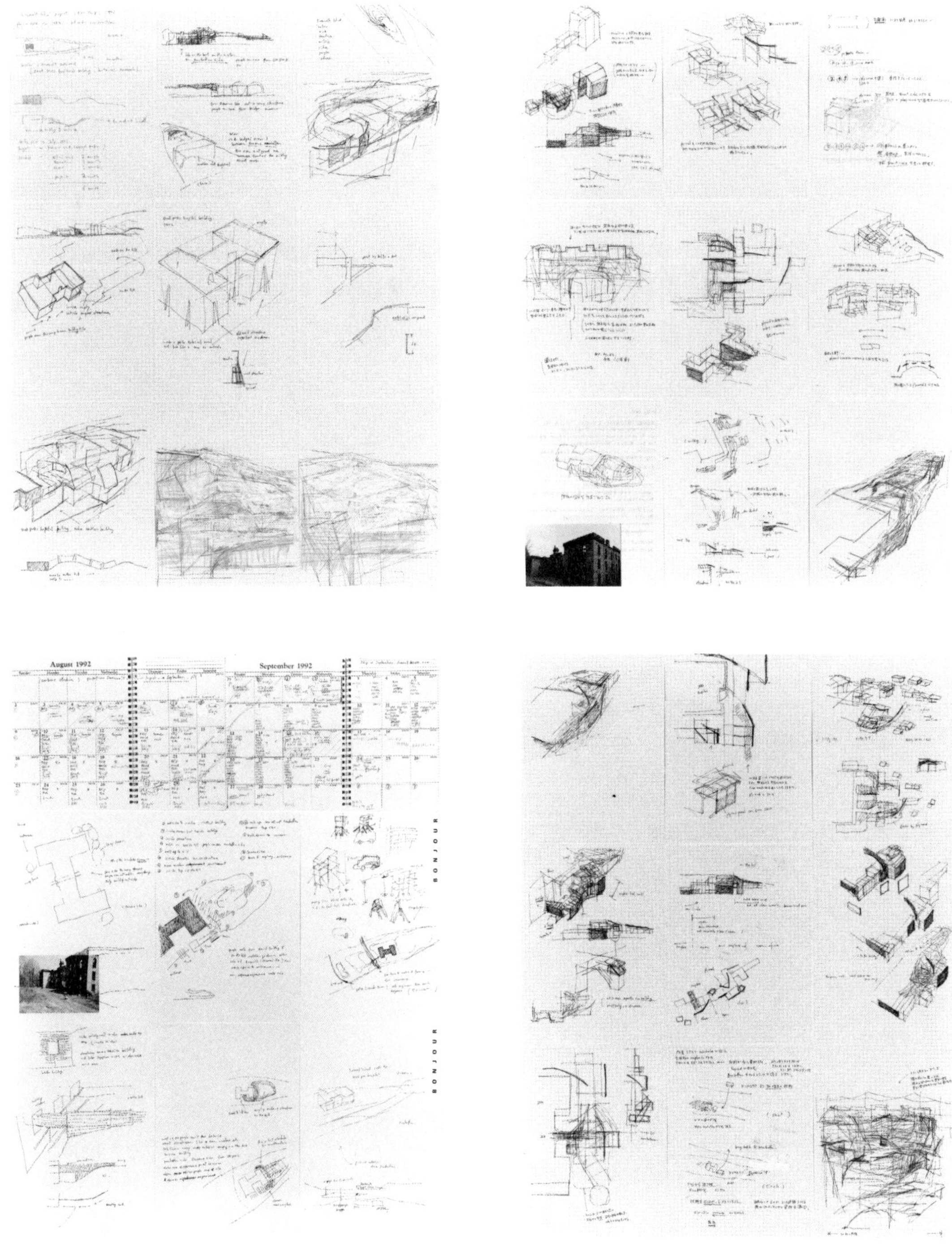

August 1992
September 1992
BONJOUR
BONJOUR

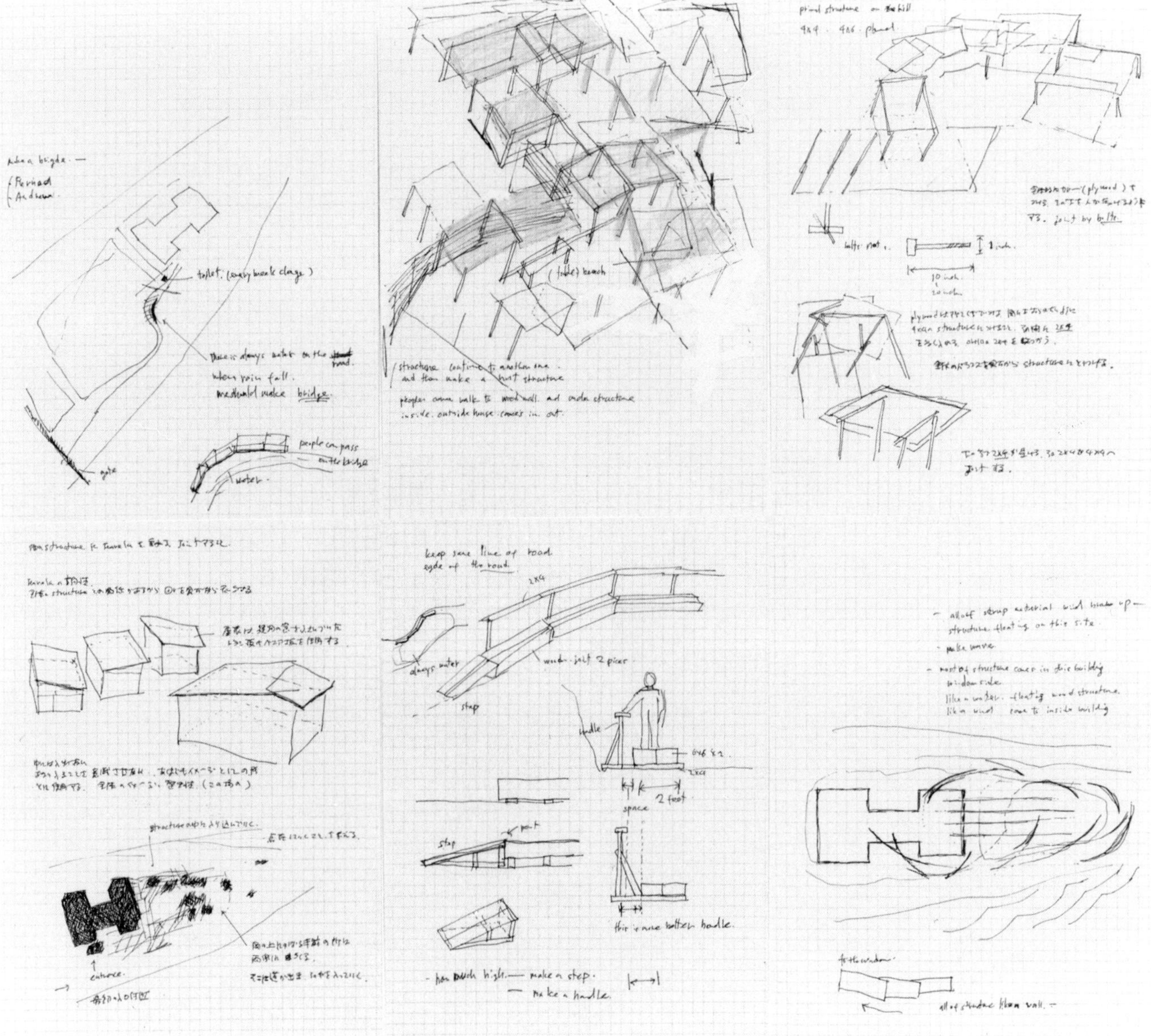
people can pass on the bridge
water
gate
(table) bench
keep same line of road
step
handle
space
2 foot
this is more better handle
make a step
make a handle
entrance

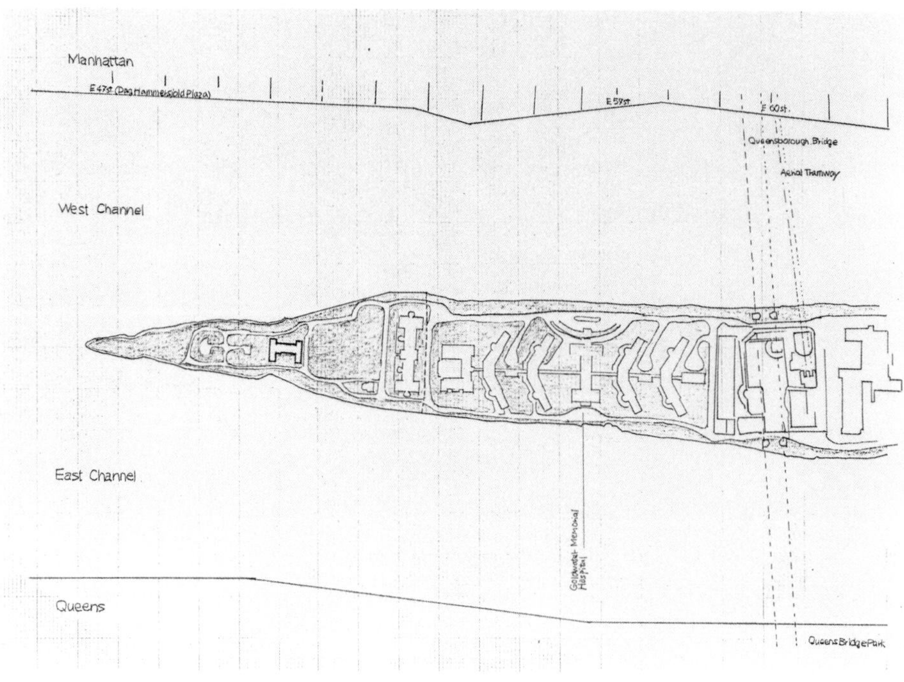
Manhattan
E 47st (Dag Hammarskjold Plaza)
E 59st
E 60st
Queensborough Bridge
Aerial Tramway
West Channel
East Channel
Goldwater Memorial Hospital
Queens
Queens Bridge Park

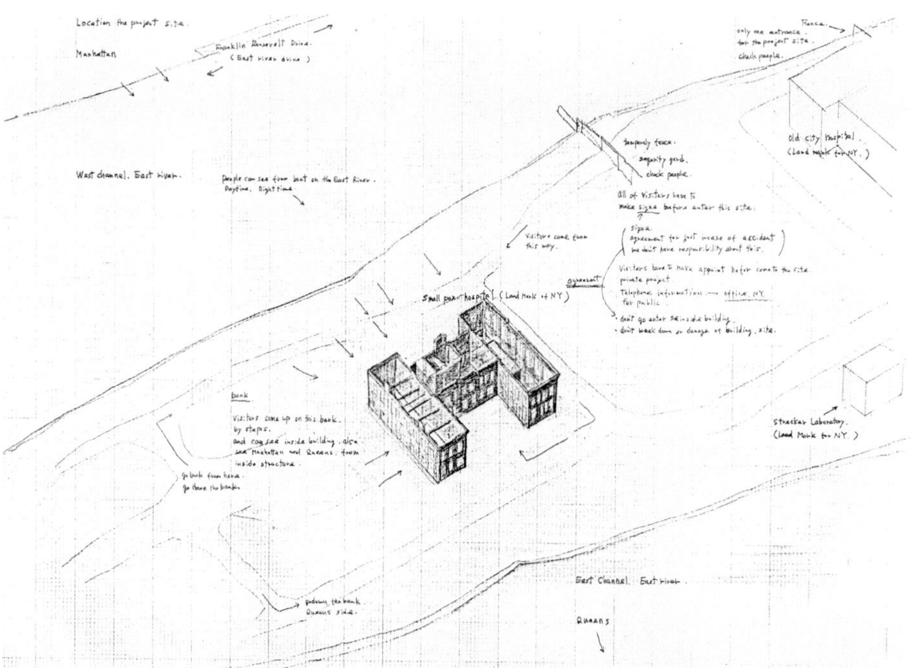
Location the project site.
Manhattan
Franklin Roosevelt Drive.
(East river drive)
Fence.
only one entrance
for the project site.
check people.
temporary fence.
security gard,
check people.
Old city hospital.
(Land mark for NY.)
West channel. East river.
People can see from boat on the East River.
Daytime. Night time
All of Visitors have to
make signs before enter this site.
sign
agreement for just incase of accident
we don't have responsibility about this.
Visitors come from
this way.
agreement
Visitors have to make appoint before come to the site.
private project.
Telephone information → office NY
for public
Small pox hospital. (Land Mark of NY)
· don't go enter inside building.
· don't break down or damage of building, site.
bank
Visitors come up on this bank.
by steps.
and can see inside building. also
see Manhattan and Queens. from
inside structure.
go back from here.
go down the bank.
Stracker Laboratory.
(Land Mark for NY.)
go down the bank
Queens side.
East Channel. East river.
Queens

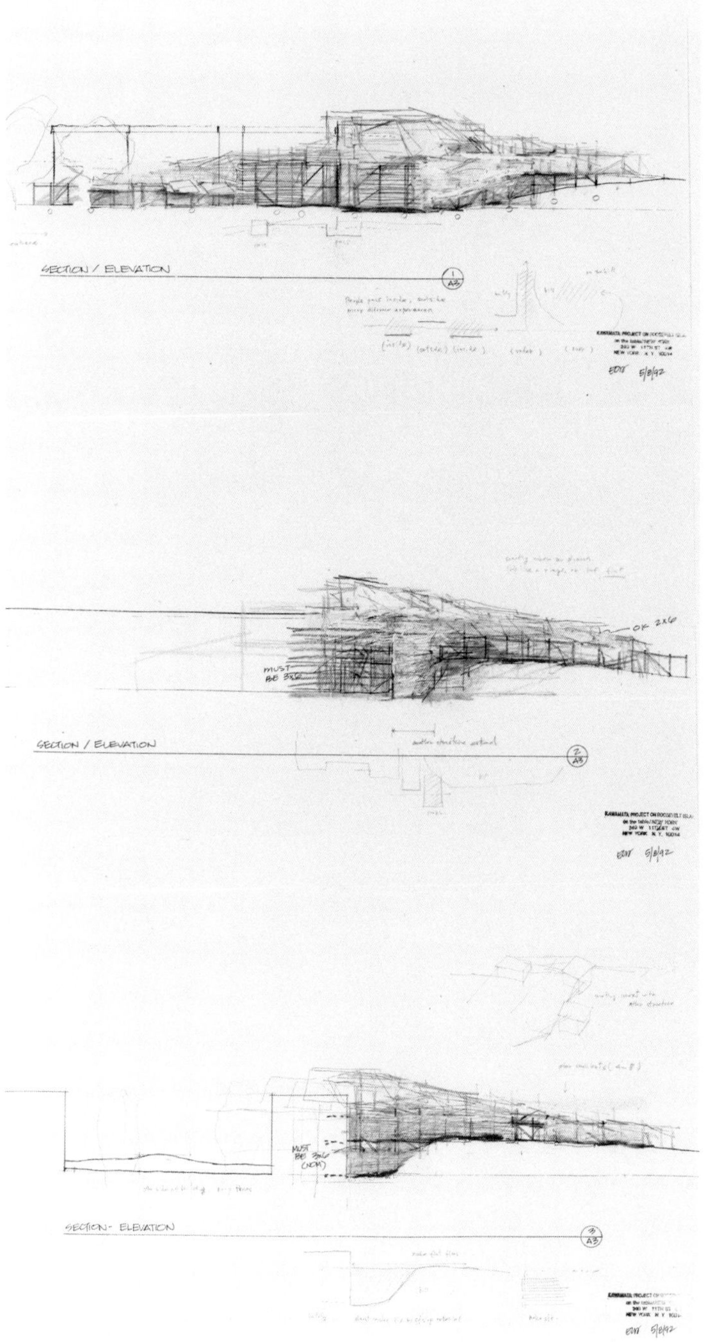
SECTION / ELEVATION
1 A3
KAWAMATA PROJECT ON ROOSEVELT ISLAND
NEW YORK N.Y.
5/8/92
OK 2X6
MUST BE 3X6
SECTION / ELEVATION
2 A3
KAWAMATA PROJECT ON ROOSEVELT ISLAND
NEW YORK N.Y.
5/8/92
MUST BE 3X6 (NOM)
SECTION - ELEVATION
3 A3
NEW YORK N.Y.
5/8/92

立ち入り禁止：建築工事

イヴーアラン・ボワ

マンハッタン、ホーランドトンネルのキャナル・ストリート側の出口付近に7年あまりも横たわっていたリチャード・セラの「ロータリー・アーク」と並んで、川俣のルーズヴェルト島プロジェクトはニューヨーク市において今まで展示された公共彫刻としては最上のものと言えるだろう。一方は不透明なカーブした壁であり、もう一方は優雅で、はかなげな、時には（マンハッタンから見ると）書のようにも映るこの二つ作品の意外な取り合わせについては後ほど話を進めるとして、まず始めに川俣の創造活動全体が公共彫刻の中でも傑出したステートメントであることを述べておきたい。今、私に20世紀におけるこのジャンルの美術史を著すだけのエネルギーと時間的余裕と気力があるとすれば、それは、わずか6章から構成されることになるだろう。まず導入部で、ロダンの「バルザック」と「カレーの市民」を中心にして歴史的な背景について述べ、第1章はブランクーシのティルグ・ジュのアトリエや住まいを含む一連の作品について述べる。第2章は、「ハイウエィ・アート」などという（実際作家自身がそう呼んだように）ひどい呼ばれ方をしているマティアス・ゲリッツのメキシコ・シティにある「サテライト・シティ」について。そして第3章はロバート・スミッソンの「サイト」「ノン・サイト」について。（パブリック・アートという概念からいささか逸脱するかもしれないが、スミッソン以外のアーティストによる様々なアース・プロジェクトについても多少補足をいれながら述べてみたい。）第4章は、ゴードン・マッタ・クラークのカットアウツについて。第5章がリチャード・セラのサイト・スペシフィックな（その場にのみ属する）作品群について。第6章で川俣のノマド的な試みについて述べる、といった次第である。

では川俣とセラの比較から始めよう。二人の作品は、見かけよりもはるかに共通点が多いが、（両者ともすぐにもオーギュスト・ショワジイーの才気に富んだ建築上の思想を想起させるのは偶然のことではないだろう。）かなり相違があるのも確かである。両者とも仮設的な仕事である。（不運な最期をとげた「ティルテッド・アーク」とは異なり、「ロータリー・アーク」は最初から一時的な作品として制作された。）しかし、セラの作品の一時性はその本質的な問題ではなく、偶然のことであり、作品そのものの構造の中に組み込まれているわけではない。（実際私自身はこの作品が恒久的なものでなかったのは、悲しむべき誤りだ思う。）作品「ロータリー・アーク」の主題は人の感性の移ろいやすさ、場と単純な形態との関わりに対しての可変的な定義であった。川俣のプロジェクトはこれには当てはまらない。そのプロジェクトの全体像は、遙か彼方から、そして正面から観察できるが、ほとんど完成すると同時に消えてしまう。セラの「ロータリー・アーク」は、まるで岩のように頑強にたたずみ、そのアイデンティティーは回りを動く人の動きとともに溶解する。これに対し川俣のプロジェクトは、ほとんどその始まりから、あたかもつかの間の残像のように思われる。(作品から受ける感覚は、実際の作品ほどに短命ではない。)セラの作品はミニマリズムをいまだに支配しているゲシュタルト的な視覚の理論、すなわち現象学的な分析から出た批判である。一方川俣はといえば、我々の都市を蝕む資本主義的な発展、衰退、再生のサイクルに対するエレジー(哀歌)なのだ。それはボードレールが書いたオースマンの詩「通行人へ(To a Passerby)」を20世紀の世紀末の10年というこの時代がもたらした病巣を描き出すさまざまな暗喩として我々が容易に読み取れるように、触知可能な崩壊の言語に見事に置き換えたものといえるだろう。[1]

川俣のこの作品にはタイトルがない点に注目してほしい。というより、他の作品の場合と同様に対象となった場所の名称がつけられているだけである。ここにもリチャード・セラの作品がサイト・スペシフィックという概念に対して、厳しく正確を期すのと根本的な違いがみられる。「ロータリー・アーク」について再考してみよう。あらゆるものがまるで奇跡のごとくその場に調整されている。すなわち、車はホーランドトンネルから飛び出すや作品のまわりを巡り、通行人は作品が設置された広い所有者のない土地を覆う砂利の上に思い切って足を踏み入れたり、作品の上空にかかったレイト・ストリートとヴァーリック・ストリートをつなぐ歩道橋の上を行ったり来たりすることになる。この作品についてセラ自身が書いたエッセイを知る者であれば、彼が作品を見られることを前提として、あらかじめいかにあらゆる微細な点までを考慮にいれていたかに感心せずにはいられないだろう。(彼のエッセイを読み、この彫刻家自身が、サイト・スペシフィックな作品について語るのに耳を傾ければ、それがすでに完成したものについてであれ、現在計画中のものについてであれ、ちょうど映画に使われる話の展開を示すスケッチを貼ったストーリーボードを思い浮かべるに違いない。)[2] セラがサイト・スペシィフィックについて語るときの真剣さに疑いを抱く者はまずあるまい。(そして「ティルテッド・アーク」の大敗北に対する彼の怒りも完全に正当化された。) しかし、なおセラが考慮にいれていない場の要素がある。歴史である。セラは彼の戸外の彫刻が見る者に開示する一時的な経験に対してはあれだけの細心の配慮を惜しまなかった。が、その関心は常に過去を含めた概念に対してではなく現在形の感覚のほうに向けられてきた。傑作のひとつ「クララ・クララ」がパリのテュイリー公園に設置された際(ああ、これもまた仮設的な作品なり!)、パリの中央軸に関する1世紀も前の論争に触れたアーバニズムに対するひとつの指標を示してはくれたが、それはあくまでも偶然の出来事であり、予期されたことではなかった。というのも、敷地はあらかじめ予定されていた場所ではなかったし、作品もサイト・スペシフィック・ワークとして発想されてはいなかった。[3]

François-Auguste-René Rodin
Monument To Balzac, 1898.

川俣の都市における大型プロジェクトは全て(彼が「フィールド・ワーク」と呼んでいる、様々な都市を放浪し、そこの荒廃した地域から拾い集めてきた廃材を使って小規模な無数の仮小屋を作る作品とは対称的に）意図的に作品が置かれた場の社会的な歴史を巻き込んでいく――少なくとも日本以外におけるプロジェクトについてはそうである。日本では建設と取り壊しという高速のリズムがあらゆる場においてある種の均質化を促し、もろもろの歴史的な痕跡を意図的に消し去ることが唯一の歴史となるような都市を生み出している。これまでのところ川俣が場の歴史を説得力を持って作品に刻み込むことをなしえた唯一のアーティストである、というのが私がこの論文で伝えたい内容である。まず彼が都市において作品の場を選ぶ際には、それぞれの場の持つ独自の歴史に対して、細心の注意を払って臨むという点に留意して欲しい。これは彼が世界的な名声を得たカッセルでの「デストロイド・チャーチ」（1987）以来のことである。（作品ごとに出版される本にその場の歴史に関するエッセイを載せるように主張したのは川俣自身であったろうと推察される。その点で最も目を見張る例はベルギーのコートリックの「ビギナージュ」、ある種の修道院で行った巨大だが親しみのもてる介入であろう。）ルーズヴェルト島のプロジェクトの場合には敷地の地理的な状況と歴史（エリザベス・フロッシュとクロゥディア・ゴールドがこの本の中で述べている）の双方が作品の意義において主要な役割を果たしている。川を隔てて国連ビルとレーヴァー・ハウス（マンハッタンで最も高級なアパートである。10年以上も前のこと、このアパートの上階の一室でお茶を飲みながらイースト・リヴァーの真っ只中に浮かぶ荒廃した細長い島の姿を見て驚いたものだった。）があり、川俣の仮小屋風の無秩序は、贅沢さと世界を制する法律に向き合うことになる。つまりこの場の排除と隔離の記憶が忘れっぽく身勝手な富める者たちと対峙するのである。そして沈黙と孤独が、大都市の混沌と交通とに対抗する。カワマタ・プロジェクトを視覚的にとらえる際のアプローチの方法さえもゲニウス・ロキ（目に見えない各々の土地にまつわる特別な力、霊的なもの、可能性）と無縁ではない。すなわち、マンハッタンからは、その船の舳先のような西側の正面だけが見えるようになっている。この作品を訪れるのには前もって予約がいる。鎖の門を開けてもらい、このプロジェクトのコーディネイターの一人に案内してもらわなくてはならないのだ――まるで牢獄にいる囚人か（実際この島は、かつて囚人たちによって占められていたのだが）、あるいは病院にいる重症の伝染病患者を訪ねるように。

もちろん、建築家たちは随分と長い間、記憶やゲニウス・ロキについて言及してきた。それらは様々な表現をとって現れた所謂ポスト・モダニズムの連中にとって60年代終わり頃から主要な命題のひとつとさえなったのである。既に普遍的で自律的な幾何学的なスペースといったモダニズム運動の夢が崩れ去ったことは明らかだった。しかし、もし建築家のあやつる言葉に十分説得力があったならば、この件に関して彼らの行為を代表する実際の建物の方に深く感動することもなかったと思う。例えばピーター・アイゼンマン、彼のウェクスナー資格美術センターは多くの観客に親しまれている。この建物に与えられた空間上の筋書きは、明快でかつ有効なものである。（立面、平面双方に表現された鋭角的に交わるふたつのグリッドのずれは調和しないままに敷地を定義づけた二つの主軸に繋がっていく――すなわち、コロンバス市全体を貫く軸線と

Constantin Brancusi
Table du silence à Tîrgu Jui, 1938.

Favela in Houston, 1991.

コロンバス市自身のグリッドの中で静かで、独自の雰囲気をもつ空間となっている大学のキャンパスの軸線にである。）しかしながらそういった筋書きに与えられたかりそめの記号は、所詮哀れなものである。アイゼンマンがその敷地内にかつてあった兵器庫の位置を示そうと地上に表した印は（複数の構造壁によって作り出されたアルカイックな廃墟のまがい物）全くのレトリックであり、解読を必要とする長いキャプションをつけたくなる。そしてこの透明感に満ちたセンターを飾る中世風のレンガのほうが歴史の謎解きとしてはもっと分かりやすいというなら、これはもうこの街の過去に対して献じられた真実の賛辞ではない。肥大したジョークそのものである。[4] 多くの建築家は歴史、記憶、あるいはそれに類することをしばしば口にするにもかかわらず、それらを相手にするだけの度量をもちえずに苦しんでいる。彼らは建てるが故に消し去ってしまうのだ。それは石やコンクリートのスラブが建築素材としてどこの場所であろうと、もともとの建築の所有者を覆いつくし、最終的に飲み込んでしまうという理由からだけではない。良きにつけ悪しきにつけ、常に実際の建築のもつ力強さが記憶を凌駕してしまうからである。川俣はそれを明確に示してくれた。そして川俣がウェクスナー・センターのオープニングの展覧会へ招待された際（テーマは、実にこの場に合った、サイト・スペシィフィシィティであった）、この出所の判明しないディズニーランド式の過去の模造品には目もくれず現在のアイゼンマンの明快なトレードマークである建物を覆う白い格子を取り上げてコンテクストに組み込んだのは、アイゼンマンの思わせ振りに刺激されたためだろう。数週間の間このミニマリストと彼の無垢のグリッドは、川俣の木の足場に寄生され、引き伸ばされ、そして逆にそれらの足場がアイゼンマンのデザインを決定しているまさにその軸に沿って引き伸ばされ、仮小屋が散在するキャンパスへと繋げられた。ヴァルター・ベンヤミンの「野蛮行為の記録とならない文明の記録などない。」という言葉はあまりにも安易に引き合いに出される引用である。しかしここで引用するのは決して飾りとしてではない。クルツィシヨフ・ウォディチェコのように、だが彼とは全く異なったやり方で、そして二人ともより直接的にあるいは控えめに暗示している。すなわち、1980年代の特徴となった都市のジェントリフィケーション計画のアリバイとして利用された文化の狂乱の中で多くの博物館が創造されたが、そのどれもがホームレスを生み出す温床のひとつとなってきたのだということを。[5]

「川俣は場所を選び抜く、そしてその選び方は巧妙である」と述べた。それは疑いようもなく、彼がよそ者であり、純化された典型としての旅人であるからだ。川俣は招かれたどの都市においても、記憶と忘却の結び目を必ず探り当てる。それは日常レベルで目にしているうちに次第に見えなくなってしまう歴史に深く根をはった乖離点である。[6] ルーツをもたない者、放浪者の原型ともいえる川俣は、そこを指し示し、しばし立ち止まって我々の社会的環境を支える根幹の部分について考えよとよびかける。これだけでも少なからぬ功績である。しかし、それだけではない。川俣が他のいかなるアーティストや建築家たちよりも、際立って効果的に我々の総体的な記憶を喚起するのはいったいなぜなのだろうか。それは川俣が我々の個人的な記憶の欠落部分をあばき、モニュメントを建てることなくこれを記念しえるからである。

デトレフ・マーティンスは川俣の都市を対象とした大型プロジェクトが与える感覚上のプロセスを次のように見事に表現している。「構築が始まる時点ではなんの反応も覚えない。やがて華々しいファンファーレがなることもなく、人々に気づかれることもなく、板材や梁が古い建築物に対して立ち現れ、あるいはもと空き地であったところに積み重ねられ始める。やがてこの堆積物の層は増大していき、もはや無視しがたいまでになる。」これが第2章である。「当惑」と呼ぶ。すなわち、「だれもが時々シティ・ホールでは奇妙なことが起こるのは承知している。しかしこれはファイルのラベルを貼りちがえるのとは訳が違う。今まで出会ったどの建設工事とも違う。足場だけで建物が存在しないのだ。なにもかもが普通でない。まるで建物の爆破による取り壊しを逆にやっているかのようだ。」[7] この章が最も長く続く。少なくとも全工程の5分の3あるいは、時としてその全てを占めることになる。が、もっと筋道を立て考えてみよう。この章があるからこそ、いったんは作品が「完成」されると、第3段階の活動へすすむことができるのだ。(論理的に「完成」されるという表現は当たっていない。かといって他にこの時期の特殊な状態をいい表せる言葉が見当たらない。)「完成」とはビルダーであり廃品回収屋である川俣がその巨大なピックアップ・スティックの山がうまく配置され、これ以上の追加を要しないと判断する時を指している。(ヨーロッパではこのゲームはミカドと呼ばれる。日本にルーツをもつゲームなのだろうか。注：棒状のピックアップスティックを任意に積み重ね、そこから一本一本、スティックの山が崩れないように順番にスティックをとっていくゲーム。)ここでやっとのことで作品を訪れる機会が与えられる。特別に作品に興味を覚え、好奇心にかられた見物人たちはついに作品の中を徘徊できるのである。といってこの時点がクライマックスというわけではない。見物人によってはプロジェクトの短い継続期間のうちの最低の部分だとさえ言うかもしれない。それから解体が始まる。それは構築に要したよりはるかに早い速度で進められる。(通常プロジェクトの期間全体の3分の1である。)しかし、最大の山場は全てが跡形もなくなった時である。川俣がその場に足を踏み入れる前と、寸分たがわぬ状態にもどった時である。いったいこれは夢だったのだろうか。この複雑な構築作業の果てに、つまり構築と解体の間のほんのつかの間の介入のためだけに何カ月もの間毎日慌ただしく動き回ったチームのあの働きぶりの後に、それを匂わせる物理的痕跡が全く残っていないとは…時間が停止してしまったのだろうか。

しかし当然のことながら痕跡は残されている。これこそが川俣のアートの核をなす部分である。痕跡は我々の心の中に存在する。そしてその場にあって永遠に痕跡を隠蔽してしまう建物とこの痕跡は張り合う必要がない。建築家は派手な装置（似非歴史、様式的引用）で我々の記憶に呼びかけることができると信じている。しかし、それらは必ずや不発に終わる。一方川俣はやってのける。彼にとっては我々のうつろいやすい記憶自体が媒体なのであり、彼が描き出そうとするものは単なるひとつの概念ではない。彼は我々の記憶を試し、執拗になじり続けるのである。一旦全てのものが消え

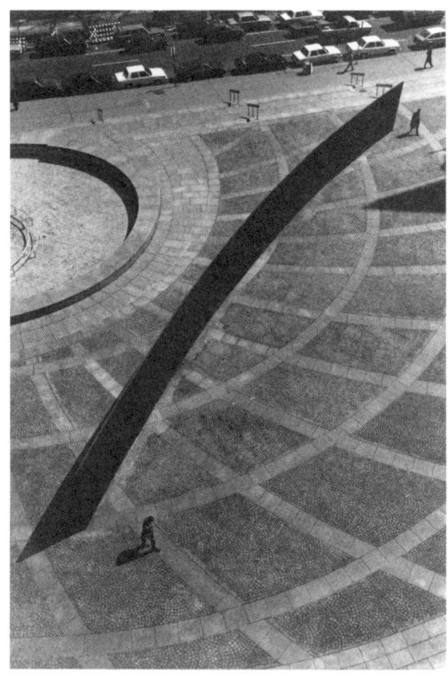

Richard Serra
Tilted Arc, 1981-1989.

去り、川俣がひとときその肉を食らうことによって地図上に書き起こされた忘れ去られていた建物の姿が介入前と同様に再び裸にされると……我々は思い起こすのである。まず川俣のおもちゃのような構造体の美しさを、そして恐らくは荒廃した建物そのもののはるか昔の荘厳な姿とそれが果たしたであろう役割を。さらに、我々は記憶をたぐり始め、未来へも思いをめぐらそうとする。この廃墟から再び何かを生み出しえないだろうか、と。川俣は言う、「グリッドへの寄生が始まり、グリッドが修復された時、秩序がよみがえる。グリッドに対する治療が完了すると、幾つかのグリッドに変化が起きている。この時こそ新しい可能性が浮かび上がる。」[8]（このアーティストはまた、癌の比喩をしばしば使って説明する。「癌が癒された時、全てはもとの通りの秩序にもどっていく。だが、癒された患者はすでに死のすれすれを経験し、もはや以前の自分ではなくなっている」と。）

私はルーズヴェルト島のカワマタ・プロジェクトを一度だけ訪れた。（構築はほぼ終了していた ――実際私は、文字どおり、「正式な開始」の数時間前に訪れたのである。）最初、私はプロジェクトを一度しか見られなかったことでひどく苛立った。（悪気があったわけではない。昨年の秋は、厳しいスケジュールを都合することが実に難しかったのだ。）だが、すぐにあまり気にならなくなった。すでにその時点でこのページを担当することを承諾していたのだが、私自身、自分のあまりの気軽さに驚いていた。私はこのプロジェクトに深く感動していたし、批評家の仕事を真剣に考えている人間である。（通常批評を書く時は、自分が書こうとする作品をよく知った上でないと書かない。）それでは、2度目の訪問をいささか躊躇している自分の気持ちをどう説明すればよかったのだろうか。答えを出すにはしばらくかかった。私はこれから亡霊となろうとしているもの、すなわち追憶になろうとしているものを相手にしていたのだ。再確認などしないほうがかえってもっと明確に触れることができるのである。繰り返しになるが、川俣が打ち建てようとしているのはモニュメントではない ――近代社会にあって、モニュンメントを建てることが、そして記憶することが、いかに不可能なことであるかを川俣は知り抜いている。[9]

私が、実際にプロジェクトを訪ねることが、つかの間のこのプロジェクトの中の最低の部分だと述べたのはもちろん誇張である。ルーズヴェルト島を訪れた者は、特に先に述べたようなかなり厳しい制限のもとで見学した場合は、その荒廃しきった島の先にある敷地のもつ荘厳さに必ずや心奪われたはずである。過去数十年にわたって打ち捨てられてきたゴミをおおう草木の茂みのまっただ中で、カモメの鳴き声と川の流れと、空の広さにすっぽりと包み込まれたようなこの場所の荘厳さに。それは、アッパー・イーストサイドのウォーターフロントのまばゆく、威嚇するような壮大なファサードに向き合うロマンティックな風景である。ここを訪れた者はだれでも、遠くから見た川俣の作品の正面の雰囲気と、ほら穴のようであったり、迷宮のように入り組んだりする板、柱、梁の集合体の様子とのギャップに驚いたはずである。その様はかつてそびえ建っていたレンウィックの建物を今やうずたかく堆積した残骸の中央の、えぐりとられたクレーターの中に沈ませたようにみせる奇妙な地形図によっていっそう強調されている。

だが、カワマタ・プロジェクトのこの部分（迷子になりそうな迷路、数え切れないほどの風景の断片、棒のジャングル、通り抜けできる通路）にその実力が発揮されているわけではない。そこがおそらくは川俣のこの作品とセラの作品との大きな違いだろう。両作品ともピラネージが提示したピクチャレスクの伝統を継承しているが、セラのほうはこの伝統の遺産を視差に関する感覚上の探求と我々の感覚的認識の不確かさとしてとらえ、一方川俣はこのヴェネチアの版画師とその継承者の作品のもっと悲劇的な面に焦点をあてた。セラのピラネージは映画的であり（セラに関してはアイゼンシュタインの偉大なエッセイに負うところが多い)、川俣のピラネージは過去と理性の黄昏を指し示すペシミスティックな歴史家である。[10]

ここまで書くと、偉大なるエンジニアにして考古学者であるショワジイーに触れた先の文章にまでもどりたくなった。彼は『建築史(Histoire de l'architecture)』を著し、これはコルビジェの座右の書となった。川俣の作り出す「雑音」の中を歩き回っているうちにショワジイーのことが浮かんだのには幾つかの理由がある。まず、この幻をみているような状態。建物の南側の正面を隠している丘から浅い谷で分離されたなだらかな小山を登った際（そしてネオ・ゴシックの廃墟から芽を吹き出した不気味な村とも見える、 複数の小さな仮小屋で川俣は南側正面を満たした）、 まるでアクロポリスの丘のプロポライエの貧者版と相対しているような心持ちになった。そしてその先にはさらにもう一つの丘があり、ここで再び私は（今度は、この「村」の屋根の高さに広がる様々なテクスチュア、色、素材を織り込んだ、あまり平らでない凍りついた海の表面が見えてきた)、ショワジイーが偉大なアテネの敷地について語る際に持ち出す「ギリシャ的なピクチャレスク」の完璧な例として極めて知的に描写された「建築的プロムナード」に近い変化を体験したのだ。さらにまた、そこにあるものはみなセラのサイト・スペシィフィックな作品の最高傑作にあてはめることが可能なものだった。

しかしここで第二の意外な局面、いわば第二の「ショワジイーイズム」が見いだせる。川俣の作品は「全て足場だけで、実際の建物がない」と非常に感覚的にデトレフ・マーティンスによって評されているが、ショワジイーはこのふたつ、足場と建築、は必ずしも別個のものではないことを提示した。比較的若い時期にショワジイーを有名たらしめたのはローマの建築様式は、経済的な理由から、レンガの仮設の足場（これ自体は安いごく基本的な木構造によって支えられている）をマッスの中に沈め、恒久的な支持体として変容させたものであろうという発見であった。[11] 明確な形ではないにしろ、川俣によって成し遂げられたと同じようなカテゴリーの逆転とよべるものがある。(そしてこれもまた足場の性質に関係する。)

Toronto Project: Colonial Tavern Park, 1989.

Sidewalk in Columbus, 1990.

そして最後のショワジイーイズムである。最後にとっておきのものを残しておいた。しかしこれは川俣の作品全般に対して多少批判を加えることになる。ショワジイーはトポロジカルな（位相的な）比較法を実践していた。例えば以下のように述べている。「控え壁の配置法には二つの全く異なったやり方が考えられる。ひとつは、こうした厄介な補助装置は外へ追い出す方法。もうひとつは逆に部屋の中に控え壁を配置する方法。中世の西洋建築であれば前者の解決法をとり、ローマやビザンティンの建築であれば後者が用いられる。双方とも長所短所がある。前者を選んだ場合は、二つの控え壁の間の空間は犠牲にしなくてはならないし、後者をとれば、この二つの控え壁の間の空間によって部屋を覆う表面は、拡大することになる。前者によれば内部空間は制限されるが、邪魔なものは取り払われより自由なものとなる。一方後者によれば、空間は広くなるが妨げるものは多くなる。」[12]

ショワジイーの方法はジョフロア・サンティレールの比較解剖の考え方を参考にしている。サンティレールはジョルジュ・キュヴィエの機能主義と対抗し、動物は骨格の外側に生命をもつ（哺乳類、鳥、魚）か、内側にもつか（虫）のいずれかであると言い切った。

このトポロジカルな空間に対する概念は川俣の作品にも働いている。(彼は「袋の内側というのは外側の表面の続きとも考えられる。」と述べており、また彼がギャラリーや美術館を離れ、公共の場へと出ていった頃、作品に対する最もショックを与えられたコメントは「部屋の内側の構造が外へはみ出してきている」「内部が裏返しになって、外に出てきたようだ」であった。)[13] 手袋のように内側を裏返すというこの挑戦的な試みがほとんどの川俣作品において建築を相手に行われている。(少なくとも私には、そう感じられる。それも非常にうまく成功していると思う。)これこそが川俣の作品によってもたらされた逆転の効果である。(そして、この効果が今度は川俣自身の個人と社会、建物とそのコンテクスト、居住者とホームレスに対する巧緻な考察全体に影響を与えているのである。）寄生された建物の内部への立ち入りを禁止された場合（通常、安全上の理由からそうなることの方が多い)、この位相的な逆転の強大な幻影がことに強まるのである。ルーズヴェルト島では特にそれが顕著であった。すなわち、レンウィックの危険な廃墟への侵入はならなかったにしても、人はその本質を見抜き、窓やドアに飛び込んでいく川俣の「癌」の触手をかいま見ることはできたはずである。外側から「裏返し」の構造をみるのは興奮を覚えるものである。しかしその中に入ることが特別に面白いわけではない。だからこそ川俣のこうした作品をたまたま正面からしか、あるいは遠くからしか見ることができなかったとしてもセラとはまた違った川俣のサイト・スペシフィックな作品を理解できるのである。しかしまた、同じ理由で私には川俣の室内の作品はかなりきどったものに見えてしまう。あまりに美しすぎる。あまりに繊細なのだ。(セラの作品が囲われた空間の中に置かれたとしても損なわれることはないだろう。）構築と解体のプロセスのわずかな合間をぬってクーパー・ユニオンにこのアーティスト自身が展示したルーズヴェルト島プロジェクトの原寸大の模型

（というよりは実際の作品の翻訳）では、中を観客は歩くことができたが、それは実際の雰囲気をつぶさに伝えるものではなかった。もし私が川俣に対して、何かアドバイスを与えることが許されるのなら——もっともそれは無理な話だが。批評家はアーティストにアドバイスなど与えるべきではない——川俣が忘却から救おうとしている建物の内部から観客をできるかぎり遠ざけておくことだと言うだろう。[14]観客は記憶につきまとう亡霊を愛でたり、これに思いをはせるために、わざわざその中に入る必要はない。

［イヴーアラン・ボワは現在ハーバード大学のヨセフ・ピリッツァー・ジュニア現代美術の教授であり、『オクトーバー』誌の編集者でもある。彼は1920年代の抽象芸術および第二次世界大戦後のアメリカ美術のについて数多くの記事を発表している。そのいくつかは1990年MITプレスから出版された彼のエッセイ集の中に収録されている。］

1．川俣に関する評論は英語で書かれたものはあまりないが、いずれも比喩的な説明に富んだ、きわめて質の高いものである。川俣による都市の介入の不規則な形式がもたらす直接的な効果として、私がとりあげている暗喩的な衝動についてここで論ずるのは適当ではない。ルーズヴェルト島プロジェクトの力強い比喩的な解釈としては、本書中のクロゥディア・ゴールドのエッセイを参照されたい。

2．リチャード・セラとクララ・ウェイアグラフによる「St.John's Rotary Arc」（1980）は、リチャード・セラによる「Interview. Etc. 1970－1980」ハドソン・リヴァー美術館（ヨンカーズ、1980）p.151－161に再録されている。

3．私のエッセイ「Stroll around Clara Clara」を参照されたい。特にテュイリー公園のインスタレーションに関する記述以降はエルンスト・ゲルハード・ギュス編集の「Richard Serra」に再録されている。リッゾーリ（ニューヨーク、1987）p.40－59。私が述べたセラの場の歴史に対する興味の欠如の中には、社会的な存在の欠如も含まれている。よってダグラス・クリンプ氏がセラの都市における作品を政治的な扇動活動のゼスチャーと解釈しているのには賛成しかねる。（ロザリンド・クラウスによる「Richard Serra/Sculpture」ニューヨーク近代美術館、ニューヨーク、1986、の中の「Serra's Public Sculpture：Redfining Site Specificity」p.40-56）1977年ドイツのボーフムに設置された彫刻「Terminal」がこの彫刻に反対したキリスト教民主党の政治的なスローガンの対象にされたという事実は、この作品自体の構造とは全く関係がない。セラはハンス・ハーケではない。

4．クリス・バーデンはこれに対してレンガ色に塗った発泡スチロール製の銃目のパターンをセンターのタワーにこの展覧会期間中はりつけて、アイゼマンのジョークを振った。「Breakthroughs：Avant－Garde Artists in Europe and America，1950－1990」リッゾーリおよびウェクスナー視覚美術センター（ニューヨークおよびコロンバス、1991）p.194－197。アイゼマンの建築を歴史化する様式に対しての評論として、私のエッセイ「Surfaces」を参照されたい。これは1993年モントリオールのカナディアン建築センターで予定されているアイゼマンに献じられる展覧会「Cities of Artificial Excavation」（人工的な発掘都市）のカタログに収録される予定である。

5．美術市場と不動産とホームレスの関係を作品の主要なテーマとしているクルツィショフ・ウォディチェコについてはデニス・ホリエー著『Krzysztof Wodiczko：Instruments，Projections，Vehicles』タピエス・ファンデーション（バルセロナ、1992）p.21-45、の中の「While the City Sleep」を参照されたい。

6．川俣のこの点については、『Kawamata Begijnhof Kortrijk』カナール・アート・ファンデーションおよび現代企画室（コートリックおよび東京、1991）p.21－45に収録されたギールト・ベカエルトによる美しいエッセイ「The Stranger」を参照されたい。

7．デトレフ・マーティンス「In Deference to Dis－Order」、『Kawamata：Toronto Project 1989』マーサー・ユニオン（トロント、1991）p.47に収録。マーティンスのエッセイは、川俣の作品に対する批評としては最高のものである。

8．「Kawamata：An Interview with Linda Genereux」『Kawamata： Toronto Project 1989』に収録。

9．ロダンの「バルザック」がその施主から拒否されたことに端を発する我々の時代のモニュメントの理論についての詳細はロザリンド・クラウスによる「Sculpture in the Expanded Field」（1978）で論じられている。これはクラウスの『The Originality of the Avant－Garde and Other Modernist Myths』MITプレス（ケンブリッジ、1985）p.277－290に再録されている。私の仮想の論文「history of public sculpture in the twentieth century」の6つタイトルの全てのヘッドラインは、ブランクーシのアトリエ、住居を含めた一連の作品群（ensemble）からスミッソンの「ノン・サイト」についてまで網羅しているが、いずれもモニュメントのコンセプトからはさらに遠ざかっている。ブランクーシとスミッソンという特別なケースについては、それぞれが歴史に対して異なった関わり方をしている。ロザリンド・クラウスの「Echelle/monumetalit—Modernisme/postmodernisme：la ruse de Brancusi」を参照のこと。これはパリのジョルジュ・ポンピドー・センターのマルギット・ロウエルによって企画された展覧会「Qu'est－ce que la sculpture moderne」のカタログ『Qu'est－ce que la sculpture moderne』（1986）p.246－253に収録されている。

10．ピラネージとセラに関しては（またショワジイーについても簡単に触れている。）、拙書『Picturesque Stroll around Clara－Clara』（前掲）を参照にされたい。川俣とピラネージについてはデトレフ・マーティンスの「In Defence To Dis－Order」（前掲）を参照のこと。

11．ショワジイーによって1869年（当時彼は28歳であった）に著された『L'art de b tir chez les Romains』デュッヒャー（パリ）は1873年に登場し、広く称賛された。私自身の長きにわたるショワジイーに関する研究は出版が予定されているアクソノメトリック投影法の歴史についての拙書に収録される。

12．オーギュスト・ショワジイー著『L'art de b tir chez les Byzantins』Librairie de la Socit Anonyme des Publicatrons Priodiques（パリ、1983）p.124

13．小池美香、正木基、村田真編、『KAWAMATA、工事中』現代企画室（東京、1987）より「インタヴュー」p.37－38。この他に川俣は、口の表皮について語った際、同じ裏返しのイメージを使っている（Genereux、前掲、p.29）。

14．ベルギーのコートリックでの川俣のプロジェクトの成功は、ここで私が述べたこととは矛盾しているかに思える。しかし、状況が全く通常の場合と異なっており、ほとんどの川俣の手法とは直接的に逆の扱い方をした。すなわち、修道院は視覚的に町から隠蔽され、（そして毎夜9時にはその小さな門が閉じられた。）川俣の足場は庭一面に、そして「町の敷地内の村」の庭や通りに拡がり、外からは見られないようになっていた。一旦修道院の中にはいるや、川俣のプロジェクトの真っ只中にいることになるのだが、依然として彼の木の板が寄生した建物の外にいるのである。

The Time Lag Inside the City

Tadashi Kawamata

When a country is developing both economically and culturally, no one stops to look back at history. The postmodern trend of the 1980's, by disguising the elements of the historical, abruptly turned history into parody. This trend showed without a doubt that it is only through existing streets and newly erected buildings that the memory of the city, or the memory of architecture, can call forth the scenes before such structures appeared. Looking at the absolute concrete of the walls of brand new buildings, one can recall their sites several months before they were constructed. However, such recollections themselves are obliterated in the violent flow of day-to-day change, thrusting the city into a constant architectural rush of new buildings.

Through the narrow discrepancies that appear under such conditions, it can sometimes seem that a single place is the only remaining element in its surrounding area. No one pays attention to this place until, amidst the dizzying changes occurring in the surrounding area, it alone is revealed by its unique time frame. In the city, one such time lag can suddenly make a place look entirely different. But this is not to say that the effect is created simply by a place's relationship with its surroundings: it can also appear that inevitabilities of one kind or another provide a place with an individual time axis.

Discrepancies in the time axis are sometimes caused by places and buildings, other times by regions or differences in the customs of residents. Actually, if the situation of the present-day city can be described as composed of people with cultures and customs from many different countries gathering and living together in a single place, some of the people in that place become one with the individual identity of the city, and others live within the national identity and customs of the countries of their birth. We often see that interposing one street in the same town brings together people of completely different languages and cultures who build their own community and continue lifestyles true to their traditional customs. However, even people with their own histories and cultures, living in a city with many other people of differing histories, display aspects of the city's own identity. Thus, a variety of gaps, many of which develop into social problems, are created in daily life. At the same time, this is precisely the reason that the city is variable, with many places changing through the cycle of re-habitation and clearance, and people moving to and fro within such cycles. Throughout the city, changes like these can show us the footprints of history, which is also forced to change. Whenever I visited New York, the ruins of the Small Pox Hospital on the southern edge of Roosevelt Island were in my mind as reflecting such footprints of history. I also thought that the ruins reflected the city of New York as it exists today.

''The Time Lag Inside the City'' is a revised version of the essay ''The Time Lag of the City,'' which appeared in April 1992 in the 370th issue of *Taiyo (The Sun)* magazine.

TAX-FREE

都市の中の時差（タイムラグ）

川俣正

その国が経済的にも文化的にも発展しているときは、だれも歴史を振り返ろうとしない。80年代のポストモダンの動きは、唐突に歴史性を装う形で歴史をパロディ化してしまった。都市の記憶、或いは建築の記憶というのは常に今現在の町並みやそこに建てられた真新しい建物を通してしか、それらがその場所に建つ前の情景を思い起こすことができないということをはからずも表している。今現在見える真新しいビルの圧倒的なコンクリートの壁を見ながら、このビルの建つ数か月前の風景を思い起こす。しかし、それすらもまた日々の暴力的な変化の流れの中で消されてしまい、常に町は真新しいビルの建築ラッシュに明け暮れる。

このような中で、わずかばかりの**ずれ**によってある場所がまわりの風景の中で一つだけ取り残されたように見えることがある。以前はだれも気にも止めなかったが、まわりが目まぐるしく変化していく中で、そこだけがまわりの時間と落差を持ったことにより顕在化してしまう。都市の中では、このように一つの時差（タイムラグ）によって突然ある場所が違った場所として見えてくることがある。しかしそれは単にまわりとの関係によってそこが浮上してきたと言うことだけではなく、何等かの必然性が固有の時間軸をその場に与えているようにも見える。

この時間軸の**ずれ**は、ある時は場所や建物、そしてある時は地域であったり、或いはそこで生活している人々の習慣の違いなどから起こることもある。実際、様々な国の文化や習慣を持つ人々が集まり、一つの場所に住んでいるのが現代の都市の状況だとすると、その中のあるものはその都市の持つ固有のアイデンティティーに同化しながら、またあるものは常に生まれ持った自国のアイデンティティーと生活習慣の中で生活している。同じ町で道路一本隔てて言葉も文化も全く違う人達がその中で自らコミュニティーを作り、自分達の伝統的な生活習慣を守って生活しているのをみかけることがよくある。しかし自国の歴史と習慣を持ちながらも多くの違った歴史を持つ人々と共に一つの都市に住むということは、当然その都市独自の生活習慣と歴史をも同時に持たざるを得ない。そのことが日々生活している上で様々なギャップを生み、しばしば社会問題となる。しかし、だからこそ町は可変的で、いろいろな場所がリハビリテーションとクリアランスとによって変化していき、人もまたその中で移動していく。

そして私たちは町のいたるところにこの様な変化によって変わらざるを得なかった歴史の痕跡を見ることができる。ニューヨークの街を訪れるたびに、ルーズヴェルト島の南端にあるこの天然痘病院跡の廃墟は、この様な歴史の痕跡を映し出しているものとして常に私の頭の中にあった。そしてその廃墟はまた、まさに現在のニューヨークの町そのものをも映し出しているように思えた。

(「都市の中の時差（タイムラグ）」は1992年4月に発行された月刊誌「太陽」No.370に掲載された「都市の時差（タイムラグ）」より抜粋・加筆されたものです。)

CATS
CATS

Banishment: Kawamata's Politics of Place

Kostas Gounis

On Roosevelt Island, the ruins of Renwick's Small Pox Hospital seem "new," freed from and strangely revived by the temporary embrace of the Kawamata project. All physical evidence of the project is now gone. In keeping with Kawamata's appreciation of transience, the Roosevelt Island project lived as a moment when our experience with the vicissitudes of space and time was given a palpable shape. Kawamata's projects in general are acts of appropriation of elements and categories that are most unyielding to domestication and representation. The project on Roosevelt Island elucidated the simultaneity and convergence of formal attributes, natural processes, and social intentionalities.

Kawamata's own ambiguous and unclassifiable "otherness" as an artist is mirrored by the choices and contingencies that went into the conception and realization of the Roosevelt Island project. Most conspicuously, the remoteness and inaccessibility of the site before, during, and after the project stood in stark contrast to the "public" nature of his intervention. Through the use of materials collected from and returned to the all-devouring social traffic of the city, Kawamata transformed the accumulation of this debris into a moment of illumination. His project dwelt on and momentarily bridged the gap between the making of obsolescence and the possibilities of repossession.

From my perspective as a social anthropologist studying homelessness in New York City, the Kawamata project is a compelling commentary on the politics of space that defines the nature of membership. Consequently, these are reflections because of, as much as about, the project.

On Institutions: Members and Strangers

Human communities come together by differentiating between members and strangers.[1] Institutions, be they codified norms or actual places, are every society's ever-growing inventory of constraints that determine the limits of membership. Our sense of belonging is grounded in a shared sense of place and time. There are several institutional arrangements that safeguard the integrity of this shared perception and facilitate the continuity of a corresponding social order. Communities, from neighborhoods to nation-states, are continually engaged in a process of consolidation through reaffirmation, reinvention, and rearrangement of the essential principles that define who their members are. We understand and experience life from within a grid of prescribed practices. Against this grid, personal and collective myths, public versions of official histories and hidden transcripts of unauthorized ones, memory and imagination are the shifting ground on which we try to define who we are. Kawamata's projects, appropriately described as "parasites," "cancers," or "viruses," have persistently attacked the seeming integrity and homogeneity of this grid.

The converse side of arrangements that bring us together is the systematic practice of exclusion. The Roosevelt Island project explored how the regulated and restricted nature of membership is bolstered through institutions that specialize in separation and displacement. Such institutions enforce the denial of community to strangers, especially when they are considered threats to the order of things. Stigma (negatively valued difference) and the fear of pollution invariably attach to these perceived predators on the established physical and symbolic securities of social being.

On Monuments and Ruins

Monuments and ruins (often, the two are interchangeable) are the tracks left by the histories of efforts to consolidate, defend, and reproduce human groups as separate and unique communities. Selectively and with a specific intentionality, these histories reinvest ruins with the elevated status of monuments, or abandon them to the erosion of nature and time. Monuments are meant to evoke continuity with a glorified past; ruins stand for failure, dead ends, and obsolescence. Kawamata's hybrid structure at the Small Pox Hospital allowed viewers a fleeting glance at the permutable nature of these processes.

As a designated landmark, the Small Pox Hospital is simultaneously a monument and a ruin. Because of this dual nature, the Kawamata structure was not allowed to touch the remains of the hospital, nor was the site of the project open to the general public, for reasons of preservation and public safety. These restrictions reflect, even if unintentionally, the practice of distancing from the messy realities of real people's lived experiences that is key to both the fabrication of monuments and the generation of ruins.

Urban ruins in the major cities of the United States mark zones of discard, territories that have been made redundant along with the people that inhabit them. Consider the epidemic of urban decay and degradation that has produced the South Bronx in New York City, downtown Detroit, and Newark, New Jersey. The physical evidence of abandonment and devastation is a loud pronouncement of unredeemable damage.[2]

Contemporary urban ruins are grim memorials to the reality of multiple epidemics that threaten the society-at-large. In New York City today, the conventional apprehension of symbolic pollution has been amplified and superseded by the dread of physical contagion. When we meet one another, we instinctively seek to establish an optimum distance of safety and comfort. Our public and private encounters with others are framed by fear—of tuberculosis and AIDS, respectively. The Kawamata project provided us with a somber reminder of the proximity between perceived fear and the practice of banishment.

On Islands of Banishment: From Lemnos to Roosevelt

Banishment is the standard social reaction to the threat of pollution and infection. Banishment has a long history. In the classical tradition, the story of Philoctetes is a compelling representation of the enduring legacy of involuntary displacement.[3] In 409 B.C., Sophocles produced *Philoctetes*, the play through which this story has survived. Listen to Odysseus describing the setting and explaining the circumstances of Philoctetes's banishment:

> This is it; the island of Lemnos and its beach
> down to the sea that surrounds it; desolate,
> no one sets foot on it; there are no houses.
> This is where I marooned him long ago,
> the son of Poias, the Melian, his foot
> diseased and eaten away with running ulcers.
> . . .
> We had no peace with him: at the holy festivals,
> we dared not touch the wine and meat; he screamed
> and groaned so, and those terrible cries of his
> brought ill luck on our celebrations; all
> the camp was haunted by him.[4]

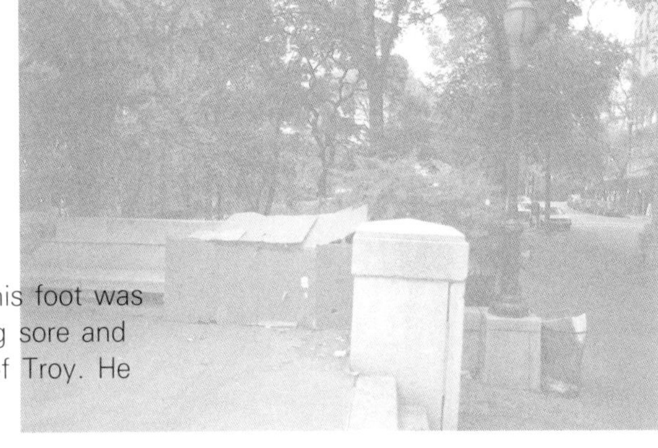

Philoctetes had joined the Achaean expedition against Troy. But his foot was bitten by a snake and would not heal. The stench of the festering sore and his horrible cries of pain spoiled the war party outside the walls of Troy. He was taken to the desolate island of Lemnos and abandoned there.

After the Kawamata Project on Roosevelt Island, I have thought of Lemnos as the mythical antecedent of a few islands around New York City, including Roosevelt. In the *AIA Guide to New York City*, Elliot Willensky and Norval White, in a twist of unintended irony, write that, "in addition to Manhattan, Staten, and Long, the city is *infested* with yet other islands" (my emphasis). Indeed, infestation has been a major concern that decided the uses, past and present, of most of these islands. Throughout the history of the city, they have housed institutions designed to protect the city from symbolic pollution and physical contagion.

On Ellis Island, the former United States Immigration Station has been reconstructed and restored as Ellis Island National Monument. Still, even as a monument to the making of America, Ellis Island depicts the experience of immigration and arrival to the U.S. with a surprising intensity: as violent dislocation from the home of origin, on the one hand, and as submission to the frightening technologies of processing for admission, on the other.

Rikers Island in the East River houses a variety of penal institutions: city jails for men and women and a local satellite of the state prison system.

Hart, a relatively unknown "other" island in Long Island Sound, east of City Island in the Bronx, is where the city's potter's field is located today. Hart Island is the final destination of people who lived on the margins of the city, and died lonely deaths on the streets and in the asylums of New York City.

Wards Island, underneath the glorious span of Triboro Bridge, is only a short distance up the East River from Roosevelt and similarly situated in the shadow of Manhattan. Wards serves as a contemporary zone of discard—in very much the way that Roosevelt Island used to in the days of the Small Pox Hospital, when it was known as Blackwell's and then as Welfare Island. Among the facilities to be found on Wards Island are a psychiatric hospital, a psychiatric unit for the "criminally insane," an 800-bed shelter for homeless men, and a psychiatric unit for children.

On each of these islands we encounter the evidence of past and present forms of banishment. Each is filled with spaces forbidden, ignored, redundant, or recycled—spaces that contain our fears, ignorance, and prejudices.

In Context: On Representation and Redemption

Across the river from Roosevelt Island, underneath the FDR drive on the east side of Manhattan, a few makeshift shacks still remain. If it weren't for the people who dwell in them, these shacks could be mistaken for Kawamata *Field Works* or a Kawamata *Favela* in New York. While the project was still standing, they looked as if they were errant parts of it, fragments that had broken off and drifted over to the Manhattan shore and were appropriated by these dwellers. Unlike the inaccessible Kawamata project, these and other similar contraptions throughout New York City—in the streets, under bridges, in subway tunnels, in parks, in abandoned buildings, and in vacant lots amidst dilapidated buildings—are true habitations, where people live lives of banishment and exposure.

Institutions, counterparts to the Small Pox Hospital that similarly may end up as ruins, continue to be integral parts of the social economy of New York City, serving the dual purpose of meeting basic needs and containing social disruptions. The psychiatric wards where hospital attendants prepare the medication trays for patients with vacant looks, incoherent speech, and ineffable needs; the AIDS wards where men and women die horrible deaths, stigmatized and often forgotten and alone; the drill floors of armories where the homeless are warehoused; the prisons that recycle inmates. People whose lived reality is a life-sentence served in installments circulate between these contemporary equivalents to the nineteenth-century asylums that were located on Roosevelt island.

The overwhelming evidence of exclusion that surrounds us is the inevitable context for assessing the social and political significance of the Kawamata project. Beyond the duly warranted praise for Kawamata's inspired contemplation of the formal attributes of time and space as they relate to the cycles of construction and destruction in the city; beyond the keen reflection on the continuities and gaps that delineate the horizons for the experience, perception, and imagination of our social realities; even beyond the explicit intent that the project serve as social commentary, or as a metaphor for the city of homelessness, AIDS, and profound polarizations—Kawamata's project raises questions that may be as difficult to articulate as are bewildering the social practices it speaks to. An immediate response to this hybrid structure would be a sense of paradox and ambivalence. Paradox because it was such an eloquent rendering of the grim artlessness of marginalization and exclusion. Ambivalence because, as a commentary on social isolation and stigma, it stood mysterious and inaccessible, detached from the lived reality of exclusion and degradation that unfolds across the river, on the streets and in the numerous institutions of New York City. Also, because of its temporariness: while the bleak realities of the city's multiple epidemics continue unabated, the Kawamata project was a transitory presence.

These peculiarities and incongruities are framed by the contemporary currency of the concern with the politics of representing "the other." The power to represent, through whatever medium, the degradations and indignities of others is, in James Agee's words, a "curious, not to say obscene and thoroughly terrifying"[5] practice fraught with the horrible consequence of reducing the immediacy of deprivation into objectifying practices and prefabricated sentiments.

On the other side, there are possibilities for redemption through participation. Philoctetes exhorted the strangers who arrived on his island of banishment to speak to him, because "[speech] is all that we can have from one another." Illuminating the many shapes of human need and speaking to the conditions that make the difference between homelessness and belonging[6] is a political category of participation entirely different from, but as important as, the kind of politics that seeks to alleviate and correct social injury. The Kawamata Project on Roosevelt Island was an inspired example of the former kind of politics—a politics that seeks to produce and represent the effects of power on the distribution of membership. The actuality of membership is a responsibility that rests with all of us.

Kostas Gounis is a social anthropologist who has studied homelessness and mental illness in New York City since 1984. He recently completed a doctoral thesis at Columbia University on "The Domestication of Homelessness," an ethnography of the New York City shelter system for homeless men.

1. Michael Walzer, *Spheres of Justice* (New York: Basic Books, 1983).

2. An exhaustive documentation of these processes in various cities of the U.S.A. is to be found in the work of Camilo Jose Vergara, a New York City-based photographer and writer.

3. My own short list of similarly powerful renderings of the experience of banishment would include *King Lear*, Daniel Defoe's *A Journal of the Plague Year*, Anton Chekhov's short story "Ward 6," Albert Camus's *The Plague*, Ibsen's *An Enemy of the People*, and almost all of Solzhenitsyn's work.

4. My quotations from *Philoctetes*, here and below, are from the translation by David Grene and Richard Lattimore in *Greek Tragedies*, volume 3 (Chicago: University of Chicago Press, 1960).

5. James Agee and Walker Evans, *Let Us Now Praise Famous Men* (Boston: Houghton Mifflin, 1941).

6. "Homelessness and Belonging" is the title of the concluding chapter in Michael Ignatieff's *The Needs of Strangers* (New York: Penguin Books, 1984), a brilliant and urgent essay "on privacy, solidarity, and the politics of being human."

追放：川俣による場をめぐる検証

コスタス・グーニス

ルーズヴェルト島にあるレンウィックのスモールポックス病院の廃墟は、カワマタ・プロジェクトによる仮設の囲い込みによって解放され、息を吹き返し、「新しく」生まれかわったかのようである。実際のプロジェクトの跡はすでにない。無常性に対する川俣の鋭い眼識によって、時空の変転をめぐる我々の体験に明確な形が与えられた時、ルーズヴェルト島プロジェクトは、かりそめの生命を得るに至った。言わば、川俣のプロジェクトは、身近なものに言い換えたり、ほかのもので置き換えたりする融通性が最もききにくい要素やカテゴリーを、みごとに表現した行為だといえる。ルーズヴェルト島プロジェクトは、因習的な属性、自然の移り変わり、そして社会的作為といったものの持つ同時性と収束性を解明したのである。

川俣自身の曖昧で分類不可能なアーティストとしての「他者性」が、ルーズヴェルト島プロジェクトのコンセプトづくり、実現化の際の判断と偶然性に現れている。最も印象的であったのは、プロジェクト実施前から最中、そして終了後にいたっても変わらないルーズヴェルト島という場のもつ遠隔性や近づき難さが、川俣の介入によってもたらされた「公共性」と純然たる対比を見せていた点である。川俣はニューヨーク市で繰り広げられる、目まぐるしいばかりの社会的動向の中でかき集められ再び元に戻された素材を使い、その破片を集積して覚醒の瞬間へと結晶させた。いわば彼のプロジェクトは、衰退をもたらすものと回復の可能性との間の深い溝に、ほんの束の間ではあるが橋渡しをしたのである。

ニューヨークのホームレス問題を研究している社会人類学者としてカワマタ・プロジェクトに接するならば、このプロジェクトは、社会の構成員の性質を定義づける「場」をめぐって展開される駆け引き（政治）に対する称賛に値いする見解とみる事ができるであろう。従って、以下に述べるのは、このプロジェクトに関しての考察ではあるが、同時にそこから派生して考えるに至った事柄についての私見でもある。

制度について：構成員と部外者

人間社会は、その構成員と部外者を区別することによってまとめ上げられている。[1] 制度というものは、それが成文化された基準であれ、あるいは一つの具体的な場所であれ、どの社会においても存在する。それは構成員とそうでないものとの境界を決定するための、増殖を続ける制約装置なのである。我々の所属意識は時間と場所の共有感覚に根差しているといえよう。こうした共有感覚の完全性を保持するためにこそ、数多くの制度的な約束事が存在し、それによって社会秩序の継続を容易にしている。地域から国家にいたるまで、共同体社会は構成員が誰なのかを定義する根本原理を再確認、再構築、再整理する過程を通して、たゆみなく統合強化されていく。我々は規定された枠組みの範囲内で人生を理解し、体験しているのにすぎない。こうした規定された枠組みに対し、我々が自ら何者であるかを定義する際の流動的な根拠となるのは、個人のあるいは集団の通念、正式なものとして公表されたてきた歴史、あるいは非公式な歴史上の記録、そして記憶と想像である。川俣のこれまでのプロジェクトは、「寄生体」や「癌」、あるいは「ウイルス」といった呼び方で的確に表現されながら、こうした枠組みのうわべだけの完璧さや同質性を執拗に攻撃し続けてきた。

我々を一つにまとめ上げる社会秩序には、制度的に除外行為を行なうという別の側面がある。構成員に規定と制限を課すという社会の本質が、いかに制度という分離と排除にたけたシステムによって支えられてきたかをルーズヴェルト・アイランドでのプロジェクトは探り出した。特に部外者たちが物事の秩序を脅かすと思われる場合、そうした制度は社会に対し部外者たちを拒絶することを強要する。社会を守るために確立された安全性を脅かす略奪者であると認識されるやいなや、部外者たちは必ず烙印（否定的な意味での差異）を押され、汚染の恐怖と結びつけられてしまう。

モニュメントと廃墟について

モニュメントと廃墟は（両者はたいてい互換可能である）人間の作る個々の集団を他とは異なる独自な共同社会として強化し、守り、繁栄させるために心を注いだ人々の努力の歴史の跡といえる。こうした歴史は特定の意図に基づいて選択され、時には廃墟をモニュメントという高尚な地位にまであらためて引き上げるが、ある時には自然や時間の淘汰に任せて見捨ててしまう。モニュメントとは、栄光に輝く過去の継続性を想起するものであり、一方廃墟が意味するものは失敗、行き詰まり、退廃である。川俣によるスモールポックス病院のハイブリッドな構築物は、こうした相互に入れ替えが可能な廃墟の特質を鑑賞者にかいま見せてくれる。

歴史的建造物に指定されたスモールポックス病院は、モニュメントであると同時に廃墟でもある。そうした二元的な性質ゆえに、保存や一般市民の安全のため、川俣の構築物が病院跡に接触することや、プロジェクトの現場を一般公開することは許可されなかった。こうした規制こそ、意図的でないにしろ、人々が現実に行なっている「厄介な現実からは身を遠ざけようとする」行為の象徴にほかならない。そしてこの行為こそモニュメントをでっちあげ、廃墟を生み出す仕組みの体質を解く鍵となる。

アメリカの主要都市に見られる都会の廃墟は、見捨てられた地域にあり、そこに住む人々とともに「あぶれもの」と判断された場所である。ニューヨーク市のサウス・ブロンクス、そしてデトロイトのダウンタウンやニュージャージーのニューアークを生み出した都市部の衰退と荒廃についての物的証拠は、もはや回復不能となった損失を声高に訴えているではないか。[2]

現代都市における廃墟は、社会全般を脅かす多くの流行病の実体を示す、不愉快なメモリアルにほかならない。今日のニューヨークでは、従来から恐れられてきた象徴的な汚染はますます拡大し、さらに疫病に対する物理的な接触感染への恐れがこれに代わろうとしている。我々は互いに出会っても、本能的にできる限り安全で快適な距離を保とうとしてしまう。公の場であれ、個人的な場であれ、他者との出会いは結核やエイズといった個々の疫病に対する恐怖のために制限されている。カワマタ・プロジェクトは、恐怖感と追放行為が隣合わせだという事実を、陰鬱にも我々に思い起こさせる。

追放の島々について：レムノスからルーズヴェルトへ

追放は、汚染や感染の脅威に対する社会の一般的な反応である。追放の歴史は長い。古典的な伝説のひとつであるピロクテーテスの物語は、長く引き継がれてきた当事者の意志に反する排除行為[3]を感動的に語っている。紀元前409年にソフォクレスは、この物語を今日に伝えることになる戯曲「ピロクテーテス」を著わした。ピロクテーテスが追放された時の状況と背景を描写したオデュッセウスの言葉に耳を傾けよう。
「ここぞまさに、四方をめぐる大海原に通じたレムノス島とその浜辺、
荒れはてた人類未踏の地。ここには人家も存在しない。
ここは遙か昔に私が彼を置き去りにした所、
メロス人ポイアスの息子を。彼の足は病に冒され、
膿を流す潰瘍に侵されていた。
・・・・・
彼といると我々は心安らかではいられなかった。聖なる祭りのときでさえ、
我々は酒や肉に手をつける勇気もなかった。それほどに彼は、
叫び呻いていた、そして彼のひどい叫びは、
我々の祝いの席に不幸をもたらした。遠征軍キャンプ全体が、
彼に悩まされた。」[4]

ピロクテーテスは、トロイア討伐のためのアカイア人の遠征に参加した。しかし彼の足は蛇に咬まれ、癒えなかった。化膿した傷から漂う嫌気がさすほどの悪臭と、ひどい苦痛の叫び声が、トロイア城壁の外に陣を構えた軍隊の士気を損なった。彼は荒涼としたレムノス島に連れて行かれ、そこに遺棄された。

ルーズヴェルト・アイランドにおけるカワマタ・プロジェクトが終了してから、ルーズヴェルト島を含むニューヨーク市周辺のいくつかの島々の、いわば神話上の先駆けとして私はレムノスを思い出した。エリオット・ウィレンスキーとノーヴァル・ホワイトは、『AIAニューヨーク市ガイドブック(AIA Guide to New York City)』の中で、本人たちも意識しないままに皮肉にもこう書いている。「マンハッタン、スタテン・アイランド、ロング・アインランド以外にも、ニューヨーク市にはまだ他の島々が**群がっている**。」(強調は著者による。群がる(infest)は病気、害虫、野獣などが群がる、はびこる、蔓延するの意。)過去、現在を問わず、この島々の利用法を決定してきた主な理由のほとんどがまさに蔓延し、群がるものへの不安であった。ニューヨーク市は歴史を通じて、象徴的な意味での汚染源と実際的な意味での接触感染から市を守るために、いくつもの施設を計画し、これらの島々に建設し続けてきた。

エリス島では合衆国移民局の古い建物が、エリス島国立モニュメントとして再建され、修復されつつある。アメリカを形づくったもののモニュメントであるにもかかわらず、エリス島は、驚くほどの強烈さで、合衆国にたどり着き、移住するという体験がどのようなものであったかを物語る。それは祖国からの決別であるとともに、入国許可を得るまでの恐るべき審査方法に服従する事実を表わしていた。

イースト・リヴァーのライカーズ島には様々な刑罰施設がある。市立男子刑務所、女子刑務所、州刑務所に付属する地元施設などがそれである。

ハート島は、ブロンクスのシティ島の東側にあり、ロング・アイランドの入江に位置する比較的無名の「別の」島だ。現在、ここには市の無縁墓地がある。ハート島は、ニューヨーク市の片隅に生きて街路や収容施設で寂しく死んだ人々が最後に行き着く場所である。

トリボロー・ブリッジの壮麗な径間のたもとに位置するワーズ島は、イースト・リヴァー沿いにルーズヴェルトから僅かに離れた所にあり、マンハッタンの陰にある。ワーズ島は現代の廃棄区域としての役割を果たしている。現在この島は、ルーズヴェルト島がブラックウェルズ島、そして後にはウェルフェア(福祉)島として知られていた頃、つまりスモールポックス病院時代のルーズヴェルト島とほぼ同じような目的で利用されている。ワーズ島には、精神病院、「精神異常犯」のための精神病施設、ホームレスの男性のための800床の収容施設、そして子供の精神病施設などがある。

これらの島々で、我々はそれぞれの過去から現在に至る追放の痕跡を目のあたりにする。島はそれぞれ禁じられ、無視され、余分とされた空間、あるいは再利用された空間でいっぱいである。それは我々の恐怖、無関心、偏見が内包された空間と言えよう。

情況のなかで：表現と救済について

ルーズヴェルト島から川を隔てた、マンハッタンのイーストサイドのFDRドライブのたもとには、一時しのぎのバラックが未だに幾つか残っている。もしもバラックがそこに住む人々のためのものでなかったなら、それらはきっと川俣の「フィールド・ワーク」や「ファヴェーラ・イン・ニューヨーク(ニューヨークのスラム)」か何かと間違えられていたかもしれない。ルーズヴェルト島のプロジェクトがまだ続行中の頃、こうしたバラックはあたかもプロジェクトの一部がさ迷い出たかのように見えたものだった。プロジェクトのどこからか裂け落ち、マンハッタンの岸辺に漂着し、ホームレスの住民たちによって流用されたもののように。川俣の接近不可能なルーズヴェルト島のプロジェクトとは異なり、街路や橋の下、地下鉄のトンネル、公園、廃墟となったビル、荒廃したビル群のはざまの空地など、ニューヨーク市のいたるところにある似たような装置は、実際の住居であり、そこで人々は追放と遺棄の人生を営んでいる。

スモールポックス病院に相当する現在の諸施設もまた、最後には同じように廃墟となる運命にあると思われるが、少なくとも当分のところはニューヨーク市の社会経済にとって必要不可欠であると言うことにはなんら変わるところがない。それらは基本的な需要を満たし、かつ社会の混乱を阻止するという、二重の目的を果たしている。無表情で支離滅裂な話し方をし、言葉にならない要求を抱えた患者たちのために、看護者が薬の盆を準備している精神病棟。男性も女性も烙印を押され、たいていは忘れ去られ、孤独のうちに恐ろしい死を迎えるエイズ病棟。ホームレスの人々が詰め込まれるように投げ込まれる兵器庫の演習用の階。被収容者たちを更正させるための牢獄。これらの施設で一生を送ることを課せられた人々にとっての現実は、19世紀にルーズヴェルト島にあった諸施設の現代版とも言えるこうした施設の間を行きつ戻りつして過ごすことであろう。

我々をとりまいている歴然たる「排除」行為がカワマタ・プロジェクトの社会的、政治的な意義を評価する上での欠かせない背景となっている。歴史と状況の中で形成された因習的な属性に対する川俣の見事な考察はまさに「折り紙付き」の正当な称賛を受けた。それは彼の考察が、この街で繰り返される構築と破壊に関するものだったからでもある。

しかし、実際の川俣の作品はそうしたものをはるかに超越している。それはまた、現実社会における我々の経験や認識、想像の限界を明確に規定した、継続やギャップに関する鋭い考察でもあるが、さらに、市の抱えるホームレス、エイズ、深刻な人々の分裂、といった諸々の問題に対する社会批判、あるいは隠喩としての役割を果たす明確な意図をも越えてしまっている。川俣のプロジェクトが問いかける問題自体、明確にするのが難かしいのかもしれない。それは、このプロジェクトが批判の対象とした

社会行為そのものが、非常に混沌としているのと重なるであろう。このハイブリッドな構築物に対してまず返ってくる反応は、逆説的な、あるいは両義的な感覚といえるだろう。社会から無視され、排除されるという容赦ない非芸術的な行為をこれほどの雄弁な方法で表現したがゆえに逆説なのである。社会的孤独と刻印に対する批評であるにもかかわらず、川をへだてニューヨークの街路や多数の施設で繰り広げられている排除や権利剝奪という生の現実から隔絶され、ミステリアスな表情で近づきがたく佇んでいるがゆえの両義性なのである。それはまた市の数多くの疫病が相も変わらず減少しないという苛酷な現実の前で、カワマタ・プロジェクトがつかのまの存在でしかありえないからでもある。

こうした特性と不調和な状況は、「他者」をどう枠にはあてはめるかということに多くの関心が払われる現代の風潮によって形作られたと言える。いかなるメディアを通してであれ、他者の退廃や屈辱的な出来事をことさらに提示しようとする傾向は、ジェイムズ・アギー曰く「実に嫌らしく、恐ろしいというよりむしろ実に奇妙な」ものである。こうした傾向は、我々自身の他者からの搾取という生々しい現実を何事をも客観視し、作為的な感慨を持つことにすり替えてしまうような恐ろしい結果を招くのである。[5]

一方、「参加する」ことによって救済への道が開かれる場合もある。ピロクテーテスは、彼が追放された島に来た見知らぬ人々に、自分に話しかけてくれるようにと熱心に訴えた。なぜなら、「“語りかけること”だけが唯一お互いに与え得るもの」だからだ。人間の要求の数多くの形態を解明すること、またホームレスであることと所属していること[6]の違いを形作る条件を論じることは、政治的なカテゴリーに属する参加方法である。もっとも、そうした参加形態は、社会的な権利の侵害を軽減し正すことを求めるといったような政治運動とは全く異なる。だがそれと同様に重要なものである。ルーズヴェルト島のカワマタ・プロジェクトは、前者の政治的活動の示唆された例である。つまり構成員の配分に対して働く力の効果を生成しつつ、なおかつ表現しようと求めた政治的活動なのである。現実の構成員の状況こそ、我々一人ひとりが負うべきものである。

［コスタス・グーニスは1984年以来、ニューヨーク市のホームレスの実態と精神病疾患を研究している社会人類学者である。最近彼は、コロンビア大学において、ニューヨーク市がホームレスを抱え込んでしまうシステムに対する民族学的考察である、「ホームレスの内在化」について博士論文を発表した。］

1. マイケル・ワルツァー「Spheres of Justice」ベイシック・ブックス（ニューヨーク、1983）

2. アメリカ合衆国の様々な都市におけるこうした経緯に関する徹底的な文献は，ニューヨーク市在住の写真家でライターのカミーロ・ホセ・ヴェルガラの著書にある。

3. 追放の体験に関する同様に強力な記述については、私の短いリストには、「リア王」、ダニエル・デフォーの「A Journal of the Plague Year」、アントン・チェーホフの短編小説「Ward 6」、アルベルト・カミュの「ペスト」、イプセンの「民衆の敵」、そしてソルジェニーツインのほとんどの作品が含まれている。

4. ここと以下の、「ピロクテーテース」の私の引用は、デイヴィッド・グレーンとリチャード・ラッティモア訳「ギリシアの悲劇、第3巻」シカゴ大学出版（シカゴ、1960）からのものである。

5. ジェイムズ・アギー、ウォーカー・エヴァンス「Let Us Now Praise Famous Men」ヒュートン・ミルフィン（ボストン、1941）

6. 「ホームレスであることと所属していること」は、マイケル・イグナティエフの「プライバシー、連帯、および人間であるための政治」について著わされた際立って説得力ある評論、「The Need of Strangers」ペンギン・ブックス（ニューヨーク、1984）の最終章のタイトルである。

Work Notes

Tadashi Kawamata

The southern tip of Roosevelt Island, home to one ruined building, is enclosed by tall fences and can be entered only by opening the location's single gate. Each morning, I and a dozen or so others opened this gate, walked through it, and went to work. While we worked, the gate was locked from the inside: no one else could enter. We labored all day, then at 5:00 p.m. came back out of the gate wearing expressions of exhaustion. For two months during New York's hot and humid summer, we took floor boards, pillars, broken doors, window frames, tables, and a variety of other scrap items, gathered from around New York City and imprinted with the mark of daily life, and worked to nail them up one by one around the ruins to put this project together. We continued with our task every day, at times covered with dust at the top of the structure, which rose to 50 feet, or bitten by mosquitoes in the tall grass around the building.

The majority of the construction work was typical carpentry, raising pillars and nailing boards. However, struggling earnestly to complete the project while looking askance at the mountain of waste materials brought in daily by two-ton trucks, I might have considered our task as never ending. The site perhaps seems to overlap the history of the ruined building itself, once a small-pox hospital, which is said to have been built stone-by-stone by convicted criminals.

Everyone involved with the project saw the model and overall sketches beforehand, but it was something of a struggle to actually stand on the site and imagine what the project would finally look like or how big it would be. This might have been because the work took place under conditions so crowded that one could not view the location from a distance. Also, with mountains of waste materials being brought in every day, it seemed that the work might go on forever. In fact, the amounts and kinds of each day's scrap gradually changed the shape and size of the project far beyond our original intentions. As work progressed, I myself was often puzzled and lost track of how we should proceed. At day's end, when I had sent everyone back out the gate, I would sometimes stay behind and ponder on the next day's work.

Every morning, before work started we bought four gallons of drinking water and six kilograms of ice cubes from a supermarket on Roosevelt Island. In the sweltering heat of August, our water cooler was always empty by the time the day's work neared completion. When we took breaks from our sweaty and dusty endeavors, we could hear the faint, varied sounds of Manhattan across the water. Our view of the city, so close but appearing as if from another world, was of skyscrapers like silhouettes on days when fog raised the humidity, or like shimmers in the air in the heat of the day. As we worked, we could see both Manhattan and the river enclosing our site through the spaces in our construction. Looking down onto the river from high spots, we could imagine ourselves standing at the prows of the boats floating by. Our work progressed in close proximity to water, from the flow of the river and the humidity of New York to the rain that fell in sudden showers.

Days of leaving my Manhattan apartment early in the morning and going to work on Roosevelt Island began. The daily commute between Manhattan Island and Roosevelt Island became another element that deepened the meaning of this project for me. One could say that, from the start, it was impossible to consider the geographical conditions and historical background of the project location without taking into account Manhattan across the river. Insurance and other problems linked to the state of the building and the surrounding area meant that public access was restricted. It turned out, however, that this restriction added to the site's history of isolation, creating a contradiction in which the project appeared close when seen from Manhattan but was difficult to reach. Actually, it was hard to view the project in its entirety while at the site, so the only way to take in the whole was to look at it from the Manhattan side. On the other hand, Manhattan seen from Roosevelt Island was truly a beautiful spectacle. In the end, this project came to completion during the round trip between these two opposing places. The round trip also went through time, between past and present history, and one of our primary goals was to see the state of present-day New York from the project site.

The project, which required about five years and proceeded completely by trial and error, has been organized in the pages of this book, which will also be used as a textbook for my next project. It could be said that this shows exactly how the end of one project is linked to the beginning of the next.

I do not know yet what kind of time nodes will be created for me by the various projects that arise one after another in this kind of sequence. Perhaps I need to sway just a little longer in this time flow.

April 1993

作業ノート

川俣正

廃墟の建物があるルーズヴェルト島の南端は、高いフェンスで閉ざされていて、ただ一か所のゲートを開けてしか中に入ることができない。毎朝私を含め十数人がそこを開けて中に入り作業をする。その間、ゲートは中から鍵が掛けられ、だれも入ることはできない。一日中作業をし、夕方5時ごろになると全員疲れた表情でこのゲートから出る。ニューヨークの蒸し暑い夏の2か月間、私たちはこの中でニューヨーク中から拾い集めてきた床板や柱、壊れたドア、窓枠、テーブルなどそれぞれに生活の跡を残した様々なスクラップを、この廃墟のまわりに一つ一つ釘で打ち付け、組み立てていく作業を行なった。ある時は50フィートの高さにまでなったこの構築物の上で埃にまみれながら、あるときは建物の脇の草深い中で藪蚊に刺されながら、毎日の作業は続けられた。

作業自体は普通の大工仕事のように柱を立てたり板を打ち付けたりすることが主な仕事だが、2トントラックで毎日運び込まれる廃材の山を横目で見ながらひたすら組み立てていくという事は、時には終りのない仕事をしているようにも思える。それはたぶん、以前は天然痘の病院であり今は廃墟となっているこの建物が、囚人の手によって一つ一つ石が積み上げられ、建てられたという歴史とどこかで重なって見えてくるからだろう。

参加したスタッフの誰もが事前にこのプロジェクトの模型や全体的なスケッチを見てはいたが、最終的にどのような形になるのか、またどのくらい大きな物になるのか、実際の現場ではなかなか想像し辛かったようだ。それは、作業している場所から離れて遠目に眺めることができないくらい密集した中で行なっていたということと、毎日廃材の山が次から次ぎへと運び込まれることでどこまでも作業が続くように思えたからではないだろうか。実際、その日その日の廃材の量と種類によってどんどん形は変化し大きさも変わってしまい、当初の予定を遙かに上回ることになってしまった。作業中は私自身、これからどの様に進めていけばいいのかわからなくなり途方にくれることもしばしばあり、作業が終わって全員をゲートの外へ出してから一人現場に残って明日からの作業を考えることも何度かあった。

毎朝作業が始まる前に、私たちは4ガロンの飲み水と6キロのアイスキューヴをルーズヴェルト島にあるスーパーマーケットで買った。8月のうだるような暑さのため、作業の終わり頃にはいつもウォータークーラーは空っぽになった。汗と埃にまみれながら作業をして一息入れたとき、対岸のマンハッタンから様々な音が遠くかすかに聞こえてくる。これ程近くにありながら全く別世界のように立ち現れるこの景観は、曇りで湿度の高い日には摩天楼がシルエットのように見え、暑い日中にはかげろうのように見えてくる。両側を川に挟まれたこの現場で作業をしている間、常にこの構築物の間から川が見え、その向こうにマンハッタンが見えた。高い所から下を見る時には川の上に浮かんだ船の突端に自分が立っているようにも思えた。川の流れとニューヨークの湿度、そして突然のシャワーのような雨など、水と深いかかわりを持ちながら作業は進んで行った。

マンハッタンのアパートを朝早く出てルーズヴェルト島の現場へ作業に通う毎日が始まり、ルーズヴェルト島とマンハッタン島との往復が、私にとってさらにこのプロジェクトの意味合いを深める要素になった。それはこの現場の持つ地理的な条件と歴史的背景が常に対岸に位置するマンハッタン抜きにしては考えられなかったということからも言えるだろう。建物や現場の状態にかかる保険の問題などから、このプロジェクトは限定された形でしか公開できなかったが、結果的にはそのことが隔離されてきたこの場所の歴史と重なり、マンハッタンから見ると近くにあるがそこへ行くのは難しいという、この場所にふさわしい状況をつくることになった。実際プロジェクトの現場ではなかなか全体が見えず、対岸のマンハッタン側から眺めることによってでしかプロジェクトの全貌を見ることができない。だが、逆に現場ではマンハッタンが実に美しく見える。

この対になった二つの場所の往復の中でプロジェクトは結果的に成立することになった。それは歴史上の過去と現在という時間の往復を意味し、同時にこの現場から現在のニューヨークの町のあり様をみることが、今回のプロジェクトの大きな目的の一つでもあった。

約5年間、いろいろな問題にぶつかりながらまったく手探りで進められたこのプロジェクトは、この記録集によって整理され、また次のプロジェクトのためのテキストとして使われていく。それはプロジェクトの終りがまさに次の始まりに繋がるという事を示しているように思える。

1993年4月

Project Bibliography

Gould, Claudia / Kawamata, Tadashi. *Kawamata Project in Roosevelt Island 1990* (brochure), Osaka: Kodama Gallery, September 1989.

Magazines

Kawamata, Tadashi. ''Roosevelt Island: Ruin as the Beginning,'' *Herumesu* No.23, February 1990, pp. 73-80.

''In the News/Reconstruction History,'' *Sculpture* Vol.9 No.2, March-April 1990, p. 12.

Kawamata, Tadashi. ''The Time Lag of the City,'' *Taiyo (The Sun)* No.370, April 1992, pp. 6-7.

''It's Time to.../...Take a Gander,'' *Metropolitan Home* Vol.XXIV No.9, September 1992.

Connors, Thomas. ''Fanfair/Wood Awakening,'' *Vanity Fair* September 1992, unpaged.

''Urban Archaeology,'' *The New Yorker* September 28, 1992, p. 10.

Lutfy, Carol. ''A Very Public Matter,'' *Tokyo Journal* October 1992, pp. 41-42.

''Art/Other Venues/Tadashi Kawamata,'' *The New Yorker* October 5, 1992, p. 36.

Murata, Makoto. ''Overseas,'' *Pia* October 15, 1992, p. 266.

Stevens, Margaret. ''A Rune on Ruins,'' *Landscape Architecture* November 1992.

Wentz, Christine. ''Kawamata: Project on Roosevelt Island,'' *Newsline* November-December 1992, p. 8.

Yanagi, Masahiko. ''Tadashi Kawamata (interview),'' *Art & Critique* No.21,

December 1992, pp. 24-31.

Fujieda, Teruo. ''Vanguard/Tadashi Kawamata,'' *Chuo-Koron* December 1992, unpaged, photo by Michio Noguchi.

Yanase, Kaoru. ''Tadashi Kawamata Roosevelt Island Project,'' *BT* No.662, December 1992, pp. 16-17.

Murata, Makoto. ''Tadashi Kawamata's Project Continues to Stimulate Environment,'' *Brutus* December 1, 1992, p. 39.

''Realized Project of Tadashi Kawamata in New York,'' *Geijutsu Shincho* Vol. 43 No. 12, December 1992.

Slatin, Peter. ''Ruins for a Ruin,'' *Artnews* December 1992, p. 16.

Branch, Mark Alden. ''A Missed Opportunity on Roosevelt Island,'' *Progressive Architecture* December 1992, p. 14.

Murphy, Jay. ''Reviews/Tadashi Kawamata/Roosevelt Island,'' *Tema Celeste* No.38 Winter, pp. 83-84.

Kitagawa, Fram. *Taiyo (The Sun)* No.378, January 1993, pp. 94-95.

Connors, Thomas. ''Kawamata: Project on Roosevelt Island,'' *Sculpture* January-February 1993, pp. 24-25.

Jodidio, Philippe. ''Bâtisseur de l'Éphémère,'' *Connaissance des Arts* March 1993, pp. 116-121, photo by Norman McGrath.

Gould, Claudia. ''Kawamata's Miracle,'' *Parkett* #35, March-April 1993, pp. 161-164.

Wentz, Christine. ''Tadashi Kawamata project op Roosevelt Island,'' *Archis* April, pp. 44-47.

Takenaka, Mitsuru. ''Tadashi Kawamata'' *Marie Claire Japon* June 1993, pp. 152-153.

Princenthal, Nancy. ''Kawamata Project on Roosevelt Island'' *Art in America* July, 1993.

Newspapers

"Artist Tadashi Kawamata: New York Project," *The Sankei Shimbun* February 6, 1992, p. 19.

"Wide Culture/'Temporary' Art, Tadashi Kawamata exhibiting models," *Hokkaido Shimbun Press* February 14, 1992, p. 10.

Hughes, Janice (Associated Press.) "Artist makes huge sculpture out of hospital," *New Haven Register* August 20, 1992.

Grimes, William. "Restoration on Roosevelt Island? No, It's Sculpture/Is It Art or Scrap Wood? The Answer Is: It's Both," *The New York Times* September 24, 1992, pp. C13, C17.

Ball, Edward. "Shelter/Re: Ruin," *The Village Voice* Vol. XXXVII No. 39, September 29, 1992, p. 99.

Tallmer, Jerry. "New life for death's dream castle," *New York Post* October 2, 1992, p. 39.

"An open installation," *USA Today* October 7, 1992.

Wallach, Amei. "Kawamata Project on Roosevelt Island," *New York Newsday* October 16, 1992, pp. 71, 74-75.

"New York's Kawamata Work: Using scrap wood," *Ehime Shimbun* October 17, 1992.

Smith, Roberta. "Manic, Inspired Carpentry," *The New York Times* October 25, 1992, Section 2, p. 33.

Mori, Tsukasa. "New York, Roosevelt Island's Kawamata Project," *The Yomiuri Shimbun* October 27, 1992, p. 22.

"Voice Listings/Art/In Brief," *The Village Voice* Vol. XXXVII No. 43, October 27, 1992, p. 83.

プロジェクト関連文献

川俣正、クロゥディア・ゴールド『KAWAMATA PROJECT IN ROOSEVELT ISLAND 1990』パンフレット、児玉画廊（大阪）、1989年9月

雑誌

川俣正「Roosevelt Island、はじまりとしての廃墟」季刊へるめす、No.23 1990年1月号、p.73－80

「In the News/Reconstructing History」隔月刊Sculpture、Vo.9 No.2 1990年3－4月号、p.12

川俣正「都市の時差（タイムラグ）」月刊太陽、No.370 1992年4月号、p.6－7

「It's Time to.../...Take a Gander」月刊Metropolitan Home、Vol.XXIV No.9 1992年9月号

トーマス・コナー「Fanfair/Wood Awakening」月刊Vanity Fair、1992年9月号、ページ付なし

「Urban Archaeology」隔週刊The New Yorker、1992年9月28日号、p.10

キャロル・ルトフィ「A Very Public Matter」Tokyo Journal、1992年10月号、p.41－42

「Art/Other Venues/Tadashi Kawamata」隔週刊 The New Yorker、1992年10月5日号、p.36

村田真「海外通信・ニューヨーク・川俣プロジェクト、ルーズベルト島は遠くにありて思うもの」週刊ぴあ、1992年10月15日号、p.266

マーガレット・スティーヴンス「A Rune on Ruins」月刊Landscape Architecture、1992年11月号

クリスティーン・ウェンツ「Kawamata： Project On Roosevelt Island」隔月刊Newsline、1992年11－12月号、p.8

柳正彦、インタビュー「川俣正」ART & CRITIQUE、No.21 1992年12月号、p.24－31

藤枝晃雄「VANGUARD・川俣正」月刊中央公論、1992年12月号、ページ付なし（撮影：野口ミチオ）

梁瀬薫「視覚化された「その場」の歴史／川俣正ルーズヴェルト島プロジェクト」月刊BT、No.662　1992年12月号、p.16－17

村田真「川俣正のプロジェクトは常に環境を刺激しつづける。」隔週刊ブルータス、1992年12月1日号、p.39

「ニューヨークに実現した川俣正のプロジェクト」月刊芸術新潮、第43巻第12号 1992年12月号、p.104

ピーター・スラティン「Ruins for a Ruin」月刊ARTnews、1992年12月号、p.16

マーク・アルデン・ブランチ「A Missed Opportunity on Roosevelt Island」月刊Progressive Architecture、1992年12月号、p.14

ジェイ・マーフィー「レビュー、Tadashi Kawamata/Roosevelt Island」月刊Tema Celeste、No.38　1993年冬号、p.83－84

北川フラム「都市への視線7／アート・ワークの新展開／ニューヨークの街より」月刊太陽、No.378 1993年1月号、p.94－95

トーマス・コナー「Kawamata： Project on Roosevelt Island」隔月刊Sculpture、1993年1－2月号、p.24－25

フィリップ・ジョディディオ「Bátisseur de l'Éphémère」月刊Connaissance des Arts、1993年3月号、p.116－121（撮影：ノーマン・マクグラス）

クロゥディア・ゴールド「Kawamata's Miracle」Parkett #35 1993年3－4月号、p.161－164

クリスティーン・ウェンツ「Tadashi Kawamata project op Roosevelt Island」月刊Archis、1993年4月号、p.44－47

竹中充「川俣正、輝ける暗黒」月刊マリ・クレール・ジャポン、1993年6月号、

p.152－153

ナンシー・プリンセンタール「Kawamata：Project on Roosevelt Island」月刊Art in America、1993年7月号

新聞

「病院を蘇らせる／造形作家・川俣正NYプロジェクト」産経新聞、1992年2月6日、p.19

「ワイドかるちゃー／夏NYで野心作／「架設」芸術の川俣正さん模型発表」北海道新聞、1992年2月14日、p.10

ジャニス・ヒューズ（AP）「Artist makes huge sculpture out of hospital」New Haven Register、1992年8月20日

ウィリアム・グリムス「Restoration on Roosevelt Island？ No, It's Sculpture/Is It Art or Scrap？ The Answer Is：It's Both」The New York Times、1992年9月24日、p.C13、C17

エドワード・ボール「Shelter/Re：Ruin」The Village Voice（Vol.XXXVII No.39）、1992年9月29日、p.99

ジェリー・テルマー「New life for death's dream castle」New York Post、1992年10月2日、p.39

「An open installation」USA Today、1992年10月7日

アメイ・ワラッチ「Kawamata Project on Roosevelt Island」New York Newsday、1992年10月16日、p.71、74－75

「アングル／NYの廃材使った川俣作品」愛媛新聞、1992年10月17日

ロバータ・スミス「Manic, Inspired Carpentry」The New York Times、1992年10月25日、Section 2、p.33

森司「NYルーズベルト島のカワマタ・プロジェクト」読売新聞、1992年10月27日

「Voice Listing/Art/In Brief」The Village Voice(Vol.XXXVII No.43)、1992年10月27日、p.83

Tadashi Kawamata

1953

born in Mikasa, Hokkaido

1979

BFA, Oil Painting Course, Fine Art Department, Tokyo Geijutsu Daigaku (Tokyo National University of Fine Arts and Music,) Tokyo

1981

MFA, Fine Art Department, Tokyo Geijutsu Daigaku, Tokyo

1984

Left Doctor Course, Fine Art Department, Tokyo Geijutsu Daigaku, Tokyo

Projects

1979

''By Land'' Tama Riverside, Tachikawa

1980

''Project Work in Takayama'' Takayama School of Architecture, Takayama

1982

apartment project ''Takara House Room 205'' Tokyo

1983

apartment project ''Otemon, Wada-So'' (Materials and Spaces Exhibition,) Fukuoka

''Project Work in Saitama'' (Shape and Spirit in Wood Work Exhibition,) The Museum of Modern Art, Saitama, Urawa

apartment project ''Slip in Tokorozawa'' Tokorozawa

apartment project ''Tetra House N-3 W-26'' Mr. and Mrs. Endo's House, Sapporo

1984

''Ginza Network'' Kaneko Art Gallery, Gallery Kobayashi, Jewellery Shop Olphe and Tokyo Gallery, Tokyo

''Okaido Installation'' collaborated with PH Studio, Okaido, Matsuyama

''Under Construction'' collaborated with PH Studio, Hillside Terrace, Tokyo

1985

''Limelight Project'' Limelight, New York

''PS1 Project'' PS1, Long Island City

1986

construction site project ''Spui'' The Hague

1987

construction site project ''La Maison des Squatters'' (Japon Art Vivant '87,) Grenoble

''Destroyed Church'' (Documenta 8,) Kassel

construction site project ''Nove de Julho Caçapava'' (The 19th Sao Paulo International Biannual Exhibition,) Sao Paulo

1988

construction site project ''Fukuroi'' Suruga Bank, Fukuroi

''Hien-So'' Higashiyama, Kyoto

1989

''Toronto Project: Colonial Tavern Park'' Toronto

''Begijnhof Sint Elisabeth'' Kortrijk

1990

''Sidewalk'' (New Works for New Spaces: Into the Nineties Exhibition,) Columbus

1991

''Favela in Houston'' (Landscape Exhibition,) Bayou Riverside, Houston

''Favela in Ottawa'' (A Primal Spirit Exhibition,) The National Gallery of Canada, Ottawa

''Favela in Ushimado'' (The 4th Biannual, Japan Ushimado Art Festival,) Ushimado

1992

''People's Garden'' (Documenta 9,) Kassel

''Project on Roosevelt Island'' Small Pox Hospital, Roosevelt Island, New York

1993

''Passaggio'' (Museo Città Eventi Exhibition,) Prato

''Public Proposals'' on Limmat River and Helmhaus, Zürich

One Man Exhibitions

1978

The 4th Room, Kanagawa Prefecture Gallery, Yokohama

1979

Lunami Gallery, Tokyo

Tamura Gallery, Tokyo (1980.)

Maki Gallery, Tokyo (1980.)

1980

Gallery Kobayashi, Tokyo (1982, 84, 86, 88, 91, 92, 93.)

ASG, Nagoya

Studio 37, Kyoto

Gallery K, Tokyo

1982

Room A, Gallery Haku, Osaka

Kaneko Art Gallery and Kaneko Art G1, Tokyo (1983, 84, 85, 86, 87, 91.)

1983

Ten Gallery, Fukuoka (1986.)

1984

Hillside Gallery, Tokyo (1986, 87, 88, 89, 90, 91, 93.)

PS1 Studio, Long Island City (1985.)

1985

Laboratory, Sapporo

1986

Area Deux Gallery, Fukuoka

Kamitori Gallery, Kumamoto

1987

Galeria Unidade Dois de Arte, Sao Paulo

1988

Storefront for Art and Architecture, New York

1989

Mercer Union, Toronto

Kodama Gallery, Osaka (1992, 93.)

Former School in Begijnhof Sint Elisabeth, Kortrijk

Galerie Brenda Wallace, Montréal (1991.)

1990

Annely Juda Fine Art, London

1992

Art Front Zürich, Zürich

Arthur A. Houghton Jr. Gallery, Cooper Union for The Advancement of Science and Art, New York

1993

Helmhaus, Zürich

Art Front Gallery, Tokyo

Group Exhibitions

1977

''Exercise 1'' Seminar Room of Tokyo Geijutsu Daigaku, Tokyo

''Athletic Meeting'' Tachikawa Citizen Hall, Tachikawa

1978

''Discussion'' Ai Gallery, Tokyo

''Exercise 2'' Seminar Room of Tokyo Geijutsu Daigaku, Tokyo

1979

''Video'' Seminar Room of Tokyo Geijutsu Daigaku, Tokyo

''Three Man Exhibition'' Seminar Room of Tokyo Geijutsu Daigaku, Tokyo

1980

''Ueno '80'' Seminar Room of Tokyo Geijutsu Daigaku, Tokyo

''Adesugata-hana-no-ayadori'' Kanagawa Prefecture Gallery, Yokohama

''Seven Scenes Show'' Tokyo Metropolitan Art Museum, Tokyo

''Photographs Exhibition'' Gallery Yamaguchi, Tokyo

''Artists To-day'' Yokohama Citizen Gallery, Yokohama

''Hara Annual 1'' Hara Museum of Contemporary Art, Tokyo

1981

''Cross of Drawings'' Gallery Parergon, Tokyo

''Two Man Exhibition'' G Art Gallery, Tokyo

''Yion'' Gryphon Gallery, Melbourne State University, Melbourne

''The First Parallelism in Art Exhibition'' Ohara School of Ikebana Center, Tokyo

''Artists To-day '81''. Yokohama Citizen Gallery, Yokohama

1982

''2 Internationale Jugendtriennale de Zeichnung (The Second International Youth Triannual of Drawings)'' Kunsthalle, Nürnberg

''La Biennale di Venezia (The Fourties Venice Biannual)'' Pavilion of Japan, Venice

''Drawings of Six Artists'' Kaneko Art Gallery, Tokyo

''Three Man Exhibition'' Gallery Haku, Osaka

1983

''Materials and Spaces'' Fukuoka Art Museum, Fukuoka

''Shape and Spirit in Wood Works'' The Museum of Modern Art, Saitama, Urawa

''Un regard sur L'Art Japonais D'Aujourd'hui (Japan Art Today)'' Musée Rath and Musée D'Art et D'Histoire, Geneve

''Fünf Zeitgenossische Künstler Aus Japan (Five Japanese Contemporary Artists)'' Kunsthalle, Düsseldorf

''Majority and Variety States'' Sea Side Koyama, Oita

''Kaneko Art '83'' Kaneko Art Gallery, Tokyo

1984

''Human Documents '84'' Tokyo Gallery, Tokyo

Tokyo Geijutsu Daigaku, Tokyo

''Echange d'Art Contemporain, Tokyo-Paris (Tokyo-Paris Contemporary Art Exchange Exhibition)'' Galerie Falideh Cadot, Paris

''Majority and Variety States in Kansai'' Studio Sette Gruppi, Osaka

''One Room Essence'' Gallery Vü, Osaka

''Exposition des affiches de la Maison Franco-Japonaise par 47 artistes japonais contemporains (Original Works of Poster Exhibition by 47 Japanese Contemporary Artists)'' Seibu Art Forum, Tokyo

1985

''Opening Exhibition 1985'' Root Gallery, Tokyo

''Echange d'Art Contemporain, Tokyo-Paris''

Asahi Gallery, Tokyo

"National and International Studio Artists' Exhibition" Clocktower, New York

"PH Studion Furniture ϕ Exhibition" Gallery Yamaguchi, Tokyo

"Perspective" Korean Cultural Service Gallery, New York

"Vision of Dream Image" Kaneko Art Gallery, Tokyo

"Wood: Between Painting and Sculpture" Hokkaido Asahikawa Museum of Art, Asahikawa

"Sculpture Japonaise Contemporain" Jullien-Cornic Galerie D'Art, Paris

"After *Tilted Arc*" Storefront for Art and Architecture, New York

1986

"Six Japanese Contemporary Artists" Cecelia Cooker Bell Gallery, Harrsville

"Imaginally Monuments" Kaneko Art Gallery, Tokyo

"White and Black" Kaneko Art Gallery, Tokyo

"Japanese Contemporary Art 3, Vol.2" Miyagi Museum of Art, Sendai

"Contatto" Sala Uno, Rome

"Prints and Drawings" Kaneko Art Gallery, Tokyo

1987

"Japon Art Vivant '87" Aix-en-Province, Marseille, and Grenoble

"Documenta 8" Kassel

"Art in Japan Since 1969; Mono-ha and Post Mono-ha" Seibu Museum of Art, Tokyo

"19a Bienal Internacional De Sao Paulo (The Nineteenth International Sao Paulo Biannual)" Sao Paulo

"Vision-Dream-Image" Kaneko Art Gallery, Tokyo

"Modern Japanese Prints" Art Front Zürich, Zürich

1988

"Drawing of Three Artists" Kaneko Art Gallery, Tokyo

"8 Drawings" Kodama Gallery, Osaka

"Tsukashin Annual '88, Japanese and Korean Artists' Art Today: Horizontal and Vertical" Tsukashin Hall, Amagasaki

"Gallery Collection '88" Kaneko Art Gallery, Tokyo

"Summer/Three Man Exhibition" Gallery Kobayashi, Tokyo

"Art in Bookshop" Art Vivant, Tokyo

"The New Urban Landscape" World Financial Center, Battery Park City, New York

"Projekt Worldfax 88: Fax The Art" Kunstraum, Neuss

1989

"Drawing Storage Exhibition" Hillside Gallery, Tokyo

"Water Painting Today" Kaneko Art Gallery, Tokyo

"From; Being; Absence" Griffin McGear Gallery, New York

"Japanese Contemporary Art in the Eighties" Heineken Village, Tokyo

"Japan-France Poster Exhibition" Yurakucho Art Forum, Tokyo

"Garden of Charity to Urban Arcadia" Urban Center, New York

"Drawing As Itself" Nathional Museum of Art, Osaka, Suita

"Japan '89" Museum van Hedendaagse Kunst, Ghent

1990

"A Primal Spirit" Hara Museum Arc, Shibukawa; Los Angeles County Museum of Art, Los Angeles; Museum of Contemporary Art, Chicago; Modern Art Museum, Fort Worth; The National Gallery of Canada, Ottawa

"The Game of Manners, Vol. 1" Contemporary Art Gallery, Art Tower Mito, Mito

"Onvoltoold Tegenwoordlge Tijd" Centraal Museum, Utrecht

"A New Necessity/First Tyne International Exhibition of Contemporary Art" Laing Art Gallery, Newcastle upon Tyne and National Garden Festival, Gateshead

"L'Art renouvelle la Ville/L'Art Contemporain et Urbanisme en France" Tsukuba Museum of Art, Tsukuba; National Museum of Art, Osaka, Suita; Sendai City Youth Cultural Center, Sendai; Fukuoka Art Museum, Fukuoka; Museum of Contemporary Art, Sapporo; Yamanashi Prefectural Museum of Art, Kofu; Yokohama

"New Works for New Spaces: Into the Nineties" Wexner Center for the Visual Arts, Columbus

"Kawamata, Charney: Two Man Exhibition" Sherbrook University, Sherbrook

1991

"Drawing Storage Exhibition" Hillside Gallery, Tokyo

"Out of Site" PS1 Museum, Long Island City

"The Landscapes/The Houston International Festival" Houston

"Sapporo Contemporary Arts 1991" Recent Gallery, Sapporo

"The Fourth Biannual/The Japan Ushimado International Festival" Ushimado

1992

"Drawing Storage Exhibition Part III" Hillside Gallery, Tokyo

"Urban Cities and Contemporary Art/Home Sweet Home in Ruins" Setagaya Art Museum, Tokyo

"Documenta 9" Kassel

"10 Artists: Contemporary Japanese Art of the

1980s-1990s/from the Acquisitions for the New Tokyo Metropolitan Art Museum'' Tokyo Metropolitan Art Museum, Tokyo

1993

''Kawamata, Suga, Selections'' Kaneko Art Gallery, Tokyo

''Transit'' The New Museum of Contemporary Art, New York

''Museo Città Eventi'' Centro per l'Arte Contemporanea Luigi Pecci, Prato

''Giappone-Anni Novanta/Proposte di 13 Artisti'' Museo del Folklore, Rome; Stadtmuseum, Düsseldorf

Other Works

1982

''A Scene'' produced by *Ryuko Tsushin* Magazine, Tokyo Geijutsu Daigaku, Tokyo

1984

''Revolution of Living Spaces'' collaborated with PH Studio, produced by *Brutus* Magazine, Tokyo

''Glass Art Akasaka'' collaborated with PH Studio, produced by Arata Isozaki and Associates, Tokyo

''Boutique Pashu'' collaborated with Super Potato, Tokyo

''Bar Ki No Hana'' collaborated with Super Potato, Tokyo

Composition for ''American Fork Art Exhibition'' collaborated with PH Studio, Laforet Museum Harajuku, Tokyo

1985

Space composition for ''Artists Book Exhibition'' Franklin Furnace, New York

Wall composition ''Chicago Artworks'' Limelight, Chicago

1986

Space composition for ''Music In Museum'' Seibu Museum of Art, Tokyo

1987

Stage set for ''Calyx'' of Lucinda Childs Dance Company, New York, touring to Kassel, Paris, Rome, and elsewhere

Composition ''I Like This'' collaborated with Ryoichi Yokota, Art Gallery Craft Salon, Seibu Department Store, Amagasaki

1988

Installation for the hall of event ''Yokohama Flush'' Mitsubishi Warehouse, Yokohama

1992

Judge for ''Sony Music Entertainment, The First Art Artists Audition '92'' Yokohama and Tokyo

Lectures

1980

Takayama School of Architecture, Takayama

1981

Praphan College of Advanced Education, Melbourne

Sydney College of Art, Sydney

1983

Studio F, Seibu Department Store, Funabashi

1984

B Semi School, Yokohama (1986, 88, 89.)

Tokyo School of Arts, Tokyo (1986.)

1986

Free Academy, The Hague

Kaneko Art Gallery, Tokyo

École des Beaux-Arts, Grenoble

1987

École des Beaux-Arts, Marseille

Vieille Charité, Marseille

École des Beaux-Arts, Paris

Fundaçao Armando Alvares Prenteado, Sao Paulo

Faculdade de Belas Artes (Art College,) Sao Paulo

1988

Fine Arts Department, Tokyo Geijutsu Daigaku, Tokyo

Akademie van Beeldende Kunsten, Rotterdam

Storefront for Art and Architecture, New York

1989

Architecture Department, University of Toronto, Toronto

Mercer Union, Toronto

Oude Dekenij, Kortrijk

Museum van Hedendaagse Kunst, Ghent

Koninklijke Academie voor Schone Kunsten, Ghent

1990

Seibu Community College, Tokyo

1992

Art Front Zürich, Zürich

Municipal Art Society, New York

New York City College, New York

Great Hall, Cooper Union for The Advancement of Science and Art, New York

Public Discussions

1980

—— at Yokohama Citizen Gallery, Yokohama

1983

with Shigeo Anzai, Akio Obigane and Makoto

Murata at Ten Gallery, Fukuoka

—— at the site of the project "Slip in Tokorozawa" Tokorozawa

with Shigeo Anzai, Jun Kawaguchi, Tomoo Shibahashi, and Makoto Murata at Dohtoku Gallery, Sapporo

1986

with Flip Bool, Raoul Bunscoten, Komar & Melamid, and George Trakas at Theater Zeebelt, The Hague

with Takashi Sugimoto at Hillside Gallery, Tokyo

with Makoto Murata and Shingo Yamano at Area Deux Gallery, Fukuoka

with Hiroshi Hayashi, Satoshi Murakami, and Makoto Murata at Kamitori Gallery, Kumamoto

1987

—— at École des Beaux-Arts, Aix-en-Provence

with Teruo Fujieda at Hillside Gallery, Tokyo

with Makoto Murata at Poppies, Tokyo

with Akio Obigane at Maison Franco-Japon (Japan-France House,) Tokyo

1988

with Fumio Nanjo at Gallery Kobayashi, Tokyo

with Kyosuke Inoue, Makoto Murata, Takashi Okunoyama, Chushiro Ota, and Hiroko Osugi at Suruga Bank, Fukuroi

with Kazuko Koike, Hiroshi Okabayashi, Akira Tatehata, and Takeshi Umehara at Hien-So, Kyoto

1990

with Howard N. Fox, Toshio Hara, and Takamasa Kuniyasu at Los Angeles County Museum of Art, Los Angeles

with Ryuji Miyamoto at Heineken Village, Tokyo

1991

with Montien Boonma at Asean Cultural Center, Tokyo

1992

with Shin-ya Izumi, Saburo Kawamoto, Koharu Kisaragi, and Chikako Oyama at Bank of Fukuoka, Fukuoka

with Hiroshi Okabayashi at Osaka Center for Contemporary Art, Osaka

with Hiroki Hasegawa, Kazukiyo Matsuba, and James G. Trulove at Pacifico Yokohama, Yokohama

1993

with Koji Taki at the lecture hall of Tokyo Metropolitan Art Museum, Tokyo

Awards

1978

Ataka Award, Tokyo Geijutsu Daigaku, Tokyo

1980

Salon de Printemps Award, Tokyo Geijutsu Daigaku, Tokyo

1982

Special Award, The Second International Youth Triannual of Drawing, Nürnberg

1984-1986

Asian Cultural Council Fellowship Grant, New York

1993

L'Association pour l'animation de Atelier Calder, Ministry of National Education and Culture, Orleans

Collections

Tokyo Metropolitan Art Museum, Tokyo

Haag Gemeentemuseum, The Hague

Musée Cantini, Marseille

Neue Galerie, Staatliche und Stadtische Kunstsammlungen, Kassel

Nissei Comprehensive Technical Center, Chiba

Kiyosato Museum of Contemporary Art, Kitakoma

Hara Museum of Contemporary Art, Tokyo

Canadian Center for Architecture, Montréal

The National Gallery of Canada, Ottawa

Adviescommisie voor Beeldende Kunst/Centrum Beeldende Kunst Utrecht, Utrecht

Musée D'Art Contemporain, Montréal

Roosevelt Island Operating Corporation, New York

New Tokyo Metropolitan Art Museum, Tokyo

New Umeda Sky Building, Osaka

Meguro Museum of Art, Tokyo

Bibliography

Individual Catalogues

1979

Kawamata, Tokyo: PH Studio.

1980

Kawamata, Tokyo: PH Studio.

1983

Kawamata, Tadashi / Miyamoto, Ryuji / Takashima, Naoyuki. *Slip in Tokorozawa*, Sapporo: Tetra House Publishing.

Endo, Kazuhiro / Manabe, Iori / Sato, Tomoya / Shibahashi, Tomoo. *Tetra House 326 Project No.1*, Sapporo: Tetra House Publishing.

1984

Anzai, Shigeo / Masaki, Hajime / Murata, Makoto / Sato, Masashi. *Tatra House 326 Project No.2*, Sapporo: Tetra House Publishing.

Under Construction (poster,) Tokyo: PH Studio and Art Front Gallery.

1986

Finkelpearl, Tom. *Kawamata Project*, Tokyo: on the table.

Takara House Room 205, 1982, Tokyo: on the table.

Tetra House N-3 W-26, 1983, Tokyo: on the table.

1987

interview by editors. *Kawamata (Under Construction,)* Tokyo: Gendaikikakushitsu Publishing.

1989

Gould, Claudia / Kawamata, Tadashi. *Kawamata Project in Roosevelt Island 1990*, Osaka: Kodama Gallery.

1990

Tadashi Kawamata / Project 1980-1990, London: Annely Juda Fine Art.

1991

Kawamata: Field Work (Japanese,) Tokyo: Kaneko Art Gallery.

Kawamata: Field Work (English,) Tokyo: on the table.

Kawamata, Tadashi. *Tower Cranes, Paris / Kawamata Urban Project with Temporary Structure*, Tokyo: Art Front Gallery.

Bekaert, Geert / de Zegher, Cathy / Kawamata, Tadashi / Tarantino, Michael. *Kawamata Begijnhof Kortrijk*, Tokyo and Kortrijk: Gendaikikakushitsu Publishing and Kanaal Art Foundation.

Donegan, Rosemary / Genereux, Linda (interview) / Mertins, Detlef / Pozel, Steven. *Kawamata: Toronto Project 1989*, Toronto: Mercer Union, A Centre for Contemporary Visual Art.

Kawamata, Tadashi. *Kawamata: Temporary Structures* Artrandom No.97, Kyoto: Kyoto Shoin Publishing.

1992

Kawamata, Tokyo: Gallery Kobayashi.

Obigane, Akio. *Kawamata: maquettes*, Osaka: Kodama Gallery, 1992.

1993

Kawamata: prefabrication, Tokyo: Gallery Kobayashi.

Bois, Yve-Alain / Frosch, Elizabeth A. / Gould, Claudia / Gounis, Kostas / Kawamata, Tadashi. *Kawamata Project on Roosevelt Island*, Tokyo and New York: Gendaikikakushitsu Publishers and on the table, inc.

Other Catalogues

1980

Haryu, Ichiro. *Hara Annual: Vision for 80s*, Tokyo: Hara Museum of Contemporary Art, unpaged.

Fujieda, Teruo. *Artists To-day*, Yokohama: Yokohama City and Yokohama City Educational Department, p. 2.

1981

Scarlett, Ken / Yamagishi, Noburo. *Yoin*, Melbourne: National Library of Australia, unpaged.

Minemura, Toshiaki. *Parallelism in Art Exhibition*, Tokyo: Ohara School of Ikebana, unpaged.

Akita, Yuri. *Artists To-day*, Yokohama: Yokohama City and Yokohama City Educational Department, unpaged.

1982

Galasso, Giuseppe. *arti visive '82: La Biennale*, Venice: La Biennale di Venezia, pp. 90-92.

Tani, Arata. *La Biennale di Venezia, Giappone 1982*, Tokyo: The Japan Foundation, unpaged.

Minemura, Toshiaki. *2. Internationale Jugendtriennale der Zeichnung*, Nürnberg: Kunsthalle Nürnberg, p. 136.

1983

Obigane, Akio. *Materials and Spaces*, Fukuoka: Fukuoka Art Museum, pp. 6-11.

Nakahara, Yusuke. *Shape and Spirit in Wood Work*, Urawa: The Modern Museum of Art, Saitama, pp. 9-12.

Harten, Jurgen / Tani, Arata. *Fünf Zeitgenossische Künstler Aus Japan*, Düsseldorf: Kunsthalle Düsseldorf, unpaged.

1984

Chiba, Shigeo / Francblin, Catherine. *Echange d'Art Contemporain, Tokyo-Paris 8+8*, Tokyo: Asahi Shimbun, pp. 96-101.

Domoto, Hisao / Jouffroy, Alain. *Exposition des affiches de la Maison Franco-Japonaise par 47 artistes japonais contemporains*, Tokyo: Maison Franco-Japonaise, p. 24.

Annual Report 1984, New York: Asian Cultural Council, pp. 11-12.

National and International Studio Programs 1984-1985, Long Island City: The Institute for Art and Urban Resources, Inc., pp. 38-39.

Minemura, Toshiaki / Nakahara, Yusuke. *Art in Japan Today II*, Tokyo: The Japan Foundation, pp. 80-83.

1985

Chiba, Shigeo. *Sculpture Japonais Contemporain*, Paris: Jullien-Cornic Galerie D'Art, unpaged.

Honma, Masayoshi. *Beauty of Wood: Between Painting and Sculpture*, Asahikawa: Hokkaido Asahikawa Museum of Art, pp. 42-43.

Cohen, C.J. *Perspective*, New York: The Korean Cultural Service Gallery, pp. 8-9.

1986

Kuwahara, Sumio. *A Scene of Contemporary Japanese Art 3: New Generation*, Sendai: Miyagi Museum of Art, p. 37.

Chiba, Shigeo / Frolet, Elisabeth / Iseki,

Masaaki / Kobayashi, Hitomi and Namikawa, Emiko. *Contatto*, Rome: Sala Uno, p. 20.

Biagini, Jean / Obigane, Akio. *Japon Art Vivant '87*, Paris: Sgraffite éditions, pp. 8-11.

1987

Jacob, Wenzel. *documenta 8* Vol.2, Kassel: documenta GmbH, pp. 118-119.

Minemura, Toshiaki / Tono, Yoshiaki. *Art in Japan since 1969: Mono-ha and Post Mono-ha*, Tokyo: The Seibu Museum of Art and Tama Art University, pp. 92-95.

Tono, Yoshiaki. *19 Sao Paulo Bienal*, Tokyo: The Japan Foundation, pp. 10-18.

Leirner, Sheil / Wiheim, Jorge. *19a Bienal Internacional De Sao Paulo*, Sao Paulo: Fundacao Bienal De Sao Paulo, p. 164.

1988

Terada, Tohru. *'88 Tukashin Annual*, Amagasaki: Tsukashin Hall, pp. 14-17.

Bazzoli, Françis / Biagini, Jean / Febvre, Jacqueline / Guillaumem, Marc / Kawamata, Tadashi. *Japon Art Vivant*, Paris: Sgraffite éditions, pp. 24-26.

Asada, Akira / Ishikawa, Kyuyo / Kakishita, Mokkan / Kawamata, Tadashi / Murata, Makoto / Osugi, Hiroko / Okabayashi, Hiroshi / Shiga, Yuji / Takahashi, Aki. *Aka-renga Final: Society, Temporary Structure, Words and Sound*, Fukuroi: Hiroko Ohsugi, pp. 23-44, 76-77.

Viatte, Germain / Vigouroux, Robert P. *L'Art Modern a Marseille La Collection du Musée Cantini*, Marseille: Musée Cantini, pp. 23, 233.

Projekt Worldfax 88: Fax The Art, Neuss: Kunstraum Neuss, unpaged.

1989

Murata, Keinosuke / Rose, Bernice / Tatehata, Akira. *Drawing As Itself*, Suita: Nathional Museum of Art, Osaka, pp. 124-127.

De Dauw, Norbert / Hoet, Jan / Nakahara, Yusuke. *Japan 1989*, Tokyo: Europalia Japan, pp. 50-55.

1990

Murata, Makoto, and others. *The Eighties*, Tokyo: Gallery Kobayashi, pp. 14-17.

Martins, Richard / Princenthal, Nancy / Yenawine, Philip. *The New Urban Landscape*, New York: Olympia & York, U.S.A. and Drenttal Doyle Partners, pp. 21, 26, 30, 32, 78-79, 115, 120-121, 127.

Nakahara, Yusuke. *The Game of Manners*, Mito: Art Tower Mito, pp. 41-44 in Vol.1, pp. 28-29 in Vol.2, p. 37 in English Edition.

L'Art renouvelle la Ville: L'Art Contemporain et Urbanisme en France, Tokyo: L'Art renouvelle la Ville Exhibition Committee, p. 143.

Fox, Howard N. *A Primal Spirit*, Tokyo and Los Angeles: Hara Museum of Contemporary Art and Los Angeles County Museum of Art, pp. 64-71.

Feij, Emilie / van Lennep, Madeleine. *Onvltooid Tegenwoordige Tijd*, Utrecht: Centraal Museum Utrecht, pp. 43-48.

McGonagle, Declan / Pohlen, Annelie. *A New Necessity*, Newcastle upon Tyne: Tyne International, cover, pp. 40-41.

Artists To-day 1969-1989, Yokohama: Yokohama Citizen Gallery, pp. 9, 93.

1991

Bremner, Ann / Gould, Claudia / Phillips, Patricia C. / Stearns, Robert. *Breakthrough/Avan-Garde Artists in Europe and America, 1950-1990/Wexner Center for the Arts*, New York: Rizzoli International Publications, pp. 176, 178, 185, 214-219, 299.

Bool, Flip / Peters, Philip. *In Situ*, The Hague: Stroom, haags centrum voor beeldende kunst, cover, pp. 50-53.

1992

Shioda, Jun-ichi. *The Urban Environment and Art in Japan/My Home Sweet Home in Ruins*, Tokyo: Setagaya Art Museum, pp. 8-10, 41-48, English text on pp. 118-120.

Documenta IX, Stuttgart and New York: Edition Cantz and Henry N. Abrams, Inc., pp. 163-164 in Vol.1, pp. 256-259 in Vol.2.

Minemura, Toshiaki. *Tempvs Victivm*, Tokyo: Ohara School of Ikebana, p. 11.

Minemura, Toshiaki, *Parallelism in Art Exhibition 1981-1991*, Tokyo: Bijutsu Shuppan-Sha, p. 15, 118.

Contribution by the Artist

1981

Graphication November, pp. 26-27.

1982

Graphication January, pp. 48-49.

Dia March 1, pp. 22-23.

1983

"Europe, Japan, Tokyo, and then Sapporo," *Dokusho Hokkaido* July 15.

The Hokkaido Shimbun Press August 27, evening.

1984

Chuo-Koron No.1183, September, p. 270.

1986

"Special Edition: New York Renessance," *Toshi Jutaku* September, pp. 37-50.

"Workshop at The Hague," *The Hokkaido Shimbun Press* October 4.

"Birds' Nest in the City Development," *The Mainichi Newspapers* October 20, p. 4.

1987

Herumesu No.13, December, pp. 65-84.

1988

Sogetsu No.176, pp. 124-125.

"From Destruction to Construction," (announcement of one man exhibition,) May, New York: Storefront for Art and Architecture.

1989

"Growing of art in the city," *Kukan* No.3, May, pp. 20-21.

1990

''Ruin as the beginning: Roosevelt Island,'' *Herumesu* No.23, February, pp. 73-80.

''Drawing '90: Beguinage Project at Kortrijk,'' *The Yomiuri Shimbun* March 3, evening, p. 9.

''Japanese Contemporary Art Exhibitions in Abroad'' *The Yomiuri Shimbun* October 15, p. 7.

1991

Raban, Jonathan / translated to Japanese by Takashima, Heigo. *Soft City*, Tokyo: Shobunsha Publishing, cover.

Post Modern and Ethnic, ed. Okabayashi, Hiroshi. Tokyo: Keiso Shobo Publishing, cover.

''Contemporary Art and Art Museum,'' *Gendai no Me* September, cover, p. 4.

''Installation work in Kyoto,'' *Kyoto Shimbun* December 13, 14 and 15.

S&E No.10, pp. 2, 7-8, 9-12, 46, 49-50.

1992

''The Time Lag of the City'' *Taiyo (The Sun)* No.370, April, pp. 6-7.

Interviews to the Artist

1980

Ikebana Ryusei No.240, April, pp. 16-17.

1984

Ki no Bunka(Culture of wood,) Tokyo: Asahi Shimbun-Sha, pp. 132-133.

1986

Bijutsu Techo No.563, June, pp. 100-105.

Atelier No.713, July, pp. 87-91.

1988

Geijutu Shincho No.459, March, pp. 60-62.

Hara Museum Review Autumn, unpaged.

''Tadashi Kawamata/Underconstruction,'' *Life Science* November, pp. 2-3, 8-13.

1989

''Tadashi Kawamata in America'' *Life Science* February, pp. 54-55.

1991

Murata, Makoto. ''In the world becoming to Disneyland,'' *Nikkei Image Crimate Forecast* No.18, pp. 54-55.

1992

Yanagi, Masahiko. ''Tadashi Kawamata'' *Art & Critique* No.21, December, pp. 24-31.

Discussions

1980

with Fujieda, Teruo. *Mizue* No.903, June, pp. 77-83.

1982

with Imai, Kinro / Tatehata, Akira. (announcement of three man exhibition,) Osaka: Gallery Haku, unpaged.

1983

with Hoshina, Toyomi. *Pia Calender* January-February, pp. 132-133.

with Anzai, Shigeo. *IAF* No.2, February, pp. 11-13.

1984

with Anzai, Shigeo / Tsukada, Seiichi. *Kikan Art* Spring, pp. 71-76.

with Morita, Yoshimitsu / Noda, Hideki / Pulvers, Roger / Sakamoto, Ryuichi. *Pia-no-Machikado*, Tokyo: Pia, Inc., pp. 22-30.

1988

with Miyake, Riichi. ''Installation as a parasite'' *Kusoh-no-gendaikenchiku(Imaginaly Contemporary Architecture,)* Tokyo: Kajima Shuppan-kai, pp. 170-181.

1991

with Okabayashi, Hiroshi. *Post Modern and Ethnic*, Tokyo: Keiso Shobo, pp. 267-283.

1992

with Iwakiri, Toru / Kitagawara, Atsushi. ''Special Feature,'' *Glass and Architecture* No.409, February, pp. 6-12.

Magazines

1980

Kitazawa, Noriaki. ''Exhibition Review,'' *Bijutsu Techo* No.465, May, pp. 229-233.

Akita, Yuri. ''Exhibition Review,'' *Bijutsu Techo* No.468, August, pp. 249-252.

1981

Akita, Yuri. *Bijutsu Nenkan* No.476, January Addition, pp. 20-24.

Ishida, Shuyo. ''Exhibition Report,'' *Bijutsu Techo* No.477, February, pp. 176-177.

Yamaguchi, Katsuhiro. *Sogetsu* No.134, February 10, pp. 97-100.

Hayami, Takashi. *Mizue* No.915, June, pp. 106-109.

Akita, Yuri. *Mizue* No.919, October, pp. 88-91.

Minemura, Toshiaki. *Ohararyu Soka* Vol.3 No.372, pp. 59-66.

1982

Haryu, Ichiro. *Shukan Shincho* No.1337, January 7, pp. 170-175.

''A scene,'' *Ryuko Tsushin* No.220, May, pp. 34-35, photo by Shigeo Anzai.

Tanaka, Kojin. *Sogetsu* No.142, June, pp. 104-107.

Tani, Arata. ''Report of Venezia Biennale,'' *Bijutsu Techo* No.502, October, pp. 80-87.

1983

Fujiuchi, Tatsuhiko / Obigane, Akio / Suga,

Akira / Yamano, Shingo. ''Tadashi Kawamata in Fukuoka,'' *IAF Journal* February.

Honma, Masayoshi. *Asahi Journal* No.1256, March 11, p. 83.

Minemura, Toshiaki. *Kikan(Seasonal) Art* Spring, pp. 92-94.

Akatsu, Tadashi. *Mizue* No.926, Spring, pp. 130-133.

Häsli, Richard. *Das Kunst Magazine* C1084E, pp. 7, 9.

Schaker, Christoph. ''Im Reich der Leere'' *Kunstforum* Bd58.2, pp. 120-130.

Hayami, Takashi. *Ikebana Ryusei* No.278, April, pp. 28-31.

Minemura, Toshiaki. *Asahi Journal* April 15.

Anzai, Shigeo. ''Installation by Tadashi Kawamata,'' *ballet dance Tes* #7-1, p. 54.

Miyamoto, Ryuji. ''Slip in Tokorozawa,'' *Toshi Jutaku* No.190, August, pp. 145-146.

Takashima, Naoyuki. ''Exhibition Review,'' *Bijutsu Techo* No.514, August, pp. 198-202.

Kate, Fumi. *ballet dance Tes* #7-4, pp. 44-45.

1984

Akita, Yuri. *Sogetsu* No.158, February, pp. 77-80.

Nakahara, Yusuke. *Asahi Journal* February 24, p. 81.

Tani, Arata. *Ikebana Ryusei* No.287, March, unpaged.

Anzai, Shigeo. *Fujin Gaho* No.968, March, p. 292.

Kondo, Yukio. *Shoten Kenchiku* Vol.29 No.3, March, p. 59.

Tono, Yoshiaki. *AD Japan* No.6, April, pp. 8-9.

Nakahara, Yusuke. *Ushio* No.300, April, p. 267.

Brutus No.93, August 1, pp. 96-97, photo by Ryuji Miyamoto.

1985

''Boutique Shin Hosokawa,'' *Japan Interior Design* No.310, pp. 18-24, 28, photo by Mitsumasa Fujitsuka.

Tanaka, Kojin. *Ikebana Ryusei* No.297, January, pp. 34-35.

Anzai, Shigeo. *Sogetsu* No.158, February, pp. 69-72.

''Underconstruction: Art by Tadashi Kawamata sticks into architecture,'' *Brutus* No.104, February 1, pp. 140-141, photo by Ryuji Miyamoto.

Callaghan, Edward. ''One Man's Junk Is Another Man's Art,'' *press release* May.

Obigane, Akio. *Asahi Journal* No.1384, August 2, pp. 35-36.

Overduin, Henk. ''Culturele confrontaties met Japan,'' *museumvisie* December, p. 148.

1986

Goldscheider, Cecile. *L'Oeil* January-Feburuary, pp. 60-65.

Takashima, Heigo. ''Tadashi Kawamata's lumber construction,'' *Nenkin-to-Jutaku* February, pp. 30-31.

Yamano, Shingo. ''Art Information, Tadashi Kawamata,'' *d-Art* #0 Summer, pp. 18-19.

van Santen, Ingrid. ''Internationale workshop zijn aanzet tot dialoog,'' *Het Biennerhof* June.

Takashima, Naoyuki. *Shoten Kenchiku* No.402, July, p. 89.

Munroe, Alexandra K. ''A Continent Away,'' *Winds* August, pp. 42-53.

Schneckenburger, Mansfred / von Wichmann-Eichhon, Jurgen Schweinbraden Freiherr. ''Urbaner kraftakt und poetische konstruktion,'' *documenta press*, October 28, pp. 3, 5.

Yamano, Shingo. *d-Art* #1 December, pp. 18-19.

1987

Kitahashi, Tomoya. ''Escape from Post-Modern,'' *Brutus* No.149, January 15, p. 135.

Comte, Sylvie. ''Empreintes sur le quartier brerriat,'' *Quartier* pp. 62-63.

Schneckenburger, Mansfred. ''über konzeption und Riehtliniender Dokumenta,'' *Hier und Jetzt* April, pp. 117-118.

Wachtel, Joachim. ''Wo stent die kunst?,'' *Die Schone Welt* June.

Bode, Peter M. ''Kraft Nach Kassel,'' *Vogue* (Germany), June.

Schwerdtle, Dieter. ''Stahl, Holz, Stein-Künstler der documenta 8,'' *documenta press* June, pp. 10-11, photo by Christina Hein.

Engagiert, Krithsche Muting. ''Die 8 Documenta in Kassel,'' *JA / Woche von der packendsten Seite* No.25, June 9, unpaged.

Christoph, Horst. ''Kunstfroh durch die Stadt,'' *Profil* No.24, June 15, unpaged.

''documenta special,'' *Wolkenratzer/Art Journal* June-July-August, pp. 16-20, 74-75, English translation on p. 120.

Thielmann, Sven. ''Kunst Fur Die Welt-Kunst Fur's Volk,'' *Prinz* July-August, p. 71.

Meyer, Ingrid. ''Documenta,'' *NIKE New Art in Europe* No.19, July-August-September, unpaged.

Takashima, Naoyuki. ''Japan Modern Art Communication,'' *Wacoa* No.7, pp. 10-13.

Hübl, Michael. *Kunstforum* Bd.90 July-September, pp. 82, 292-293.

Takashima, Naoyuki. ''Art Now 31: Destroyed Church,'' *Asahi Journal* No.1492, August 7, p. 30, photo by Shigeo Anzai.

West, Thomas. ''Republic of Ready-Mades'' *Art International* Autumn, pp. 82-88.

Henry, Clare. ''International Platform Documenta 8,'' *Alba* Autumn, pp. 34-37.

Ashton, Dore. ''Documenta of What,'' *art Magazine* September, pp. 17-20.

Nanjo, Fumio. ''From the site of Documenta 8,'' *Subaru* Vol.9 No.10, September, pp. 132-143.

Fry, Edward F. / Nanjo, Fumio. ''Collapse of

Post-Modernism,'' *Subaru* Vol.9 No.10, September, pp. 125-129.

Fujieda, Teruo. ''Documenta 8 News,'' *Bijutsu Techo* No.585, September, pp. 26-27, 59.

Marmer, Nancy. ''Documenta 8: The Social Dimension?,'' *Art in America* September, pp. 128-140.

Shikata, Yukiko. ''Document of Documenta Exhibition,'' *Brutus* September 1, p. 94.

Matchesini, Annamaria. ''Para chocar a populacao,'' *Visao* September 23, pp. 44-45,

Takashima, Naoyuki. ''Return to System of Painting,'' *Nikkei Image Climate Forecast* No.2, October, pp. 60-62.

Cameron, Dan. ''Documenta 8 Kassel,'' *Flash Art International* October, pp. 61-68.

Smith, Shaw. ''Documenta 8,'' *New Art Examiner* Vol.15 No.2, October, pp. 22-28.

Frank, Peter. ''Documenta 8,'' *Sculpture* November-December, pp. 20-25.

Tani, Arata. *Sogetsu* No.30, December, p. 13.

Schwarze, Dirk. ''Documenta 8,'' *Kunstforum* December 1987-January 1988, p. 244.

1988

Murata, Makoto. ''Christo and Tadashi Kawamata,'' *Kokoku* January-February, pp. 2-3.

Takashima, Naoyuki. ''Kawamata Annual,'' *Mono Magazine* Vol.7 No.4, February 2, p. 135.

Iijima, Yoichi. ''Lumber's 'Papier Collé','' *Shin-Kenchiku* March, p. 319.

Tatehata, Akira. *AC* No.5, March, pp. 1-3.

Yamazaki, Hitoshi. *AC* No.5, March, p. 8.

Kurabayashi, Yasushi. *Bijutsu Techo* No.593, April, p. 202.

Peters, Philip. ''Japan Hout,'' *Magasijn* No.17, May, pp. 20-21.

Koplos, Janet. ''Review: Tadashi Kawamata,'' *Art in America* May, pp. 194-195.

Welling, Dolf. ''Rotterdam- zet de kunsten op een sokkel,'' *De Stad Als Podium* May, pp. 12-17.

Roberts, James. ''Review: Tadashi Kawamata,'' *Artscribe International* No.70, Summer, p. 89.

Koplos, Janet. ''Mono-ha and The Power of Materials,'' *New Art Examiner* June, pp. 29-32.

Peters, Philip. ''Tadashi Kawamata,'' *Artefactum* Vol.5 No.24, June-August, pp. 10-13, English translation on p. 55, photo by Leo van der Kleij.

Kinoshita, Osahiro. *Misho* September, pp. 16-17.

Yoshiga, Yoshisuke. ''Temporary Constructing and Dismantling, Hien-So,'' *Sansai* No.492, September, pp. 120-121.

Takashima, Naoyuki. *icon* Vol.13, September, pp. 44-45, photo by Yoshio Shiratori.

Tatehata, Akira. ''Tadashi Kawamata's 'Hien-So' project,'' *Shoten Kenchiku* No.429, September, p. 121.

McCormick, Calro. ''On the waterfront,'' *Paper* October, p. 17.

Murata, Makoto. ''Art Today,'' *Ikebana Ryusei* October, p. 39.

Takashima, Naoyuki. *Nikkei Woman* October, pp. 144-145.

Masaki, Motoi. ''Constructs with Footwork/Tadashi Kawamata,'' *BT (Bijutsu Techo)* No.600, October, pp. 128-129, 137-138.

Sugiura, Takao. ''Hien-So, Under Construction, Tadashi Kawamata,'' *AC* No.8, pp. 34-35.

Campbell, Robert. ''Sharkin and Dreck,'' *AJ* November 9, pp. 94-95.

O'Brien, Rodney. ''Shivering Timbers: Tadashi Kawamata,'' *Intersect* December, pp. 24-25.

Nakahara, Yusuke. *Sogetsu* No.181, December, pp. 13-20.

1989

Koplos, Janet. ''Japan's Contemporary Arts,'' *Sumitomo Corporation News* No.72, January, pp. 2-7.

Shelter, Gimme ''New Urban Landscape'' *Design (U.S.A.)* January, pp. 81-82.

Yanase, Kaoru. ''New Urban Landscape, Suggestion to City,'' *BT* No.606, March, pp. 86-93.

Aihara, Yumi. *Brutus* No.200, April 1, p. 9.

Phillips, Patricia C. ''Added Attraction,'' *Artforum International* May, pp. 108-112.

Anzai, Shigeo. *Sogetsu* No.185, August, pp. 17-24.

Freedman, Adele. ''Fastforward,'' *Canadian Art* Vol.6 No.3, Autumn, p. 54.

Harris, Pamela. ''Kawamata's Toronto Project,'' *Azume Magazine* Vol.6 No.59, September, unpaged.

Sandiford, Judith / Weihs Ronald. ''The Endless Project,'' *Work Seen* Vol.1 No.2, September-October, pp. 7-8.

Deonandan, Ray. ''Ball Crowd Illuminates Riotou Architecture,'' *The Varsity* Vol.110 No.11, October 2, p. 13.

Dobrocnik, Frank. ''Modern Art Pussles Yonge Street Crowd,'' *The Eyeopener* October 21, unpaged.

Rhodes, Richard. ''Toronto: Tadashi Kawamata/Mercer Union,'' *Artforum International* November, p. 162.

Bekaert, Geert. ''Tadashi Kawamata's ontmoetingen in Gent en Kortrijk,'' *Archis* December, p. 2.

Braet, Jan. ''Het Kawamata-projekt,'' *Knack* December 13, pp. 150-153.

Kobayashi, Hitomi. ''Interior Coordination,'' *Wacoa* No.17, December 15, pp. 28-31.

1990

Okabayashi, Hiroshi. ''Ruin as a longing,'' *Kenchiku Zasshi* Vol.105 No.1294, January, pp. 36-37.

Shinohara, Motoaki. "Trans Art Map," *Yuriika* Vol.22 No.2, February, pp. 142-149.

Marcelis, Bernard "Tadashi Kawamata" *art press* No.144, February, p. 96.

Herstatt, Claudia. "Neuer Kragen fur den alten Begijnhof von Kortrijk," *Kunst Magazine* February, p. 25.

Tatehata, Akira. *Nikkei Art* No.17, February, pp. 193-196.

Legris, Peter. "Kawamata & Aesthetics of Radicalism," *a/r/c* Vol.1 No1, Spring, pp. 34-35.

Theriault, Normand. "Visual Art Review / Tadashi Kawamata," *Parachute* No.58, pp. 37-38.

Freedman, Adele. "Jammed Session," *Toronto Life* March, pp. H7-H12.

Malis, Liesbeth. "Opdrachtkunst Verkeerd Geinterprepeerd," *de Architect* March, pp. 28-29.

Hume, Christpher. "The Politics of Public Art," *Toronto Star Sunday Magazine* March 10, pp. M10-M19.

"In the News/Reconstruction History," *Sculpture* Vol.9 No.2, March-April, p. 12.

Roos, Robbert. "15 Imaginaire projecten voor Utrecht," *Beelding* No.2, unpaged.

Vaizey, Marina. "Annely Juda Fine Art," *Galleries* May.

Currah, Mark. "Visual Art/Tadashi Kawamata," *City Limits* No.450, May 17-24, p. 74.

Kent, Sarah. "Tadashi Kawamata," *Time Out* No.1030, May 16-23, p. 31.

Nicholson, Chuck. "Toward a Spiritual Whole," *Artweek* Vol.21 No.26, August, p. 13.

Mikami, Yutaka / editors. "Directory of Japanese Arts," *BT* Vol.142 No.627, September, pp. 36-37, 59, 61.

Hatton, Brian. "Reveiw: Tadashi Kawamata/Annely Juda," *Artscribe International* September-October, p. 81.

Clothier, Peter. "A Primal Spirit," *Artspace* September-October, pp. 50-54.

Heatney, Eleanor. "Report from New Castle / Cultingan Engaged Public Art," *Art in America* October, pp. 54-57.

Plagens, Peter "Invention Is the Mother of..." *Newsweek* October 1, pp. 70L-70N.

Plagens, Peter "Palms and Circumstance" *Newsweek* October 20, p. 64.

Ellenberger, Michel. "Tadashi Kawamata/batisseur du provisoire," *art press* No.153, pp. 50-54.

Nesbitt, Lois E. "New Works for New Spaces: Into the Nineties," *Newsline* December 1990-January 1991, p. 8.

1991

Dery, Louise. "Triptyque: Musée-Artste-Environment," *Muse* Vol.VIII No.4, Winter, pp. 61-63, English translation on pp. 64-66.

Ueda, Takahiro. *Studio Voice* Vol.181, January, p. 39.

Bois, Yve-Alain. "In situ: Site-Specific Art In And Out of Context," *The Journal of Art* January, p. 30.

Okabayashi, Hiroshi. "Multi-media Work, No.2," *hiroba* No.322 February, pp. 60-63.

Yanase, Kaoru. "New Works for New Spaces: Into the Nineties," *BT* Vol.43 No.635 March, pp. 143-149.

Koplos, Janet. "Material Meditation," *Art in America* March, pp. 95-101.

Fryer-Kohles, Jeanne C. "Review: 'New Works for New Spaces: Into the Ninties," *New Art Examiner* March, p. 37.

Herstatt, Claudia. "Kunst aus Brettern," *Zeitmagazin* No.10, March 1, pp. 76-83.

Connors, Thomas. "Review/Ohio/New Works for New Spaces: Into the Nineties," *Sculpture* March-April, pp. 63-64.

Anzai, Shigeo / Shinoda, Tatsumi. "Seeing and Taking about Contemporary Art," *Sogetsu* No.195 April, pp. 90-96.

Okabayashi, Hiroshi. "An Essay on Tadashi Kawamata: Wall, Space, Form of Occupation," *Mizue* No.959, Summer, pp. 14, 40-49.

Tanigawa, Atushi. "Topography of Contemporary Art," *Taiyo (The Sun)* No.362, August, p. 27.

Takashima, Naoyuki. "Homme Let's: Art," *Ryuko Tsushin Homme* No.19 September, p. 25.

Lowitz, Leza. "Review: Tadashi Kawamata," *Sculpture* November-December, p. 60.

Okabayashi, Hiroshi. "Multi-media Work, No.12," *hiroba* No.332, December, pp. 54-57.

Takashima, Heigo. *FS (Fukuoka Style)* Vol.2, pp. 14-17.

1992

Ord, Douglas. "Kawamata's Sheds / Débats Issues," *Parachute* No.65, January-February-March, pp. 64-68.

Sakai, Yuko. "The World of Tadashi Kawamata," *Nikkei Architecture* No.426, March 16, pp. 263-265.

Takashima, Naoyuki. "Tadashi Kawamata," *BT* Vol.44 No.652, April, pp. 105-118.

Betsky, Aaron. "Violated Perfection," *a+u* April, pp. 106-107.

Kobayashi, Hitomi / Murata, Makoto. "Artists File," *Wave* #33, May 25, pp. 30-31, 98-99, 143, 145.

Schlagheck, Irma. "Documenta IX / Riskanter Balanceakt mit 186 Artisten," *art Das Kunstmagazin* No.6, June, pp. 36-37, 46.

Kitagawa, Fram. *Taiyo (The Sun)* No.373, July, pp. 158-159.

Adcock, Craig. "Documenta IX," *Teme Celeste* No.37-38, Autumn, pp. 84-86.

Raap, Jürgen. "Documenta campague de soldes," *art press* No.172, September, pp. 66-67.

"It's Time to.../...Take a Gander," *Metropolitan Home* Vol.XXIV No.9,

September, unpaged.

Connors, Thomas. ''Fanfair/Wood Awakening,'' *Vanity Fair* September, unpaged.

Freiburger, H.C. *Rokugatsu no Kaze (June Wind)* September, pp. 21-22.

Madoff, Steven Henry. ''Review/Documenta IX: More is A Mess,'' *Artnews* September, p. 131.

''Urban Archaeology'' *The New Yorker* September 28, p. 10.

Hixson, Kathryn / McWilliams, Martha. ''The way to Docu-drama,'' *New Art Examiner* October, pp. 12-15.

Lutfy, Carol. ''A Very Public Matter,'' *Tokyo Journal* October, pp. 41-42.

''Art / Other Venues / Tadashi Kawamata'' *The New Yorker*, October 5, p. 36.

Murata, Makoto ''Overseas'' *Pia* October 15, p. 266.

Stevens, Margaret. ''A Rune on Ruins'' *Landscape Architecture* November.

Peters, Philip. ''En Route,'' *Kunst & Museum Journaal* Vol.4, November 2, pp. 25-32.

---. ''Die Documenta Als Kunstwerk,'' *Kunstforum* Bd.119, pp. 461-465.

Wentz, Christine. ''Kawamata: Project on Roosevelt Island,'' *Newsline* November-December, p. 8.

Fujieda, Teruo. ''Vanguard / Tadashi Kawamata,'' *Chuo Koron* December, unpaged, photo by Michio Noguchi.

Yanase, Kaoru. ''Kawamata Tadashi, Roosevelt Island Project,'' *BT* No.662, December, pp. 16-17.

''Realized Project of Tadashi Kawamata in New York,'' *Geijutsu Shincho* Vol.43 No.12, December, p. 104.

Slatin, Peter. ''Ruins for a Ruin,'' *Artnews* December, p. 16.

Branch, Mark Alden. ''A Missed Opportunity on Roosevelt Island,'' *Progressive Architecture* December, p. 14.

Murata, Makoto. ''Tadashi Kawamata's Project Continues To Stimulate Environments,'' *Brutus* December 1, p. 39.

1993

Murphy, Jay. ''Reviews / Tadashi Kawamata / Roosevelt Island,'' *Tema Celeste* No. 38, Winter, pp. 83-84.

Kitagawa, Fram. *Taiyo (The Sun)* No.378, January, pp. 94-95.

Connors, Thomas. ''Kawamata: Project on Roosevelt Island,'' *Sculpture* January-February, pp. 24-25.

Suga, Akira. *BT* No.665, February, pp. 261-270.

''Best 10: Art after the Would War,'' *Geijutsu Shincho* Vol.44 No.2, February, cover, pp. 4, 5, 27, 39, 45, 46, 48, 50, 53, 54, 56, 62-63.

Jodidio, Philippe. ''Bâtisseur de L'Éphémére,'' *Connaissance des Arts* March, pp. 116-121, photo by Norman McGrath.

Gould, Claudia. ''Kawamata's 'Miracle','' *Parkett* #35, March-April, pp. 161-164.

Wentz, Christine. ''Tadashi Kawamata project op Roosevelt Island,'' *Archis* April, pp. 44-47.

Akasaka, Hideto. ''Tadashi Kawamata, People's Garden'' *Shukan Asahi* April 2, p. 161.

Princenthal, Nancy. *Art in America* July.

Newspapers

1980

Fujieda, Teruo. *Nippon Dokusho Shimbun* No.2064, July 7.

Fujieda, Teruo. *Nippon Dokusho Shimbun* No.2067, July 28.

Saint-Gilles, Amaury. ''Hara Annual Show On'' *Daily Yomiuri* December 11.

Tono, Yoshiaki. ''Art: 1980 Best 5,'' *The Asahi Shimbun* December 15, evening, p. 9.

Thoren, Barbara. ''This Week in Art,'' *The Japan Times* December 21.

1981

Nakamura, Keiji. *Nippon Dokusho Shimbun* (Kansai,) October 20.

1982

Chiba, Shigeo. *Nippon Dokusho Shimbun* May 31.

Nakahara, Yusuke. ''Art: This Year,'' *Nippon Dokusho Shimbun* (Kansai,) December 17, p. 9.

1983

Obigane, Akio. ''What is 'Materials and Spaces Exhibition','' *Nishi-Nihon Shimbun* February 23.

Tanaka, Kojin. ''Review: 'Shape and Spirit in Wood Work','' *The Mainichi Newspapers* March 12, p. 5.

Saint-Gilles, Amaury. ''Art: People and Places,'' *Mainichi Dairy News* May 28.

Sato, Tomoya. ''Art as a footwork,'' *Dokusho Hokkaido* October 15.

1986

Tanaka, Kojin. *The Mainichi Newspapers* May 16.

Oiivier, Ed. ''Slooppand 'Ingepakt' door Japanse Kunstenaar,'' *Haagsche Courant* June 12.

Olivier, Ed. ''Eindelijk gebeurt er eens wat,'' *Haagsche Courant* July 2.

Chiba, Shigeo. ''Frontier of Beauty Vol.6 No.5,'' *Tokyo News* July 10, p. 3.

Sanda, Haruo. ''Free Footwork,'' *The Mainichi Newspapers* August 7, evening.

1987

Mango, Lorenzo. ''Due Monstre Romane Tornano A Proporci Il 'Cuore Tematico' Dell Arte Orientale,'' *Paese Sera* January 5, p. 9.

Micacchi, Dario. ''Scultori acrobatici: nove installatori giapponesi in mostra,'' *l'Unita*

January 18.

Bilardello, Enzo. ''Nove giovani giapponesi,'' *Corriere Della Sela* January 19.

Waleson, Heidi. ''Lucinda Childs Tiptoes Toward Ballet,'' *New York Newsdays* May 10.

Dunning, Jennifer. ''The Stage As Element Of Dance,'' *The New York Times* May 11.

Anderson, Jack. ''The Dance: 3 Works By Childs,'' *The New York Times* May 14.

Schwarze, Dirk. ''Das Gebaude offnen,'' *Hessische Niedersachsiscfhe Allgemeine* May 23.

Jowitt, Deborah. ''Lucinda Childs' Calyx,'' *The Village Voice* June 2.

Orzechwski, Lothar. ''Die visuelle aschine,'' *Hessische Niedersachsische Allgemeine* June 11.

Kronthaler, Helmut. ''documenta 8 Jenseits der Postmoderne?,'' *Laudshuter Zeitung* June 11.

Rainer, Wolfgang. ''Gaz sanfte Signale,'' *Stuttgarter Zeitung* June 13.

Berichtet, Haberl / Gerhard, Horst. ''Kuckuckseier in der Stadt,'' *Kleine Zeitung* June 14.

Hollenstein, Roman. ''Besinnung der kunst auf ihre historesche und soziale Dimension,'' *Reue Burcher Zeitung* June 16.

Giessler, Ursula. ''Kunst kritisiert Kassel,'' *Saabrucker Zeitung* June 17.

Kipphoff, Petra. ''Das hohe Fest der Beliebigkeit,'' *Die Zeit* June 19.

Muller, Bertram. ''Lichtschein auf Horror und poesie,'' *Geist und Leben* June 20.

Buck, Ernst. ''Alles ist moglich!,'' *Offenbach-Post* June 20-21.

Schulz, Bernard. ''Buhnenbilder der Zerstreuungskultur,'' *Weltspiegel* (Berlin,) June 21.

Breerette, Genevieve. ''Les pieds dans le meuble,'' *Le Monde* June 21-22.

Michaelis, Rolf. ''Augentheater,'' *Die Zeit* June 25.

Huylebroeck, Paul. ''Achtste Dokumenta: als geen andre...,'' *Zutphen Dagblad* June 27.

Schwarze, Dirk. ''Eingriffe in die Stadt,'' *Hessische Niedersachsische Allgemeine* July 8.

Freese, Uwe. ''Der Geruch des Spektalularen fehlt in diesem Jahre,'' *Holsteinischer Courier* July 9.

Lobeck, Rolf. ''Im Augenblick des Kräftesammelns,'' *Deutsche Volkszeitung* July 10.

Brackert, Gisala. ''Kalte Engel raunen vom Ende der Zeit,'' *Deutsches Allgemeines Sonntagsblatt* July 12, p. 21.

Stachelhaus, Heiner. ''Buhne fur ein Verwertungs-Spektakel,'' *NRZ*, July 12, photo by Friedhelm Zigler.

Marzluf, Arnuf. ''Installateure der Postmoderne,'' *Allgemeine Beitung* August 4.

Muller-Mehlis, Reinhard. ''Die Macher und ihre Hatschelkinder,'' *Bayernkurier* August 15.

Geduldig, Gernot. ''Luxus-Auto und vier Guillotinen,'' *Aachener Nachrichten* August 22.

Goncalves Filho, Antonio. ''Kawamata, um japones muito louco,'' *Folha De S. Paulo* September 11.

Goncalves Filho, Antonio. ''O demolidor Kawamata chega para a Bienal,'' *Folha De S. Paulo* September 11.

Amarante, Leonor. ''De pernas pro ar,'' *O Estado De S. Paulo* September 11.

Martinho, Tete. ''Visuais Arte Sobre Ruinas,'' *jarnal de tarde* September 12.

Ramos, Calros. ''Pau para toda obra '' *O Globo* September 16.

Koplos, Janet. ''Looking at Inside and Outside,'' *Asahi Evening News* December 9.

1988

Bentivoglio, Leonetta. ''Il segno di Lucinda Childs,'' *la Repubblica Danza* January 19, p. 1.

Murakami, Kei. ''Tadashi Kawamata's 'Under Construction,'' *The Senken* February 2, p. 1.

Depondt, Paul. ''Een zacht geluid dringt door tot de stadsjungle,'' *de Volkskrant* May 7.

Brenson, Michael. ''Kawamata: From Destruction to Construction,'' *The New York Times* May 20.

Levin, Kim. ''Kawamata,'' *The Village Voice* May 31.

Horsley, Carter B. ''Provocative peek into future,'' *New York Post* October 13.

Smith, Roberta. ''A Wide-Ranging Spread Of Artists and Installations,'' *The New York Times* November 4.

Kramer, Hilton. ''Sculpture Show a Lachrymose Valentine to a Bygone Era,'' *The New York Observer* November 7.

Hess, Elizabeth. ''Captive of Industry?,'' *The Village Voice* November 15.

1989

Hume, Christpher. ''Art Stopper,'' *Toronto Star* March 9.

Bently Mays, John. ''Kawamata Installation To Be A First,'' *The Globe and Mail* No.43496, May 2, p. A25.

Freedman, Adele. ''Is It A Disturbance? Public Art? No, It's A Parasite,'' *The Globe and Mail* July 15, p. C13.

Balfour-Bowen, Lisa. ''Art in Our Park,'' *Toronto Sun* August 19-20, p. S20.

Genereux, Linda. ''Visual Terrorism,'' *Metropolis* Vol.2, No.15, August 24.

Hume, Christopher. ''Whirlwind of changies public art scene,'' *Toronto Star* August 25, p. E3.

Freedman, Adele. ''Watch for the rare but possible: recognition of young talent,'' *The Globe and Mail* September 9.

De Kexzer, Laurens. ''Japan kunst van vandaag,'' *De Gentenaar* October 27.

Wesseling, Janneke. ''Modern Japanse Kunst staat voor een dilemma,'' *NRC Handelsblad*

November 11, p. 6.

Lecluyse, Filip. ''Japanner 'emballeert' kortrijks begijnhof met houten planken,'' *Gazet van Antwerpen* November 25-26, p. 7.

De Cauter, Lieven. ''Kawamata pakt Begijnhof in,'' *De Standaad* December 21.

Balfour-Bowen, Lisa. ''Visually Speaking... Best of 89,'' *Toronto Sun* December 31, p. S10.

1990

Whetstone, David. ''An uplifting idea for river skyline,'' *The Journal* January 15.

Dagbland, Velouws. ''Imaginaire projecten in het Centraal Museum Utrecht,'' *Vazdias* March 8.

Courant, Meppeler. ''Ingebeelde kunst in Utrecht,'' *Vazdias* March 14.

Okuda, Yu. *The Sankei Shimbun* March 15, p. 19.

Jones, Derek. ''A Primal Spirit,'' *Asahi Evening News* No.11239, March 16.

Figee, Thea. ''Expositie vol dromen over de stad in Centraal Museum,'' *Utrecht Nieuwsblad/NZC* March 30.

Silva, Arturo. ''A primal spirit,'' *The Daily Yomiuri* April 12.

Feaver, William. ''In paradise upon Tyne,'' *The Observer* May 20.

Paterson, Rose. ''Artistic fog on the Tyne?,'' *Daily Teregraph* May 30, p. 6.

Wilson, William. ''Japanese Art Exhibition: A Rare Find,'' *Los Angeles Times Calender*, June 17.

Berland, Dinah. ''Japan's 'Primal Spirit' is a sensual feast,'' *Press Teregram* (Long Beach,) June 24, p. S2.

Chiba, Shigeo. ''Seasonal Article: Contemporary Art,'' *Tokyo News* July 3, p. 9.

Lutfy, Carol. ''Contemporary Japanese Art Makes Jump to U.S.,'' *The Asian Wall Street Journal* July 13-14.

Hendryson, Cindy. ''Lots more two by four,'' *The Ohio State Lantern* September 27, p. 9.

Wong, Lois J. '' 'Sidewalk' repaired for show,'' *The Ohio State Lantern* October 3.

1991

Lowitz, Leza. ''Shelter in the Storm / The 'Field Work' of Tadashi Kawamata,'' *Asahi Evening News* March 22.

Johnson, Patricia C. ''Landscapes on the Bayou,'' *Houston Chronicle* April 25.

Gunn, Jeanelle. ''Sculptor uses what he can get his hands on,'' *The Daily Couger* April 25.

Chadwick, Susan. ''Simple shack - complex art,'' *The Houston Post* April 27.

Sanda, Haruo. ''Art'' *The Mainichi Newspapers* June 21, evening.

Baele, Nancy. ''This Is Art?,'' *The Ottawa Citizen* June 22.

Bronkskill, Jim. ''Gallery exhibit raises hackle,'' *The Globe and Mail* June 26.

Sugawara, Norio. ''Face of Tomorrow No.280/Tadashi Kawamata,'' *The Yomiuri Shimbun* July 4, evening.

Freedman, Adele. ''By Design,'' *The Globe and Mail* July 6.

Hart, Matthew. ''But is it art? Must be, Ottawa hates it,'' *The Globe and Mail* July 6.

Lehmann, Henry. ''Kawamata's hovels draw observers into fields of broken dreams,'' *The Gazette* July 6.

Baele, Nancy. ''Primal Spirit quick to make headlines,'' *The Gazette* July 6.

Cron, Marie-Michèle. ''Le passage du temp/Tadashi Kawamata,'' *Le Devoir* July 6.

Sanda, Haruo. ''New El Dorado/Installation work of Tadashi Kawamata,'' *The Mainichi Newspapers* December 10.

Shibusawa, Kazuhiko. ''World/Ruin with scrap wood of Artist Tadashi Kawamata,'' *The Sankei Shimbun* December 12, p. 15.

1992

''Artist Tadashi Kawamata: New York Project,'' *The Sankei Shimbun* February 6, p. 19.

''Wide Culture/'Temporary' Art, Tadashi Kawamata exhibiting models,'' *The Hokkaido Shimbun Press* February 14, p. 10.

Shioda, Jun-ichi. ''Tadashi Kawamata's Installation in the courtyard of Setagaya Museum of Art,'' *The Asahi Shimbun* April 16, evening.

Gimelson, Deborah. ''Art Diary,'' *The New York Observer* June 1, p. 21.

Lück, Jürgen. ''Kunst kämpft mit Holz (köpfen),'' *Extra Tip* (Kassel,) June 11, p. 5.

Gauville, Hérve/Lebovici, Elisabeth. ''Arts / La Documenta Se Mouille,'' *Liberation* June 18.

Breerttel, Genevieve. *Le Monde* June 18.

Tilroe, Anna. ''Bazar van grootse, erbarmelijke lichamen,'' de *Volkskrant* June 19.

Smith, Roberta. ''A Small Show Within an Enormous One,'' *The New York Times* June 22, p. C13.

Tatehata, Akira. ''Culture,'' *The Asahi Shimbun* July 1, p. 18.

Sugawara, Norio. ''Documenta IX: Report 4'' *The Yomiuri Shimbun* July 3, evening.

Kimmelman, Michael. ''Art Review/At Documenta, It's Survival Of the Loudest,'' *The New York Times* July 5.

Levin, Kim. ''Jan Who? Docu What?,'' *The Village Voice* July 14, pp. 95-96.

Hughes, Janica (Associate Press.) ''Artist makes huge sculpture out of hospital,'' *New Haven Register* August 20.

Grimes, William. ''Restoration on Roosevelt Island? No, It's Sculpture/Is It Art or Scrap Wood? The Answer Is: It's Both,'' *The New York Times* September 24, pp. C13, C17.

Ball, Edward. ''Shelter/Re: Ruin,'' *The Village Voice* Vol. XXXVII, No. 39, September 29, p. 99.

Tallmer, Jerry. ''New life for death's dream castle,'' *New York Post* October 2, p. 39.

''An open installation'' *USA Today* October 7.

Wallach, Amei. ''Kawamata Project on Roosevelt Island'' *New York Newsday* October 16, pp. 71, 74-75.

''New York's Kawamata Work: Using Scrap Wood,'' *Ehime Shimbun* October 17.

Smith, Roberta. ''Manic, Inspired Carpentry,'' *The New York Times* October 25, Section 2, p. 33.

Mori, Tsukasa. ''New York, Roosevelt Island's Kawamata Project,'' *The Yomiuri Shimbun* October 27, p. 22.

''Voice Listings/Art/In Brief,'' *The Village Voice* Vol. XXXVII, No. 43, October 27, p.83.

Takashima, Naoyuki. ''Best 5 of 1992,'' *The Yomiuri Shimbun* December 16, evening, p. 17.

Sugawara, Norio. *The Yomiuri Shimbun* December 16, evening, p. 17.

1993

Tempestini, Riccard. ''Il Pecci 'trasferice' nei vicoli del centro,'' *Il Tirreno* February 19.

Bruni, Vannessa. ''Una mostra all'aperto per favvivare gli angoli più pittoreschi del centro,'' *Il Tirreno* February 24.

Riccomini, Franco. ''L'arte dentro la città,'' *La Nazione* February 24.

Sato, Takao. *The Hokkaido Shimbun Press* February 28, p. 6, photo by Kuniomi Matsubara.

Other Publications

Pia Graphity Tokyo: Pia Co., Ltd., 1984, p. 66.

Nakahara, Yusuke. ''Opening Exhibition/ Drawing Installation/Tadashi Kawamata,'' (announcement of one man exhibition) Tokyo: Gallery Kobayashi Annex, 1984, unpaged.

Portraits/Autumn and Winter Collection New York: Jun Co. Ltd., 1985, pp. 8-9.

Betsky, Aaron. *Violated Perfection* New York: Rizzoli International Publication, Inc., 1990, pp. 106-107.

Freedman, Adele. *Sight Lines* Donmille/Toronto: Oxford University Press, 1990, pp. 211-215.

Chiba, Shigeo. *Present Point of Art* Tokyo: Goryu Shoin, 1990, pp. 237-239.

Shinohara, Motoaki. *Transart Apparatus* Tokyo: Shiso-sha, 1991, pp. 205-207.

Art of Showa/Chronicle of Art Vol.6, Tokyo: Mainichi Newspapers, 1991, p. 196, 206.

Pia Galleries Collection Tokyo:Pia, Ltd., 1991, p. 25, 28, 32, 37, 44, 57.

川俣　正

1953

北海道三笠市生れ

1979

東京藝術大学美術学部油画科卒業

1981

東京藝術大学大学院美術研究科終了

1984

東京藝術大学大学院美術研究科後期博士課程中退

プロジェクト

1979

「By Land」多摩川河岸、立川

1980

「プロジェクト・ワーク・イン・高山」高山建築学校、高山

1982

アパートメント・プロジェクト「宝ハウス205号室」東京

1983

アパートメント・プロジェクト「大手門・和田荘」(素材と空間展) 福岡

「プロジェクト・ワーク・イン・埼玉」(木のかたちとエスプリ展) 埼玉県立近代美術館、浦和

アパートメント・プロジェクト「Slip in 所沢」所沢

アパートメント・プロジェクト「テトラハウスN−3 W−26」遠藤宅、札幌

1984

「銀座ネットワーク」かねこ・あーとギャラリー〜コバヤシ画廊〜ジュエリーショップ・オルフェ〜東京画廊、東京

「松山・大街道インスタレーション」川俣正＋PHスタジオ、大街道、松山

「工事中」川俣正＋PHスタジオ、ヒルサイド・テラス、東京

1985

「ライムライト・プロジェクト」ライムライト、ニューヨーク

「PS1プロジェクト」PS1、ロング・アイランド・シティ

1986

コンストラクション・サイト・プロジェクト「スプイ」デン・ハーグ

1987

コンストラクション・サイト・プロジェクト「ラ・メゾン・デ・スクォッター」(ジャポン・アール・ヴィヴァン '87) グルノーブル

「デストロイド・チャーチ」(第8回ドクメンタ) カッセル

コンストラクション・サイト・プロジェクト「ノヴァ・デ・ジュルホ・カサパーヴァ」(第19回サンパウロ国際ビエンナーレ) サンパウロ

1988

コンストラクション・サイト・プロジェクト「袋井駅前プロジェクト」駿河銀行、袋井

「比燕荘」東山、京都

1989

「トロント・プロジェクト、コロニアル・タヴァン・パーク」トロント

「ビギンホフ・セント・エリザベス」コートリック

1990

「サイドウォーク」(New Works for New Spaces: Into the Nineties展) コロンバス

1991

「ファヴェーラ・イン・ヒューストン」(ランドスケープ展) バヨウ川岸、ヒューストン

「ファヴェーラ・イン・オタワ」(プライマル・スピリット展) カナダ国立美術館、オタワ

「ファヴェーラ・イン・牛窓」(第4回ビエンナーレ、牛窓国際芸術祭) 牛窓

1992

「ピープルズ・ガーデン」(第9回ドクメンタ) カッセル

「プロジェクト・オン・ルーズヴェルト・アイランド」スモール・ポックス病院跡、ルーズヴェルト・アイランド、ニューヨーク

1993

「パッサジオ」(Museo Città Eventi展) プラート

「パブリック・プロポーザルス」リマット川及びヘルムハウス、チューリッヒ

個展

1978

神奈川県民ギャラリー第4室、横浜

1979

ルナミ画廊、東京

田村画廊、東京 (1980)

真木画廊、東京 (1980)

1980

コバヤシ画廊、東京 (1982、84、86、88、91、92、93)

1981

ASG、名古屋

スタジオ37、京都

ギャラリィK、東京

1982

ギャラリー白・A室、大阪

かねこ・あーとギャラリー及びかねこ・あーとGI、東京（1983、84、85、86、87、91）

1983

天画廊、福岡（1986）

1984

ヒルサイド・ギャラリー、東京（1986、87、88、89、90、91、93）

PS1スタジオ、ロング・アイランド・シティ（1985）

1985

ラボラトリー、札幌

1986

エリア・ドゥ・ギャラリー、福岡

上通ギャラリー、熊本

1987

ガラリア・ウニダデ・ドイス・デ・アルテ、サンパウロ

1988

ストアフロント・フォー・アート・アンド・アーキテクチュア、ニューヨーク

1989

マーサー・ユニオン、トロント

児玉画廊、大阪（1992、93）

ビギンホフ・セント・エリザベス内学校跡、コートリック

ギャルリ・ブレンダ・ウォレス、モントリオール（1991）

1990

アネリー・ジュダ・ファイン・アート、ロンドン

1992

アート・フロント・チューリッヒ、チューリッヒ

アーサー・A・ヒュートン・ジュニア・ギャラリー、クーパー・ユニオン、ニューヨーク

1993

ヘルムハウス、チューリッヒ

アート・フロント・ギャラリー、東京

グループ展

1977

「演習1」東京藝術大学美術学部演習室、東京

「競技会」立川市民会館、立川

1978

「DISCUSSION」藍画廊、東京

「下地の上塗りに及ぼす影響（演習2）」東京藝術大学美術学部演習室、東京

1979

「VIDEO」東京藝術大学美術学部演習室、東京

「三人展」東京藝術大学美術学部演習室、東京

1980

「Ueno'80」東京藝術大学美術学部演習室、東京

「艶姿華彩（あですがたはなのあやどり）」神奈川県民ギャラリー、横浜

「展出された七景」東京都美術館、東京

「写真展」ギャラリー山口、東京

「今日の作家［感情と構成］展」横浜市民ギャラリー、横浜

「第1回ハラ・アニュアル」原美術館、東京

1981

「ドローイングの交叉」画廊パレルゴン、東京

「二人展」Gアート・ギャラリー、東京

「余韻」グリフォン・ギャラリー、メルボルン州立大学、メルボルン

「第1回平行芸術展」東京小原流会館、東京

「今日の作家展」横浜市民ギャラリー、横浜

1982

「第2回インターナショナル・ユース・ドローイング・トリエンナーレ」クンストハーレ、ヌールンベルグ

「第40回ヴェネチア・ビエンナーレ」日本館、ヴェニス

「6人のドローイング」かねこ・あーとギャラリー、東京

「三人展」ギャラリー白、大阪

1983

「素材と空間展」福岡市美術館、福岡

「木のかたちとエスプリ展」埼玉県立近代美術館、浦和

「今日の日本美術展」ラース美術館、歴史博物館、ジュネーヴ

「五人の日本現代美術作家展」クンストハーレ、デュッセルドルフ

「多数多様態展」レストラン Sea Side Koyama、大分

「かねこ・あーと '83」かねこ・あーとギャラリー、東京

1984

「ヒューマン・ドキュメンツ'84」東京画廊、東京

「博士課程研究発表展合同展」東京藝術大学美術学部陳列館、東京

「パリー東京・現代美術交流展」ギャルリ・ファリデ・カド、パリ

「多数多様態展 IN KANSAI」スタジオ・セッテ・

グルッピ、大阪

「ONE ROOM ESSENCE」（ゲスト出品）ギャラリー・ビュウ、大阪

「現代日本47作家ポスター原画展」西武アート・フォーラム、東京

1985

「1985年オープニング展」ルート・ギャラリー、東京

「パリー東京・現代美術交流展」有楽町朝日ギャラリー、東京

「ナショナル・インターナショナル・スタジオ・アーティスツ展」クロックタワー、ニューヨーク

「PHスタジオ家具Φ展」ギャラリー山口、東京

「パースペクティヴ」コリアン・カルチュラル・サーヴィス・ギャラリー、ニューヨーク

「架想モニュメント展」かねこ・あーとギャラリー、東京

「木の美・絵画と彫刻のあいだ展」北海道立旭川美術館、旭川

「日本の現代彫刻展」ジュリアン・コーニック・ギャラリー・デゥアール、パリ

「アフター『ティルティッド・アーク』」ストアフロント・フォー・アート・アンド・アーキテクチュア、ニューヨーク

1986

「6人の日本現代美術作家展」シシリア・クッカー・ベル・ギャラリー、ハールスヴィル

「架想モニュメント展」かねこ・あーとギャラリー、東京

「白と黒展」かねこ・あーとギャラリー、東京

「現代日本の美術3、戦後生まれの作家たち・第2期」宮城県美術館、仙台

「コンタット、接触」サラ・ウノ、ローマ

「版画・ドローイング展」かねこ・あーとギャラリー、東京

1987

「ジャポン・アール・ヴィヴァン '87」エクサンプロヴァンス～マルセイユ～グルノーブル

「第8回ドクメンタ」カッセル

「もの派とポストもの派の展開」西武美術館、東京

「第19回サンパウロ国際ビエンナーレ」サンパウロ

「架想モニュメント展」かねこ・あーとギャラリー、東京

「近代日本版画展」アート・フロント・チューリッヒ、チューリッヒ

1988

「3人のドローイング展」かねこ・あーとギャラリー、東京

「8・ドローイング展」児玉画廊、大阪

「つかしん・アニュアル'88、日本・韓国作家による『美術の現在』水平と垂直」つかしん・ホール、尼崎

「ギャラリー・コレクション展'88」かねこ・あーとギャラリー、東京

「SUMMER・3人展」コバヤシ画廊、東京

「アート・イン・ブックショップ」アール・ヴィヴァン、東京

「ニュー・アーバン・ランドスケープ展」ワールド・ファイナンシャル・センター、バテリー・パーク・シティ、ニューヨーク

「プロジェクト・ワールドファックス88」クンストラウム・ネウス、ネウス

1989

「ドローイング倉庫展」ヒルサイド・ギャラリー、東京

「今日の水彩展」かねこ・あーとギャラリー、東京

「From； Being； Absence」グリフィン・マックギア・ギャラリー、ニューヨーク

「JAPANESE CONTEMPORARY ART IN THE 80's」ハイネケンヴィレッジ、東京

「日仏会館ポスター展」有楽町アート・フォーラム、東京

「Garden of Charity to Urban Arcadia」アーバン・センター、ニューヨーク

「ドローイングの現在」国立国際美術館、吹田

「ジャパン'89」ゲント現代美術館、ゲント

1990

「プライマル・スピリット」ハラ・ミュージアム・アーク、渋川～ロサンジェルス・カウンティー美術館、ロサンジェルス～シカゴ現代美術館、シカゴ～フォート・ワース近代美術館、フォート・ワース～カナダ国立美術館、オタワ

「作法の遊戯、第1期」現代美術ギャラリー、水戸芸術館、水戸

「Onvoltoold Tegenwoordlge Tijd」セントラル美術館、ユトレヒト

「『ニュー・ネセシティー』第1回タイン国際現代美術展」ニューキャッスル及びゲーツヘッド

「芸術が都市をひらくーフランスの芸術と都市計画」茨城県つくば美術館、筑波～国立国際美術館、吹田～仙台市青年文化センター、仙台～福岡市美術館、福岡～札幌芸術の森美術館、札幌～山梨県立美術館、甲府～横浜

「New Works for New Spaces／Into the 90s」ウェクスナー視覚美術センター、コロンバス

「Kawamata、Charney、二人展」シェアブルック大学、シェアブルック

1991

「ドローイング倉庫展」ヒルサイド・ギャラリー、東京

「Out of Site」PS1ミュージアム、ロング・アイランド・シティ

「ランドスケープ」ヒューストン国際フェスティバル、ヒューストン

「Sapporo Contemporary Arts 1991」リーセント・ギャラリー、札幌

「第4回ビエンナーレ、牛窓国際芸術祭」牛窓

1992

「ドローイング倉庫展　PART III」ヒルサイド・ギャラリー、東京

「都市と現代美術、廃墟としてのわが家」世田谷美術館、東京

「第9回ドクメンタ」カッセル

「特別展示1980－90年代の現代日本美術－東京都新美術館収蔵作品より」東京都美術館企画展示室、東京

1993

「カワマタ、スガ、セレクション」かねこ・あーとギャラリー、東京

「トランジット」ニュー・ミュージアム、ニューヨーク

「Museo Città Eventi」ルイジ・ペッチ現代美術センター、プラート

「90年代の日本、13人のアーティストの提言」フォルクローレ美術館、ローマ～スタッドミュージアム、デュッセルドルフ

その他

1982

「A Scene」月刊誌流行通信企画、東京藝術大学構内、東京

1984

「住居空間革命」隔週刊誌ブルータス企画、川俣正＋PHスタジオ制作、東京

「グラス・アート・赤坂」内装、磯崎新アトリエ企画、川俣正＋PHスタジオ制作、東京

「ブティーク・パシュ」内装、川俣正＋スーパー・ポテト、東京

「バー・木の花」内装、川俣正＋スーパー・ポテト、東京

「アメリカン・フォーク・アート展」のための会場構成、川俣正＋PHスタジオ制作、ラフォーレ・ミュージアム原宿、東京

1985

「アーティスト・ブック展」のための会場構成、フランクリン・ファーナス、ニューヨーク

「ライムライト・シカゴ」のためのアートワーク、ライムライト、シカゴ

1986

「ミュージック・イン・ミュージアム」のための会場構成、西武美術館、東京

1987

「ルシンダ・チャイルズ・ダンス・カンパニー公演『キャリックス』」のための舞台装置、ニューヨーク～カッセル～パリ～ローマ、他、巡回

「I LIKE THIS」横田良一とのコラボレーション、西武百貨店つかしん店美術画廊工芸サロン、尼崎

1988

「横浜フラッシュ」のための会場構成、三菱倉庫、横浜

1992

「ソニー・ミュージック・エンタテインメント・第1回アート・アーティスト・オーディション」審査員、横浜及び東京

講義

1980

高山建築学校、高山

1981

プラファン大学大学院、メルボルン

シドニー美術大学、シドニー

1983

西武百貨店スタジオF、船橋

1984

Bゼミ・スクール、横浜（1986、88、89）

東京芸術専門学校（TSA）、東京（1986）

1986

フリー・アカデミー、デン・ハーグ

かねこ・あーとギャラリー、東京

エコール・デ・ボザール、グルノーブル

1987

エコール・デ・ボザール、マルセイユ

ヴュイエ・シャリテ、マルセイユ

エコール・デ・ボザール、パリ

フンダション・アルマンド・アルヴェレス・ペンテアド、サンパウロ

ファルダデ・デ・ベラス・アルテス（美術大学）、サンパウロ

1988

東京藝術大学美術学部、東京

アカデミー・ヴァン・ビールデンデ・クンステン、ロッテルダム

ストアフロント・フォー・アート・アンド・アーキテクチュア、ニューヨーク

1989

トロント大学建築学科、トロント

マーサー・ユニオン、トロント

オウデ・デケニー、コートリック

ゲント現代美術館、ゲント

コニンクリーケ・アカデミー・ヴォー・ション・クンステン、ゲント

1990

西武コミュニティー・カレッジ、東京

1992

アート・フロント・チューリッヒ、チューリッヒ

市営美術協会、アーバン・センター、ニューヨーク

ニューヨーク・シティ・カレッジ、ニューヨーク

グレート・ホール、クーパー・ユニオン、ニューヨーク

座談会

1980

横浜市民ギャラリー、横浜

1983

安斎重男、帯金章郎、村田真。天画廊、福岡

プロジェクト「Slip in 所沢」会場、所沢

安斎重男、川口淳、柴橋伴夫、村田真。道特画廊、札幌

1986

ラウル・ブンショーテン、クーマー・アンド・メラミッド、ジョージ・トラカス、フィリップ・ブール。シアター・ズィーベルト、デン・ハーグ

杉本貴志。ヒルサイド・ギャラリー、東京

村田真、山野真悟。エリア・ドゥ・ギャラリー、福岡

林浩、村上哲、村田真。上通ギャラリー、熊本

1987

エコール・デ・ボザール、エクサンプロヴァンス

藤枝晃雄。ヒルサイド・ギャラリー、東京

村田真。ポピーズ、東京

帯金章郎。日仏会館、東京

1988

南條史生。コバヤシ画廊、東京

井上恭介、大杉弘子、太田忠四郎、奥之山隆、村田真。駿河銀行、袋井

梅原猛、岡林洋、小池一子、建畠晢。比燕荘、京都

1990

國安孝昌、原俊夫、ハワード・N・フォックス。ロサンジェルス・カウンティー美術館、ロサンジェルス

宮本隆司。ハイネケン・ヴィレッジ、東京

1991

モンティエン・ブンマー。アセアン文化センター、東京

1992

泉真也、大山千賀子、川本三郎、如月小春。福岡市都市景観賞第5回記念シンポジウム、福岡銀行、福岡

岡林洋。大阪現代美術センター、大阪

松葉一清、ジェイムズ・G・トゥルーラブ、長谷川祐己。パシフィコ横浜会議センター、横浜

1993

多木浩二、木下勇、久保覚。東京都美術館講堂、東京

授与

1978

安宅賞、東京藝術大学美術学部、東京

1980

サロン・ド・プランタン賞、東京藝術大学大学院美術研究科、東京

1983

第2回インターナショナル・ユース・ドローイング・トリエンナーレ特別賞、ヌールンベルグ

1984−1986

アジアン・カルチュラル・カウンシル・フェローシップ、ニューヨーク

1993

フランス教育及び文化省アトリエ・カルダー、オルレアン

コレクション

東京都美術館、東京

ハーグ市美術館、デン・ハーグ

カンティーニ美術館、マルセイユ

カッセル市ノイエ・ギャラリー、カッセル

ニッセイ総合技術センター、千葉

清里現代美術館、北巨摩

原美術館、東京

カナディアン建築センター、モントリオール

カナダ国立美術館、オタワ

ユトレヒト市絵画彫刻芸術センター、ユトレヒト

モントリオール現代美術館、モントリオール

ルーズヴェルト・アイランド・オペレーティング・コーポレーション、ニューヨーク

東京都新美術館、東京

新梅田スカイビル、大阪

目黒区美術館、東京

関連文献

個人カタログ

1979

「KAWAMATA」PHスタジオ(東京)

1980

「KAWAMATA」PHスタジオ（東京）

1983

川俣正、高島直之、宮本隆司「SLIP IN　所沢」テトラハウス出版局（札幌）

遠藤一博、佐藤友哉、柴橋伴夫、真鍋庵「TETRA HOUSE 326 PROJECT No.1」テトラハウス出版局（札幌）

1984

安斎重男、佐藤真史、中森敏夫、まさきはじめ、村田真「TETRA HOUSE 326 PROJECT No.2」テトラハウス出版局（札幌）

「工事中」（ポスター）PHスタジオ＋アート・フロント・ギャラリー（東京）

1986

トム・フィンケルパール「KAWAMATA PROJECT」on the table（東京）

「TAKARA HOUSE ROOM 205, 1982」on the table（東京）

「TETRA HOUSE N－3 W－26, 1983」on the table（東京）

1987

「KAWAMATA・工事中」現代企画室（東京）

1989

川俣正、クロゥディア・ゴールド「KAWAMATA PROJECT IN ROOSEVELT ISLAND」児玉画廊（大阪）

1990

「Tadashi Kawamata／Project 1980－1990」アネリー・ジュダ・ファイン・アート（ロンドン）

1991

川俣正「Field Work」（和文）、かねこ・あーとギャラリー（東京）

川俣正「Field Work」（英文）、on the table（東京）

川俣正「Tower Cranes, Paris／Kawamata／Urban Project with Temporary Structure」アート・フロント・ギャラリー（東京）

川俣正、キャシー・ドゥ・ジグハー、マイケル・タランティーノ、ギールト・ベカエルト「KAWAMATA BEGIJNHOF KORTRIJK」現代企画室（東京）及びカナール・アート・ファンデーション（コートリック）

リンダ・ジェネルゥ（インタヴュー）、ローズマリー・ドゥネガン、スティーヴン・ポゼル、デトレフ・マーティンス「Kawamata：Toronto Project 1989」マーサー・ユニオン現代視覚美術センター（トロント）

川俣正「KAWAMATA／Temporary Structure」Artrandom No.97、京都書院（京都）

1992

「KAWAMATA」コバヤシ画廊（東京）

帯金章郎「KAWAMATA maquettes」児玉画廊（大阪）

1993

「KAWAMATA prefabrication」コバヤシ画廊（東京）

川俣正、コスタス・グーニス、クロゥディア・ゴールド、エリザベス・A・フロッシュ、イヴーアラン・ボア「Project on Roosevelt Island（1992）」現代企画室（東京）及び on the table, inc.（ニューヨーク）

その他のカタログ

1980

針生一郎「HARA ANNUAL：VISION FOR 80s」原美術館（東京）、ページ付なし

藤枝晃雄「今日の作家展」横浜市及び横浜市教育委員会（横浜）、p.2

1981

ケン・スカーレット、山岸信郎「YOIN」オーストラリア国立図書館（メルボルン）、ページ付なし

峯村敏明「平行芸術展」財団法人小原流（東京）、ページ付なし

秋田由利「今日の作家展」横浜市及び横浜市教育委員会（横浜）、ページ付なし

1982

ギュセッペ・ガラッソ「arti visive '82：La Biennale」La Biennale di Venezia（ヴェニス）、p.90－92

たにあらた「La Biennale di Venezia, 1982 Giappone」国際交流基金（東京）、ページ付なし

峯村敏明「2. Internationale Jugendtriennale der Zeichnung」クンストハーレ（ヌールンベルグ）、p.136

1983

帯金章郎「素材と空間展」福岡市美術館（福岡）、p.6－11

中原佑介「木のかたちとエスプリ展」埼玉県立近代美術館（浦和）、p.9－12

たにあらた、ユルゲン・ハルテン「FÜNF ZEITGENOSSISCHE KÜNSTLER AUS JAPAN」クンストハーレ・デュッセルドルフ及びアウトレン（デュッセルドルフ）、ページ付なし

1984

千葉成夫、キャサリン・フランブリン「パリー東京現代美術交流展」朝日新聞社（東京）、p.96－101

アラン・ジョフロワ、堂本尚郎「現代日本47作家ポスター原画展」日仏会館（東京）、p.24

「ANNUAL REPORT 1984」アジアン・カルチュラル・カウンシル（ニューヨーク）、p.11－12

「NATIONAL AND INTERNATIONAL STUDIO PROGRAMS 1984－1985」The Institute for Art and Urban Resources, Inc.（ロング・アイランド・シティ）、p.38－39

中原佑介、峯村敏明「ART IN JAPAN TODAY II」国際交流基金、（東京）、p.80－83

1985

千葉成夫「Sculpture Japonais Contemporain」ジュリアン・コーニック・ギャラリー・デゥ・ア

ール（パリ）、ページ付なし

本間正義「木の美・絵画と彫刻のあいだ展」北海道立旭川美術館（旭川）、p.42－43

C.J.コーヘン「PERSPECTIVE」コリアン・カルチュラル・サーヴィス・ギャラリー（ニューヨーク）、p.8－9

1986

桑原住雄「現代日本の美術・3／戦後生まれの作家たち」宮城県美術館（仙台）、p.37

井関正昭、千葉成夫、並河恵美子＋小林ひとみ、エリザベス・フローレット「CONTATTO」サラ・ウノ（ローマ）、p.20

帯金章郎、ジャン・ビアジーニ「JAPON ART VIVANT '87」スグラフィト・エディション（パリ）、p.8－11

1987

ウェンゼル・ヤコブ「documenta 8」ドクメンタGmbH（カッセル）、Vol.2　p.118－119

東野芳明、峯村敏明「もの派とポストもの派の展開」西武美術館及び多摩美術大学（東京）、p.92－95

東野芳明「19 Sao Paulo Bienal」国際交流基金（東京）p.10－18

ヨルグ・ウィヘイム、セイル・レイアナー「19a Bienal Internacional De Sao Paulo」サンパウロ・ビエンナーレ・ファンデーション（サンパウロ）、p.164

1988

寺田透「'88 TSUKASHIN ANNUAL／美術の現在」つかしんホール（尼崎）、p.14－17

マーク・ギローム、フランセ・バッゾーリ、ジャン・ビアジーニ、ジャクリン・ファブレ、川俣正「JAPON ART VIVANT」スグラフィト・エディション（パリ）、p.24－26

浅田彰、石川九楊、大杉弘子、岡林洋、柿下木冠、川俣正、志賀雄二、高橋アキ、松枝到、村田真「赤レンガファイナル／社会・仮説的構築物・文字・音」大杉弘子（袋井）、p.23－44、76－77

ジャーマン・ヴィアッテ、ロベルト・P・ヴィグルゥ「L'Art Moderne a Marseille La Collection du Musée Cantini」カンティーニ美術館（マルセイユ）、p.23、233

「Projekt Worldfax 88：Fax The Art」クンストラウム（ネウス）、ページ付なし

1989

建畠晢、村田慶之輔、バーニス・ローズ「ドローイングの現在」国立国際美術館（吹田）、p.124－127

ノベルト・デゥ・ドウ、中原佑介、ヤン・フート「Japan 1989」ヨーロパリア・ジャパン（東京）、p.50－55

1990

村田真、他「The Eighties」コバヤシ画廊（東京）、p.14－17

リチャード・マーティンス、ナンシー・プリンセンタール、フィリップ・イェナウィン「The NEW URBAN LANDSCAPE」オリンピア・アンド・ヨークU.S.A.及びドレンタル・ドイル・パートナー（ニューヨーク）、p.21、26、30、32、78－79、115、120－121、127

中原佑介「作法の遊戯」水戸芸術館（水戸）、Vol.1－p.41－44、Vol.2－p.28－29、英語版－p.37

「芸術が都市をひらく－フランスの芸術と都市計画」「芸術が都市をひらく」展実行委員会（東京）、p.143

ハワード・N・フォックス「A Primal Spirit」原美術館（東京）及びロサンジェルス・カウンティー美術館（ロスアンジェルス）、p.64－71

エミリィ・フェイ、マデレイン・ヴァン・レネップ「Onvoltooid Tegenwoordige Tijd」ユトレヒト・セントラル美術館（ユトレヒト）、p.43－48

アネリー・ポーレン、ディクラン・マクゴナグル「A New Necessity」タイン・インターナショナル（ニューキャッスル・アポン・タイン）、表紙、p.40－41

「今日の作家展1964－1989」横浜市民ギャラリー（横浜）、p.9、93

1991

クロゥディア・ゴールド、ロバート・スターンズ、パトリシア・C・フィリップ、アン・ブレムナー「BREAKTHROUGH：Avant-Garde Artists in Europe and America 1950－1990/ Wexner Center for the Arts」リッゾーリ・インターナショナル出版（ニューヨーク）、p.176、178、185、214－219、229

フリップ・プール、フィリップ・ペータース「In Situ」ストローム・ハーグ美術センター（デン・ハーグ）、表紙、p.50－53

1992

塩田純一「都市と現代美術／廃墟としてのわが家」世田谷美術館（東京）、p.8－10、41－48、118－120（英文）

「Documenta IX」エディション・カンツ（ステュットガルト）及びヘンリー・N・アブラムス出版（ニューヨーク）、Vol.1－p.163－164、Vol.2－p.256－259

峯村敏明「TEMPVS VICTVM」小原流企画部（東京）、No.（p.）11

峯村敏明「平行芸術展1981－1991」美術出版社（東京）、p.15、118

執筆

1981

「コピーはハリボテであるということ」月刊GRAPHICATION、11月号、p.26－27

1982

「当たりをつけると一挙に見える」月刊GRAPHICATION、1月号、p.48－49

「はりぼてとしての現代への試み」月刊ダイヤ、3月1日号、p.22－23

1983

「ヨーロッパ・日本・東京・そして札幌」読書北海道、7月15日

「空間造形－場のかかわりについて」北海道新聞、8月27日夕刊

1984

「作品を作るということより、ことがらを作るということににている」月刊中央公論、9月号　第1183号、p.270

1986

「特集／ニューヨーク・ルネサンス」月刊都市住宅、9月号、p.37−50

「ハーグのワークショップ（公開制作）」北海道新聞、10月4日

「都市計画の中の"鳥の巣"」毎日新聞、10月20日、p.4

1987

挿図、季刊へるめす、No.13　12月、p.65−84

1988

挿図、月刊草月、No.176、p.124−125

「From Destruction to Construction」（同名の個展案内状）5月、ストアフロント・フォー・アート・アンド・アーキテクチュア（ニューヨーク）

1989

「都市に増殖するアート細胞」FP別冊月刊Kukan、第3号　5月号、p.20−21

1990

「Roosevelt Island、はじまりとしての廃墟」季刊へるめす、No.23　1月号、p.73−80

「ドローイング'90／コートリックのビギナージュ・プロジェクト」読売新聞、3月3日夕刊、p.9

「画一化する日本現代美術の海外展」読売新聞、10月15日夕刊　第41083号、p.7

1991

ジョナサン・ラバン著、高島平吾訳「住むための都市」晶文社（東京）、表紙作品写真

岡林洋編「ポスト・モダンとエスニック」勁草書房（東京）、表紙デザイン

「現代美術と美術館」現代の眼、No.442　9月号、国立東京近代美術館（東京）、表紙写真、p.4

「きょうと文化考・京都でのインスタレーション（上）」京都新聞、12月13日、p.7

「きょうと文化考・京都でのインスタレーション（中）」京都新聞、12月14日、p.6

「きょうと文化考・京都でのインスタレーション（下）」京都新聞、12月15日、p.7

挿図、月刊S&E、No.10、p.2、7−12、46、49−50

1992

「都市の時差」月刊太陽、No.370　4月号、p.6−7

インタビュー

1980

「「囲み込む」制度としての空間へ」月刊いけ花龍生、第240号　4月号、p.16−17

1984

「なぜ木で表現するか」木の芸術シリーズ「木の文化」朝日新聞社（東京）、p.132−133

1986

「作家訪問」月刊美術手帖第563号　6月号、p.100−105

「日本美術の国際化へ向けて」月刊アトリエ第713号　7月号、p.87−91

1988

「作品が工事現場風なのはなぜ?」月刊芸術新潮、通巻459号　3月号、p.60−62

Hara Museum Review、原美術館（東京）、秋号

「特集ARTの生態／川俣正・工事中」月刊ライフサイエンス、第15巻第11号　通巻243号　11月号、p.2−3、8−13

1989

「川俣正inアメリカ」月刊ライフサイエンス、第16巻第2号　通巻246号　2月号、　p.54−55

1991

村田真「ディズニーランド化する世界の中で」日経イメージ気象観測、No.18

1992

柳正彦「川俣正」ART & CRITIQUE、No.21　12月号、p.24−31

対談

1980

藤枝晃雄「現代との対話　PART　II−8／空間を埋めることについて」季刊みづゑ、第903号　6月号、p.77−83

1982

今井偉郎、建畠晢「操作とでっち上げ」ギャラリー白（大阪）、案内状、ページ付なし

1983

保科豊巳「ART　GALLERY／新春画廊オープニング展」ぴあCALENDER　1−2月合併号、p.132−133

安斎重男「熱血対談:振り返って福岡」IAF通信、No.2　2月号、p.11−13

1984

安斎重男、塚田誠一「展望:街角・装置・川俣正」季刊アート、春号、p.71−76

坂本龍一、島本脩二、野田秀樹、森田芳光、ロジャー・パルバース「いまを感じる、表現する」ぴあの街角、p.22−30

1988

三宅理一「寄生としてのインスタレーション」「空想の現代建築」鹿島出版会（東京）、p.170−181

1991

岡林洋「対談:川俣vs岡林」「ポスト・モダンとエスニック」勁草書房（東京）、p.267−283

1992

岩切徹、北川原温「新世紀の冒険者たち」GA、No.409　2月号、p.6−12

雑誌

1980

北沢憲昭「展評」月刊美術手帖、第465号　5月号、p.229−233

秋田由利「展評」月刊美術手帖、第468号　8月号、p.249−252

1981

秋田由利「美術における脱ー体系の動き」美術年鑑、月刊美術手帖1月号増刊476号、p.20−24

石田秀洋「展覧会レポート・独自性への展望」月刊美術手帖、第477号　2月号、p.176−177

山口勝弘「住まい＝芸術ー建築と環境への問いかけ」月刊草月、No.134　2月10日号、p.97−100

早見堯「仕切ることで結合される空間」季刊みづゑ、第915号　6月号、p.106−109

秋田由利「<木>と<彫刻>を巡って」季刊みづゑ、第919号　10月号、p.88−91

峯村敏明「平行芸術展を企画して」月刊小原流挿花、第3巻通巻372号　11月号、p.59−66

1982

針生一郎「知らなくても天才といわれるこの人たち」週刊新潮、第1337号　1月7日号、 p.170−175

「A Scene」月刊流行通信、No.220　5月号、p.34−35（撮影:安斎重男）

田中幸人「変容する空間」月刊草月、No.142　6月号、p.104−107

たにあらた「ヴェネツィア・ビエンナーレ報告」月刊美術手帖、第502号　10月号、p.80−87

1983

帯金章郎、管章、藤内龍彦、山野真悟「特集・川俣正in福岡」IAF通信、2月号

本間正義「木の持つ力や美しさをどう表現するか」週刊朝日ジャーナル、通巻1256号　3月11日号、p.83

峯村敏明「背後にある裏面」季刊アート、春号、p.92−94

赤津侃「素材の木が語る相手のない対話」季刊みづゑ、第926号　春号、p.130−133

リチャード・ハスリ「UNFRAGE」月刊Das Kunst Magazine No.C−1084E、p.7、9

クリストフ・シャッカー「Im Reich der "Leere"」月刊　Kunstforum、Bd58.2、p.120−130

早見堯「インスタレーションにおける"場"の意味」月刊いけ花龍生、No.278　4月号、p.28−31

峯村敏明「高水準をしめした福岡市美術館・素材と空間展」週刊朝日ジャーナル、4月15日号

安斎重男「川俣正のインスタレーション」ballet dance TES、7−1号、p.54

宮本隆司「Slip In 所沢」月刊都市住宅、第190号8308、p.145−146

高島直之「展評」月刊美術手帖、第514号　8月号、p.198−202

佳手芙美「装置であることを拒否したインスタレーション」ballet dance TES、7−4号、p.44−45

1984

秋田由利「木による柔軟な空間の創出」月刊草月、No.158　2月号、p.77−80

中原佑介「文化ジャーナル・美術／インスタレーションとしてのいけばな」週刊朝日ジャーナル、2月24日号、p.81

たにあらた「展評」月刊いけ花龍生、No.287　3月号、ページ付なし

安斎重男「ジュエリーショップと現代アートとの珍しい出会い」月刊婦人画報、通巻968号　3月号、p.292

近藤幸夫「風景を蹂躙する巨人」月刊商店建築、第29巻第3号　3月号、p.59

東野芳明「現代美術への展望と疑問」AD Japan、No.6　第2巻第4号　4月号、p.8−9

中原佑介「日本をリードする 208人／世界に活躍する新感覚アーチスト」月刊潮、4月号　通巻300号、p.267

「居住空間革命・廃材からの発想」隔週刊ブルータス、第93号　8月1日号、p.96−97（撮影:宮本隆司）

1985

「ブティック・シン・ホソカワ」Japan Interior Design、No.310、p.18−24、28（撮影:藤塚光政）

田中幸人「連載:感性の祖形／融通無碍の空間ー1」月刊いけ花龍生、No.297　1月号、p.34−35

安斎重男「実用性を伴うインスタレーション」月刊草月、No.158　2月号、p.69−72

「工事中ー建築にからみつく川俣正のアート」隔週刊ブルータス、No.104　2月1日号、p.140−141（撮影:宮本隆司）

エドワード・カラガン「One Man's Junk Is Another Man's Art」（press release）、5月

帯金章郎「ART:文化'85」週刊朝日ジャーナル、通巻1384号　第27巻第32号　8月2日号、p.35−36

ヘンク・オーヴァーダン「Culturele confrontaties met Japan」museumvisie、12月号、p.148

1986

セシル・ゴールドシェイダー「Sculptures Japonais D'Aujourd'hui」隔月刊L'OEIL、1−2月号、p.60−65

高島平吾「川俣正の板材構築」月刊年金と住宅、2月号、p.30−31

山野真悟「ART INFORMATION」d−ART、創刊準備号#0　夏号、p.18−19

イングリッド・ヴァン・サンテン「Internationale workshop zijn aanzet tot dialoog」Het Biennerhof、6月号

高島直之「意識としてのインスタレーション」月刊商店建築、第402号　7月号、p.89

アレクサンドラ・K・マンロゥ「A Continent Away」月刊Winds、8月号、p.42－53

マンスフレッド・シュネッケンブルガー、ユルゲン・シュワインブラーデン・フレイハール・ヴォン・ウィッチマン・アイッコン「Urbaner kraftakt und poetische konstruktion」documenta press、10月28日号、p.3、5

山野真悟「思考するインスタレーション」d－ART、創刊号#1　12月、p.18－19

1987

北橋朋也「ポストモダンからの脱出」隔週刊ブルータス、第149号　1月15日号、p.135

シルヴィエ・コムテ「EMPREINTES SUR LE QUARTIER BRERRIAT」QUARTIERS、p.62－63

マンスフレッド・シュネッケンブルガー「über konzeption und Riehtliniender Dokumenta」月刊 Hier und Jetzt、4月号、p.117－118

ジョアチム・ヴァチテル「Wo stent die kunst?」Die Schone Welt、6月号

ピーター・M・ボーデ「Kraft Nach Kassel!」月刊 ヴォーグ（ドイツ）、6月号

ディエター・シュウェルドル「Stahl, Holz, Stein－Künstler der documenta 8」documenta press、6月号、p.10－11（撮影：クリスティーナ・ヘイン）

クリスシェ・ムーチング・エンガギェト「Die 8 Documenta in Kassel」JA／Die woche von der packendsten Seite、No.25　6月9日号、ページ付なし

ホルスト・クリストフ「Kunstfroh durch die Stadt」Profil、No.24　6月15日号、ページ付なし

「documenta special」季刊Wolkenratzer Art Journal、6－7－8月号、p.16－20、74－75、120（英訳）

スヴン・ティエルマン「Kunst Fur Die Welt－Kunst Fur's Volk」PRINZ、7－8月号、p.71

イングリッド・メヤー「Documenta」Nike, New Art in Europe、No.19　7－8－9月号、ページ付なし

ミッシェル・ヒュブル、Kunstforum Bd.90、7－9月号、p.82、292－293

高島直之「日本モダンアート通信」月刊WACOA、No.07、p.10－13

高島直之「高島直之の表紙招待席／Art Now（31）川俣正『Destroyed Church 1987』」週刊朝日ジャーナル、第1492号　8月7日号、p.30（撮影：安斎重男）

トーマス・ウエスト「Republic of Ready－Made」季刊 Art International、秋号、p.82－88

クレア・ヘンリー「INTERNATIONAL PLATFORM DOCUMENT 8」季刊 Alba、秋号、p.34－37

ドアー・アッシュトン「Documenta of What?」月刊art Magazine、9月号、p.17－20

南條史生「ドクメンタ8の現場から」月刊すばる、第9巻第10号　9月号、p.132－143

エドワード・F・フライ＋南條史生「ポストモダニズムの崩壊」月刊すばる、第9巻第10号　9月号、p.125－129

藤枝晃雄、他「ドクメンタ8速報」月刊美術手帖、第585号　9月号、p.26－27、59

ナンシー・マーマー「Documanta 8: The Social Dimension?」月刊Art In America、9月号、p.128－140

四方幸子「ドクメンタ展ドキュメント」隔週刊ブルータス、9月1日号、p.94

アンナマリア・マットチェシニ「Para chocar a populacao」Visao、9月23日号、p.44－45

高島直之「<絵画>のシステムへの回帰」月刊日経イメージ気象観測、No.2　10月号、p.60－62

ダン・カメロン「DOCUMENTA 8 KASSEL」月刊Flash Art International、10月号、p.61－68

シャウ・スミス「DOCUMENTA 8」月刊New Art Examiner、Vol.15　No.2　10月号、p.22－28

ピーター・フランク「DOCUMENTA 8」隔月刊Sculpture、Vol.6　No.6　11－12月号、p.20－25

たにあらた「身体的作用を受けやすい素材」月刊草月、No.30　12月号、p.13

ダーク・シュワルツ「Documenta 8」月刊Kunstforum、1987年12月－1988年1月号、p.244

1988

村田真「クリストと川俣正」隔月刊広告、1－2月号、p.2－3

高島直之「KAWAMATA ANNUAL 川俣正」月刊MONOマガジン、第7巻第4号　2月2日号、p.135

飯島洋一「板によるパピエ・コレ」月刊新建築、3月号、p.319

建畠晢「彫刻の失敗」月刊AC、No.5　3月号、p.1－3

山崎均「まき散らされた眼球－川俣正の光学」月刊AC、No.5　3月号、p.8

倉林靖「展評」月刊美術手帖、第593号　4月号、p.202

フィリップ・ペータース「Japan Hout」Magazijn、No.17　5月号、p.20－21

ジャネット・コプロス「Review／Tadashi Kawamata」月刊Art in America、5月号、p.194－195

ドルフ・ウェリング「Rotterdam－zet de kunsten op een sokkel」De Stad Als Podium、5月号、p.12－17

ジェイムズ・ロバーツ「Review」月刊Artscribe International、第70号　夏号、p.89

ジャネット・コプロス「Mono－ha and The Power of Materials」月刊 New Art Examiner、6月号、p.29－32

フィリップ・ペータース「Tadashi Kawamata」季刊 Artefactum、第5巻第24号　6－8月号、p.10－13、55（英訳）（撮影：レオ・ヴァン・ダー・クレイ）

木下長宏「車輪の花・廃材の花」月刊未生、9月号、p.16－17

吉賀好之「仮設構築と解体『比燕荘』」月刊三彩、

9月号　第492号、p.120－121

高島直之「反転した不可視の＜家＞、痕跡としての記憶」月刊icon、Vol.13　9月号、p.44－45（撮影：白鳥美雄）

建畠晢「川俣正の『比燕荘』プロジェクト」月刊商店建築、第429号　9月号、p.121

カルロ・マコーミック「On the waterfront」Paper、10月号、p.17

村田真「アート・トゥディ」月刊いけ花龍生、10月号、p.39

高島直之「丸太の木組みでアート領域を広げる」月刊日経Woman、10月号、p.144－145

正木基「フットワークで構築する」月刊BT、第600号　10月号、p.128－129、137－138

杉浦隆夫「比燕荘『工事中』－川俣正」月刊AC、No.8、p.34－35

ロバート・キャンベル「Sharkskin and Dreck」AJ、11月9日号、p.94－94

ロドニー・オブライエン「Shivering Timbers: Tadashi Kawamata」Intersect、12月号、p.24－25

中原佑介「現代の表現・第4回／絵画的と彫刻的と」月刊草月、No.181　12月号、p.13－20

1989

ジャネット・コプロス「Japan's Contemporary Arts」Sumitomo Corporation News、No.72　1月号、p.2－7

ギム・シェルター「New Urban Landscape」Design（U.S.A.）、1月号、p.81－82

梁瀬薫「New Urban Landscape／都市への提案」月刊BT、第606号　3月号、p.86－93

相原由美「場との共同作業を証明する・記録されたギャラリーと現代美術」隔週刊ブルータス、通巻第200号　4月1日号、p.9

パトリシア・C・フィリップス「Added Attraction」月刊Artforum International、5月号、p.108－112

安斎重男「社会との接点から生じた行為」月刊草月、No.185　8月号、p.17－24

アデーレ・フリードマン「Fastforward」季刊Canadian Art、第6巻第3号　秋号、p.54

パメラ・ハリス「Kawamata's Toronto Project」Azume Magazine、第6巻第59号　9月号

ジュディス・サンディフォード、ロナルド・ウェイス「The Endless Project」隔月刊Work Seen、第1巻第2号　9－10月号、p.7－8

ロイ・ディオナンダン「Ball Crowd Illuminates Riotou Architecture」The Varsity、第110巻11号　10月2日号、p.13

フランク・ドブロクニック「Modern Art Pussles Yonge Street Crrowd」週刊Eyeopener、10月21日号、ページ付なし

リチャード・ロドス「TORONTO／TADASHI KAWAMATA MERCER UNION」月刊Artforum International、11月号、p.162

ギールト・ベカエルト「Tadashi Kawamata's ontmoetingen in Gent en Kortrijk」月刊Archis、12月号、p.2

ヤン・ブラエット「Het Kawamata－projekt」週刊Knack、12月13日号、p.150－153

小林ひとみ「特集＝インテリア・コーディネーション／現代美術普及に向けて」月刊WACOA、No.17　12月15日発行、p.28－31

1990

岡林洋「憧れとしての廃虚」月刊建築雑誌、Vol.105　No.1294　1月号、p.36－37

篠原資明「総展望＝90年代カルチュア・マップ／トランスアート・マップ」月刊ユリイカ、第22巻第2号　2月号、p.142－149

ベルナール・マルセリス「TADASHI KAWAMATA」月刊art press、No.144　2月号、p.96

クラウディア・ハーシュタット「Neuer Kragen furden alten Beginenhof von Kortrijk」art Magazine、2月号、p.25

建畠晢「続・現代美術視／問いかける"場"、換気する"場"」月刊にっけい・あーと、第17号　2月号、p.193－196

ピーター・レグリス「Kawamata & Aesthetics of Radicalism」季刊a／r／c、Vol.1　No.1　春号、p.34－35

ノーマンド・セリオルト「Artsvisuels／Visual Art Review／Tadashi Kawamata」季刊Parachute、No.58、p.37－38

アデーレ・フリードマン「Jammed Session」週刊Toronto Life Homes、3月号、p.H7－H12

リエスベス・マリス「OPDRACHTKUNST VERKEERD GEINTERPRETEERD」月刊de Architect、3月号、p.28－29

クリストファー・ヒューム「The Politics of Public Art」週刊Toronto Star Sunday Magazine、3月10日号、p.M10－M19

「In the News／Reconstructing History」隔月刊Sculpture Vo.9, No.2、3－4月号、p.12

ロベルト・ロース「15 Imaginaire projecten voor Utrecht」Beelding、No.2、ページ付なし

マリナ・ヴァイゼイ「Annely Juda Fine Art」月刊Galleries、5月号

マーク・カラー「Visual Arts／TADASHI KAWAMATA」週刊City Limits Magazine、No.450　5月17－24日号、p.74

サラ・ケント「Tadashi Kawamata」週刊Time Out、No.1030　5月16－23日、p.31

チャック・ニコルソン「Toward a Spiritual Whole」月刊Artweek、Vol.21　No.26　8月号、p.13

三上豊＋編集部「気になる日本のアーティスト」月刊BT、第42巻第627号　9月号、p.36－37、59、61

ブライアン・ハットン「REVIEW, LONDON／Tadashi Kawamata」月刊Artscribe Internationale、9－10月号、p.81

ピーター・クロセイアー「A Primal Spirit」月刊Artspace、Vol.14　No.6　9－10月号、p.50－54

エレナー・ヒートニー「Report From New Castle／Cultingan Engaged Public Art」月刊Art in America、10月号、p.54－57

ピーター・プラゲン「Invention Is the Mother of....」週刊Newsweek、10月20日号、p.70L－70N

ピーター・プラゲン「Palms and Circumstance」週刊Newsweek、10月20日号、p.64

ミッシェル・エレンバーガー「Tadashi Kawamata／batisseur du provisoire」月刊art press、No.153、p.50－54

ルイス・E・ネスビット「New Works For New Spaces： Into The Nineties」隔月刊Newsline、1990年12月－91年1月号、p.8

1991

ルイーズ・デリー「Triptyque：Musee-Artiste-Environment」季刊Muse、Vol.VIII No.4　冬号、p.61－63(仏文)、64－66(英文)

上田高弘「ポストモダンの建築ドローイングと＜アート＞の相姦」月刊スタジオ・ヴォイス、Vol.181　1月号、p.39

イヴーアラン・ボア「In Situ： Site－Specific Art In And Out of Context」月刊The Journal of Art、1月号、p.30

岡林洋「マルチメディア・ワーク／第2回、川俣正」月刊hiroba、No.322　2月号、p.60－63

梁瀬薫「New Works for New Spaces： Into the Nineties」月刊BT、第635号　3月号、p.143－149

ジャネット・コプロス「Material Meditation」月刊Art in America、3月号、p.95－101

ジーン・C・フライアー・コールス「Review：『New Works for New Spaces：Into the Nineties』」月刊New Art Examiner、3月号、p.37

クラウディア・ハーシュタット「Kunst aus Brettern」週刊Zeitmagazin、No.10　3月1日号、p.76－83

トーマス・コナー「Review／New Works for New Spaces： Into the Nineties」隔月刊SCULPTURE、3－4月号、p.63－64

安斎重男＋篠田達美「現代美術を見る、そして語る［5］／インスタレーションと美術館」月刊草月、No.195　4月号、p.90－96

「特集『絵画と建築のあいだ』」、岡林洋「川俣正論－壁面・空間・生業形態」季刊みづゑ、No.959　夏号、p.14、40－49

谷川渥「現代美術のトポグラフィー」月刊太陽、No362　8月号、p.27

高島直之「既製の空間を食い破る。」季刊流行通信オム、No.19　秋号、p.25

レザ・ローウィッツ「Reviews」隔月刊Sculpture、11月－12月号、p.60

岡林洋「マルチメディア・ワーク／第12回」月刊hiroba、No.332　12月号、p.54－57

高島平吾「特集・北九州ルネサンス／八幡＝スペースワールドと鉄の都」FS（フクオカ・スタイル）、Vol.2、p.14－17

1992

ダグラス・オルド「KAWAMATA'S SHEDS／Débats Issues」季刊 Parachute、No.65　1－2－3月号、p.64－68

サカイ優佳子「アート／川俣正の世界／モノの一過性と連続制テーマに」月刊日経アーキテクチュア、No.426　3月16日号、p.263－265

高島直之「現代をになう作家たちXV／川俣正／境界線の開閉と閾の形成」月刊BT、第652号　4月号、p.105－118

アーロン・ベトスキー「ヴァイオレイテド・パーフェクション、第5章・破片と凶器」月刊a＋u、4月臨時増刊号、p.106－107

小林ひとみ、村田真「特集アーティスト・ファイル」Wave、#33　5月25日、p.30－31、98－99、143、145

イルマ・シュラグヘック「Documenta IX／Riskanter Balanceakt mit 186 Artisten」月刊art、No.6　6月号、p.36－37、46

北川フラム「都市への視点1／地名はうたう－都市軸再考／アーバン・デザインとの距離の取り方」月刊太陽、No.373　7月号、p.158－159

グレッグ・アドコック「Documenta IX」季刊Tema Celeste、No.37－38 秋号、p.84－86

ユルゲン・ラープ「Documenta campague de soldes」月刊 art press、No.172　9月号、p.66－67

「It's Time to...／... Take a Gander」 月刊Metropolitan Home、Vol.XXIV, No.9　9月号

トーマス・コナー「Fanfair／Wood Awakening」月刊Vanity Fair、9月号、ページ付なし

H.C.フライバーガー「フライバーガーのニューヨーク情報」六月の風、9月号、p.21－22

スティーヴン・ヘンリー・マドフ「Review／Documenta IX： More is A Mess」月刊ARTnews、9月号、p.131

「Urban Archaeology」隔週刊The New Yorker、9月28日号、p.10

マーサ・マクウィリアムス、カテリン・ヒクソン「The Way to Docu－drama」月刊New Art Examiner、10月号、p.12－15

キャロル・ルトフィ「A Very Public Matter」Tokyo Journal、p.41－42

「Art／Other Venues／Tadashi Kawamata」隔週刊The New Yorker、10月5日号、p.36

村田真「海外通信・ニューヨーク・川俣プロジェクト、ルーズベルト島は遠くにありて思うもの」週刊ぴあ、10月15日号、p.266

マーガレット・スティーヴンス「A Rune on Ruins」月刊Landscape Architecture、11月号

フィリップ・ペータース「En Route」Kunst & Museum Journaal、 Vol.4　11月2日号、p.25－32

――「Die Documenta Als Kunstwerk」月刊Kunstforum、 Bd.119、p.461－465

クリスティーン・ウェンツ「Kawamata： Project On Roosevelt Island」隔月刊Newsline、11－12月号、p.8

藤枝晃雄「VANGUARD・川俣正」月刊中央公論、12月号、ページ付なし（撮影：野口ミチオ）

梁瀬薫「視覚化された「その場」の歴史／川俣正ルーズヴェルト島プロジェクト」月刊BT、 No.662　12月号、p.16－17

「ニューヨークに実現した川俣正のプロジェクト」月刊芸術新潮、第43巻第12号　12月号、p.104

ピーター・スレイティン「Ruins for a Ruin」月刊ARTnews、12月号、p.16

マーク・アルデン・ブランチ「A Missed Opportunity on Roosevelt Island」月刊Progressive Architecture、12月号、p.14

村田真「川俣正のプロジェクトは常に環境を刺激しつづける。」隔週刊ブルータス、12月1日号、p.39

1993

ジェイ・マーフィー「Tadashi Kawamata/Roosevelt Island」季刊Tema Celeste、No.38 冬号、p.83－84

北川フラム「都市への視線7／アート・ワークの新展開／ニューヨークの街より」月刊太陽、 No.378　1月号、p.94－95

トーマス・コナー「Kawamata： Project on Roosevelt Island」隔月刊Sculpture、1－2月号、p.24－25

菅章「BT創刊650号記念・芸術評論募集入選作発表『アンチ・メーシスの文脈、川俣正におけるコンテクストの意味』」月刊BT、第665号　2月号、p.261－270

「特集・アンケート／戦後美術ベストテン!」月刊芸術新潮、第44巻第2号　2月号、表紙、 p.4、5、27、39、45、46、48、50、53、54、56、62－63

フィリップ・ジュディディオ「Bâtisseur de L'Éphémére」月刊Connaissance des Arts、3月号、p.116－121（撮影：ノーマン・マクグラス）

クロゥディア・ゴールド「Kawamata's Miracle」Parkett #35　3－4月号、p.161－164

クリスティーン・ウェッツ「Tadashi Kawamata project op Roosevelt Island」月刊Archis、4月号、p.44－47

赤坂英人「BUNKA STADIAM／川俣正／ピープルズ・ガーデン」週刊朝日、4月2日号、p.161

ナンシー・プリンセンタール、月刊Art in America、7月号

新聞

1980

藤枝晃雄「ドグマからの自律的文脈・素材の扱い方の新しさ」日本読書新聞（第2064号）、7月7日

藤枝晃雄「迎合する『ドグマ』なき論難へ」日本読書新聞（第2067号）、7月28日

アムリー・サンージェル「Hara Annual Show On」 Dairy Yomiuri、 12月11日

東野芳明「美術－'80回顧・ベスト5」朝日新聞、12月15日夕刊、p.9

バーバラ・トーレン「The Week in Art」The Japan Times、12月21日

1981

中村敬治「推敲されつくした空間の占拠」日本読書新聞（関西）、10月20日

1982

千葉成夫「いまあらたな『獅子の時代』に」日本読書新聞（第2159号）、5月31日

中原佑介「美術・今年の収穫」日本読書新聞、（関西）、 12月17日、p.9

1983

帯金章郎「『素材と空間展』とは何か」西日本新聞（九州）、2月23日

田中幸人「展評／木の形とエスプリ展」毎日新聞、3月12日、p.5

アムリー・サンージェル「ART：People And Places」Mainichi Dairy News、5月28日

佐藤友哉「フットワークとしての芸術」読書北海道、10月15日

1986

田中幸人「都市の裏側の存在を隠諭化」毎日新聞、5月16日

エド・オリヴィエ「Slooppand 'Ingepakt' door Japanse Kunstenaar」Haagsche Courant、6月12日

エド・オリヴィエ「Eindelijk gebeurt er eens wat」Haagsche Courant、7月2日

千葉成夫「美のフロンティア6・⑤」東京新聞、7月10日、p.3

三田晴夫「自在なフットワーク」毎日新聞、8月7日夕刊

1987

ローレンツォ・マンゴ「Due Mostre Romane Tornano A Proporci il "Cuore Tematico" Dell' Arte Orientale」 Paese Sera（ローマ）、1月5日、p.9

ダリオ・ミカッシ「Scultori acrobatici：nove installatori giapponesi in mostra」l'Unita（ローマ）、1月18日

アンヅォ・ビラリデッロ「Nove giovani giapponesi」Corriere Della Sera（ローマ）、1月19日

ヘイディ・ワレソン「Lucinda Childs Tiptos Toward Ballet」The New York Newsday、5月10日

ジェニファー・ダニング「The Stage As Element Of Dance」The New York Times、5月11日

ジャック・アンダーソン「The Dance：3 Works By Childs」The New York Times、5月14日

ダーク・シュワルツ「Das Gebaude offnen」Hessische Niedersachsische Allgemeine （カッセル）、5月23日

デボラ・ジョーウィット「Lucinda Childs's Calyx」The Villege Voice、6月2日

ロザル・オーゼチュウスキィ「Die visuelle Maschine」Hessische Niedersachsische Allgemeine（カッセル）、6月11日

ヘルムット・クロンザラー「documenta 8 Jenseits der Postmoderne?」Landshuter Zeitung、6月11日

ウォルフガング・レイナー「Ganz sanfte Signale」Stuttgarter Zeitung、6月13日

ホルスト・ゲルハード、ハベル・ベリチテット「Kuckuckseier in der Stadt」Kleine Zeitung、6月14日

ローマン・ホルンステイン「Besinnung der Kunst auf ihre historische und soziale Dimension」Reue Burcher Zeitung、6月16日

ウルスラ・ギエスラー「Kunst kritisiert Kassel」Saabrucker Zeitung、6月17日

ペトラ・キプホフ「Das hohe Fest der Beliebigkeit」Die Zeit、6月19日

ベルトラム・ミュラー「Lichtschein auf Horror und Poesie」Geist und Leben、6月20日

エルンスト・ブック「Alles ist moglich」Offenbach－Post、6月20－21日

バーナード・シュルツ「Buhnenbilder der Zerstreuungskultur」Weltspiegel（ベルリン）、6月21日

ジェネヴィエヴ・ブリーレット「Les pieds dans le meuble」Le Monde、6月21－22日

ロルフ・ミカエリス「Augentheater」Die Zeit、6月25日

ポール・ヒュイルブロク「Achtste Dokumenta：als geen andre...」Zutphens Dagblad、6月27日

ダーク・シュワルツ「Eingriffe in die Stadt」Hessische Niedersachsische Allgemeine、7月8日

ウイィ・フレース「Der Geruch des Spektakularen fehlt in diesem Jahre」Holsteinischer Courier、7月9日

ロルフ・ロベック「Im Augenblick des Kraftesammelns」Deutsche Volkszeitung、7月10日

ジサラ・ブラッカート「Kalte Engel raunen vom Ende der Zeit」Deutsches Allgemeines Sonntagsblatt、7月12日、p.21

ヘイナー・スタチェハウス「Buhne fur ein Verwertungs－Spektakel」NRZ、7月12日（撮影：フリードヘルム・ジングラー）

アルナフ・マルツルフ「Installateure der Postmoderne」Allgemeine Beitung、8月4日

リチャード・ミュラー・メリス「Die Macher und ihre Hatschelkinder」Bayernkurier、8月15日

ゲルノット・ゲデゥルヂング「Luxus－Auto und vier Guillotinen」Aachener Nachrichten、8月22日

アントニオ・ゴンカルベス・フィルホ「Kawamata, um japones muito louco」Folha De S. Paulo、9月11日

アントニオ・ゴンカルベス・フィルホ「O demolidor Kawamata chega para a Bienal」Folha De S. Paulo、9月11日

レーノー・アマランテ「De pernas pro ar」O Estado De S. Paulo、9月11日

テテ・マルティンホ「Visuais Arte Sobre Ruinas」jarnal de tarde（サンパウロ）、9月12日

カルロ・ラモス「Pau para toda obra」O Globo、9月16日

ジャネット・コプロス「Looking at Inside and Outside」Asahi Evening News、12月9日

1988

レオネッタ・ベンティヴォグリオ「Il segno di Lucinda Childs」la Repubblica Danza、1月19日、p.1

村上ケイ「川俣正の『工事中』」繊研新聞、2月2日

ポール・デュポント「Een zacht geluid dringt door tot de stadsjungle」de Volkskrant、5月7日

マイケル・ブレンソン「Kawamata：From Destruction to Construction」The New York Times、5月20日

キム・レヴィン「Kawamata」The Village Voice、5月31日

カーター・B・ホースレイ「Provocative peek into future」New York Post、10月13日

ロバータ・スミス「A Wide－Ranging Spread Of Artists and Installations」The New York Times、11月4日

ヒルトン・クラマー「Sculpture Show a Lachrymose Valentine to a Bygone Era」The New York Observer、11月7日

エリザベス・ヘス「Captive of Industry？」The Village Voice、11月15日

1989

クリストファー・ヒューム「Art Stopper」Toronto Star、3月9日

ジョン・ベントリー・メイス「Kawamata Installation To Be A First」The Glove and Mail、5月2日（通巻43496号）、 p.A25

アデーレ・フリードマン「Is It A Disturbance？ Public Art？ No, It's A 'Parasite'」The Glove and Mail、7月15日、p.C13

リサ・バルフォー・ボーウェン「Art in Our Parks」Toronto Sun、8月19－20日、p.S20

リンダ・ジェネルゥ「Visual Terrolism」Metropolis、Vol.2, No.15、8月24日

クリストファー・ヒューム「Whirlwind of changehies public art scene」Toronto Star、8月25日、p.E3

アデーレ・フリードマン「Watch for the rare but possible：recognition of young talent」The Glove and Mail、9月9日

ローレン・デゥ・ケクスザー「Japanse kunst van vandaag」De Gentenaar、10月27日

ジャネク・ウェッセリング「Moderne Japnse Kunst staat voor een dilemma」NRC Handelsblad、11月11日、p. 6

フィリップ・レクリュス「Japanner "emballeert" kortrijks begijnhof met houten planken」Gazet Van Antwerpen、11月25－26日、p.7

リーヴェン・デゥ・コーター「Kawamata pakt Begijnhof in」De Standaad、12月21日

リサ・バルフォー・ボーウェン「Visually Speaking... Best of 89」Toronto Sun、12月31日、p.S10

1990

デイビッド・ウェットストン「An uplifting idea for river skyline」The Journal、1月15日

ヴェルゥス・ダグブランド「Imaginaire projecten in het Centraal Museum Utrecht」Vazdias、3月8日

メッペラー・コーラント「Ingebeelde kunst in Utrecht 」Vazdias、3月14日

奥田裕「まぎれもない"日本人のアート"ロサンゼルス・カウンティ美術館の選んだ10人」産経新聞、3月15日、p.19

デレク・ジョーンズ「A Primal Spirit 」Asahi Evening News（No.11239）、3月16日

セア・フィギー「Expositie vol dromen over de stad in Centraal Museum」Utrchts Nieuwsblad／NZC、3月30日

オーシュロ・シルヴァ「a primal spirit」The Daily Yomiuri、4月12日

ウィリアム・フィーヴァー「In paradise upon Tyne」The Observer、5月20日

ローズ・パターソン「Artistic fog on the Tyne？」Daily Telegraph、5月30日、p.6

ウィリアム・ウィルソン「Japanese Art Exhibition：A Rare Find」Los Angeles Times Calender、6月17日

ディナ・バーランド「Japan's 'Primal Spirit' is a sensual feast」Press Telegram（ロング・ビーチ）、6月24日、p.S2

千葉成夫「季評現代美術」東京新聞、7月3日、p.9

キャロル・ルトフィ「Contemporary Japanese Art Makes Jump to U.S.」The Asian Wall Street Journal、7月13−14日

シンディ・ヘンリソン「Lots more two by four」The Ohio State Lantern、9月27日、p.9

ルイス・J・ウォング「'Sidewalk' repaired for show」The Ohio State Lantern、10月3日

1991

レザ・ローウィッツ「Shelters in the Storm／The 'Field Work' of Tadashi Kawamata」The Asahi Evening News、3月22日

パトリシア・C・ジョンソン「Landscapes on the Bayou」 Houston Chronicle、4月25日

ジーネル・ガン「Sculptor uses what he can get his hands on」The Daily Couger、4月25日

スーザン・チャドウィック「Simple shack−complex art」The Houston Post、4月27日

三田晴夫「美術／見えざる構造を顕現」毎日新聞、6月21日夕刊

ナンシー・バエル「This Is Art？」The Ottawa Citizen、6月22日

ジム・ブロンスキル「Gallery exhibit raises hackle 」The Globe and Mail、6月26日

菅原教夫「あすの顔No.280・川俣正・空間に架構する想念」読売新聞、7月4日夕刊

アデーレ・フリードマン「By Design」The Globe and Mail、7月6日

マセユウ・ハート「But is it art？ Must be, Ottawa hates it」The Globe and Mail、7月6日

ヘンリー・レーマン「Kawamata's hovels draw observers into field of broken dreams」The Gazette、7月6日

ナンシー・バエル「Primal Spirit quick to make headlines」The Gazette Montreal、7月6日

マリーミシェル・クロン「Le passage du temps／Tadashi Kawamata」Le Devoir（ケベック）、7月6日

三田晴夫「現代美術のWhy・新しい黄金郷・川俣正のインスタレーション」毎日新聞（第41559号）、12月10日夕刊

渋沢和彦「都市に増殖する小屋群／美術家・川俣正が構築する廃墟の世界」産経新聞、12月12日、p.15

1992

「病院を蘇らせる／造形作家・川俣正NYプロジェクト」産経新聞、2月6日、p.19

「ワイドかるちゃー／夏NYで野心作／「架設」芸術の川俣正さん模型発表」北海道新聞、2月14日、p.10

塩田純一「美の裏方・学芸員から／物置？／何かな？川俣正のインスタレーション＝世田谷美術館中庭」朝日新聞、4月16日夕刊

デボラ・ギムルソン「Art Diary」The New York Observer、6月1日、p.21

ユルゲン・リュック「Kunst kampft mit Holz (kopfen) 」Extra Tip、6月11日、p.5

エリザベス・レボヴィッチ、エルヴェ・ゴーヴィル「Arts／La Documenta Se Mouille」Liberation、6月18日

ジェネヴィエヴ・ブリーテル Le Monde、6月18日

アンナ・ティルロン「Bazar van grootse, erbarmelijke lichamen」de Volkskrant、6月19日

ロバータ・スミス「A Small Show Within an Enormous One」The New York Times、6月22日、p.C13

建畠哲「道の芸術への賭け・ドクメンタ展を見て」朝日新聞、7月1日、p.18

菅原教夫「ドクメンタIX／報告4」読売新聞、7月3日夕刊

ミッシェル・キムルマン「Art View／At Documenta, It's Survival Of the Loudest」The New York Times、7月5日

キム・レヴィン「Jan Who？ Docu What？」The Villege Voice、7月14日、p.95−96

ジャニス・ヒューズ「Artist makes huge sculpture out of hospital」Associate Press／New Haven Register、8月20日

ウィリアム・グリムス「Restoration on Roosevelt Island？ No, It's Sculpture／Is It Art or Scrap？The Answer Is：It's Both」The New York Times、9月24日、p.C13、C17

エドワード・ボール「Shelter／Re：Ruin」The Village Voice（Vol.XXXVII, No.39)、9月29日、p.99

ジェリー・トールマー「New life for death's dream castle」New York Post、10月2日、p.39

「An open installation」USA Today、10月7日

アメイ・ワラッチ「Kawamata Project on Roosevelt Island」New York Newsday、10月16日、p.71、74−75

「アングル／NYの廃材使った川俣作品」愛媛新聞、10月17日

ロバータ・スミス「Manic, Inspired Carpentry」The New York Times、10月25日、Section 2、p.33

森司「NYルーズベルト島のカワマタ・プロジェクト」読売新聞、10月27日、p.22

「Voice Listing／Art／In Brief」The Village Voice(Vol.XXXVII No.43)、10月27日、p.83

高島直之「美術／四氏が選んだベスト5」読売新聞、12月16日夕刊、p.17

菅原教夫「美術／日本の閉鎖せいに風穴」読売新聞、12月16日夕刊、p.17

1993

リカルド・テンペスティーニ「Il Pecci "trasferisce" nei vicoli del centro」Il Tirreno、2月19日

ヴァネッサ・ブルーニ「Una mostra all'aperto per ravvivare gli angoli più pittoreschi del centro」Il Tirreno、2月24日

フランコ・リコミーニ「L'arte dentro la città」La Nazione、2月24日

佐藤孝雄「造型作家川俣正さん／作って壊す"一時的な美"」北海道新聞、2月28日、p.6（撮影：松原国臣）

その他の出版物

ぴーぷるあいてむ・ぴあ事典／ぴあグラフティ、ぴあ株式会社（東京）、1984、p.66

中原佑介「開廊記念、ドローイング・インスタレーションー川俣正」（個展案内）コバヤシ画廊アネックス（東京）、1984

『PORTRAITS／Autumn and Winter Collection』ジュン株式会社（ニューヨーク）、1985、p.8−9

アーロン・ベトスキー『Violated Perfection』リッゾーリ・インターナショナル出版（ニューヨーク）、1990、p.106−107

アデーレ・フリードマン『Slight Lines』オクスフォード大学出版（ドン・ミルス／トロント）、1990、p.211−215

千葉成夫『美術の現代地点』五柳書院（東京）、1990、p.237−239

篠原資明『トランスアート装置』思想社（東京）、1991、p.205−207

『昭和の美術 Vol.6』毎日新聞社（東京）、1991、p.196、206

『ぴあギャラリーコレクション』ぴあ株式会社（東京）、1991、p.25、28、32、37、44、57

Photograph Credits

Hisayasu Kashiwagi, Tokyo: pp. 2-3, 7, 33, 39, 57-62, 94-95, 117-119, 128-129, 137, 142, 158, 167.

Andrew Moore, New York: pp. 53, 91-93, 115-116.

on the table, Tokyo: cover, pp. 8-28, 34-38, 40-49, 54-56, 73-80, 83 (below), 87, 89, 96-114, 120-126, 131-134, 138-141, 143-157, 203.

Hirshhorn Museum and Sculpture Garden, Smithsonian Institution, Washington D.C.:
François-Auguste-René Rodin, *The Burghers of Calais*, 1886/cast 1930s-before 1947, bronze, 79 3/8 × 80 7/8 × 77 1/8 inch. Gift of Joseph H. Hirshhorn, 1966, p. 65.
François-Auguste-René Rodin, *Monument To Balzac*, 1898/cast 1954-1965, bronze, 106 × 43 × 50 3/8 inch. Gift of Joseph H. Hirshhorn, 1966, p. 82.

Richard Serra, New York:
Richard Serra *St. John's Rotary Arc*, 1980, Cor-ten steel, 12 × 200 feet. Holland Tunnel Exit, New York, p. 66 (above).
Richard Serra *Tilted Arc*, 1981, Cor-ten streel, 12 × 120 × 1 1/2 feet. Installed at Federal Plaza, New York; destroyed in 1989 by US Government. Photo: Anne Chauvet, p. 85.

Holly Solomon Gallery, New York:
Gordon Matta-Clark, *Conical Intersect*, 1975, p. 69.

John Weber Gallery, New York:
Robert Smithson, *A Non-Site*, 1968, wood, limestone, 16 1/2 × 82 × 110 inch. Franklin, New Jersey, 1968, p. 66 (below).

Estelle Carley Jackson, Boston:
Mathias Goeritz (in collaboration with Luis Barragan), *The Towers of Satellite City*, 1957, painted concrete, height of tallest tower: 190 feet. City planner of Satellite City: Mario Pani, p. 67.

Musée National d'Art Moderne/Centre Georges Pompidou, Paris:
Constantin Brancusi *Table du silence à Tîrgu Jui* 1938, p. 83 (above).

Kawamata Project on Roosevelt Island

執筆：
川俣正
コスタス・グーニス
クロゥディア・ゴールド
エリザベス・A・フロッシュ
イヴ-アラン・ボワ

編集：
木村稔
小池美香
阪野光慶

アン・ブレムナー
近藤直美

デザイン監修：
有賀強

翻訳：
速水葉子
ダニエル・ジョン・オブライエン
神谷百代
郷随佳
鈴木恭子

発行人：
北川フラム

発行元：

現代企画室
東京都千代田区猿楽町2-2-5 興新ビル302
電話 03.3293.9539　ファクス 03.3293.2735

on the table, inc.
249 West 11th Street 4W,
New York, New York 10014 U.S.A.
電話 212.924.2104　ファクス 212.633.9685

発売元：現代企画室

1993年6月25日　初版第1刷発行

定価7,210円（本体7,000円）

印刷所：
アーテクッス博進堂